# A Special Message from The Globe Pequot Press

The Globe Pequot Press is proud to present the third edition of *The Complete Guide to National Park Lodges,* which is written by our intrepid park experts, David and Kay Scott, who have been our park authors for more than twenty years.

But this book is special to us for another reason. Globe Pequot has been publishing books on the national parks for many years. We have helped thousands and thousands of people discover our nation's most sacred treasures. And while we are very proud of our part in this, we are also well aware that with park attendance at an all-time high, the parks themselves have suffered from excessive wear and tear. We feel that if we are going to contribute to the damage to parks by directing visitors to them, we also want to help offset that damage by directing funds to the parks.

The Globe Pequot Press therefore will donate $1 from the sale of each copy of this book directly to the National Parks Conservation Association, a nonprofit organization. This money will help NPCA protect parks from damaging development; monitor and inventory natural and historic resources; and develop financial and transportation plans; and keep destructive and disruptive activities out of the parks.

If you would like to donate to the National Parks Conservation Association, please send a check or money order to:

National Parks Conservation Association
1776 Massachusetts Ave., N.W.
Washington, D.C. 20036

The Globe Pequot Press is committed to helping preserve our national parks and ensuring that they will remain wonderful places to visit for generations to come.

The Staff of the Globe Pequot Press

# HELP KEEP THIS GUIDE UP TO DATE

Every effort has been made by the authors and editors to make this guide as accurate and useful as possible. However, many things can change after a guide is published—establishments close, phone numbers change, facilities come under new management, and so on.

We would love to hear from you concerning your experiences with this guide and how you feel it could be improved and be kept up to date. While we may not be able to respond to all comments and suggestions, we'll take them to heart, and we'll also make certain to share them with the authors. Please send your comments and suggestions to the following address:

The Globe Pequot Press
Reader Response/Editorial Department
P.O. Box 480
Guilford, CT 06437

Or you may e-mail us at:

editorial@globe-pequot.com

Thanks for your input, and happy travels!

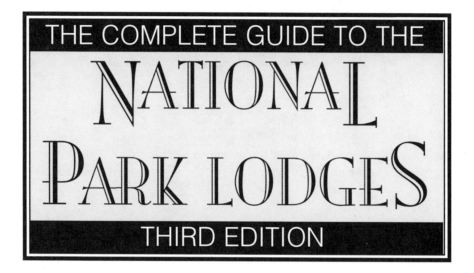

# THE COMPLETE GUIDE TO THE
# NATIONAL PARK LODGES
## THIRD EDITION

*by*

DAVID L. SCOTT

KAY W. SCOTT

The
Globe
Pequot
Press

GUILFORD, CONNECTICUT

Other Globe Pequot Press books by
David L. Scott and Kay Woelfel Scott

*Guide to the National Park Areas: Eastern States*

*Guide to the National Park Areas: Western States*

*Cover photo by Tom Alger; cover photo inset by Keith Walklet.*
*Cover design by Adam Schwartzman*
*Text design by Nancy Freeborn*
*Text illustrations by Carole Drong*

ISSN: 1537-3312
ISBN: 0-7627-1197-3

Manufactured in the United States of America
Third Edition/First Printing

# CONTENTS

Alphabetical List of Lodges      xi
Introduction      xiii

| | Page Number | Map Number* |
|---|---|---|
| **ALASKA** | | |
| **Glacier Bay National Park and Preserve** | 1 | 30 |
| Glacier Bay Lodge | 3 | |
| **ARIZONA** | | |
| **Canyon de Chelly National Monument** | 5 | 18 |
| Thunderbird Lodge | 7 | |
| **Glen Canyon National Recreation Area** | 9 | 14 |
| Wahweap Lodge | 9 | |
| Bullfrog Resort | 12 | |
| Halls Crossing | 13 | |
| Hite Marina | 13 | |
| **Grand Canyon National Park** | 14 | 17 |
| **SOUTH RIM** | 15 | |
| Bright Angel Lodge | 17 | |
| El Tovar Hotel | 19 | |
| Kachina Lodge/Thunderbird Lodge | 21 | |
| Maswik Lodge | 22 | |
| Moqui Lodge | 24 | |
| Yavapai Lodge | 25 | |
| **NORTH RIM** | 27 | |
| Grand Canyon Lodge | 27 | |
| **CALIFORNIA** | | |
| **Death Valley National Park** | 31 | 8 |
| Furnace Creek Inn | 33 | |
| Furnace Creek Ranch | 35 | |
| Panamint Springs Resort | 38 | |
| Stovepipe Wells Village | 39 | |
| **Lassen Volcanic National Park** | 42 | 5 |
| Drakesbad Guest Ranch | 42 | |
| **Sequoia National Park/ Kings Canyon National Park** | 46 | 7 |
| Cedar Grove Lodge | 48 | |
| Grant Grove Village | 49 | |
| Stony Creek Lodge | 52 | |
| Wuksachi Village and Lodge | 54 | |

* Map numbers correspond with numbers on the map on pages vi–vii.

Lake Superior

21

22

Minnesota

Wisconsin

Lake Huron

Lake Michigan

Michigan

Lake Ontario

New York

Vermont

Maine

New Hampshire

Massachusetts

Rhode Island

Connecticut

Iowa

Illinois

Indiana

Ohio

Lake Erie

33

Pennsylvania

New Jersey

Delaware

Missouri

Kentucky

West
Virginia

25

Virginia

Maryland

24

23

Tennessee

26

North Carolina

Arkansas

South
Carolina

ıa

Mississippi

Alabama

Georgia

Louisiana

27

Florida

28

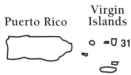

Puerto Rico

Virgin
Islands

31

| | Page Number | Map Number |
|---|---|---|
| **Yosemite National Park** | **56** | **6** |
| **YOSEMITE VALLEY LODGING** | **58** | |
| Ahwahnee | 59 | |
| Curry Village | 61 | |
| Housekeeping Camp | 63 | |
| Yosemite Lodge | 64 | |
| **LODGING OUTSIDE YOSEMITE VALLEY** | · **66** | |
| Wawona Hotel | 66 | |
| Tuolumne Meadows Lodge | 69 | |
| White Wolf Lodge | 71 | |

## COLORADO
| | | |
|---|---|---|
| **Mesa Verde National Park** | **74** | **15** |
| Far View Lodge | 74 | |

## FLORIDA
| | | |
|---|---|---|
| **Everglades National Park** | **78** | **28** |
| Flamingo Lodge, Marina, and Outpost Resort | 78 | |

## GEORGIA
| | | |
|---|---|---|
| **Cumberland Island National Seashore** | **81** | **27** |
| Greyfield Inn | 83 | |

## HAWAII
| | | |
|---|---|---|
| **Hawaii Volcanoes National Park** | **86** | **29** |
| Volcano House | 87 | |

## KENTUCKY
| | | |
|---|---|---|
| **Mammoth Cave National Park** | **90** | **24** |
| Mammoth Cave Hotel | 90 | |

## MICHIGAN
| | | |
|---|---|---|
| **Isle Royale National Park** | **94** | **22** |
| Rock Harbor Lodge | 96 | |

## MINNESOTA
| | | |
|---|---|---|
| **Voyageurs National Park** | **98** | **21** |
| Kettle Falls Hotel | 100 | |

## MISSOURI
| | | |
|---|---|---|
| **Ozark National Scenic Riverways** | **103** | **23** |
| Big Spring Lodge | 105 | |

## MONTANA
| | | |
|---|---|---|
| **Glacier National Park** | **107** | **9** |
| Apgar Village Lodge | 109 | |
| Glacier Park Lodge | 111 | |
| Lake McDonald Lodge | 113 | |
| Many Glacier Hotel | 115 | |

|  | Page Number | Map Number |
|---|---|---|
| Prince of Wales Hotel | 117 | |
| Rising Sun Motor Inn | 120 | |
| Swiftcurrent Motor Inn | 122 | |
| Village Inn | 124 | |

## NEVADA

| **Lake Mead National Recreation Area** | **126** | **16** |
|---|---|---|
| Cottonwood Cove Resort | 128 | |
| Echo Bay Resort | 129 | |
| Lake Mead Resort | 131 | |
| Lake Mohave Resort at Katherine Landing | 133 | |
| Temple Bar Resort | 134 | |

## NORTH CAROLINA

| **Blue Ridge Parkway** | **137** | **26** |
|---|---|---|
| Bluffs Lodge | 139 | |
| Peaks of Otter Lodge (VA) | 141 | |
| The Pisgah Inn | 143 | |
| Rocky Knob Cabins (VA) | 145 | |

## OHIO

| **Cuyahoga Valley National Park** | **147** | **33** |
|---|---|---|
| The Inn at Brandywine Falls | 149 | |

## OREGON

| **Crater Lake National Park** | **151** | **3** |
|---|---|---|
| Crater Lake Lodge | 153 | |
| Mazama Village Motor Inn | 155 | |
| **Oregon Caves National Monument** | **157** | **4** |
| Oregon Caves Lodge | 157 | |

## SOUTH DAKOTA

| **Badlands National Park** | **162** | **19** |
|---|---|---|
| Cedar Pass Lodge | 164 | |

## TEXAS

| **Big Bend National Park** | **167** | **20** |
|---|---|---|
| Chisos Mountains Lodge | 167 | |

## U.S. VIRGIN ISLANDS

| **Virgin Islands National Park** | **171** | **31** |
|---|---|---|
| Cinnamon Bay Campground | 173 | |

## UTAH

| **Bryce Canyon National Park** | **175** | **13** |
|---|---|---|
| Bryce Canyon Lodge | 177 | |

| | Page Number | Map Number |
|---|---|---|
| **Zion National Park** | 179 | 12 |
| Zion Lodge | 180 | |

## VIRGINIA

| | Page Number | Map Number |
|---|---|---|
| **Shenandoah National Park** | 183 | 25 |
| Big Meadows Lodge | 185 | |
| Lewis Mountain Cabins | 187 | |
| Skyland | 189 | |

## WASHINGTON

| | Page Number | Map Number |
|---|---|---|
| **Mount Rainier National Park** | 191 | 2 |
| National Park Inn | 193 | |
| Paradise Inn | 195 | |
| **North Cascades National Park/Lake Chelan National** | | |
| **Recreation Area/Ross Lake National Recreation Area** | 197 | 32 |
| North Cascades Stehekin Lodge | 199 | |
| Stehekin Valley Ranch | 201 | |
| **Olympic National Park** | 205 | 1 |
| Kalaloch Lodge | 205 | |
| Lake Crescent Lodge | 208 | |
| Lake Quinault Lodge | 210 | |
| Log Cabin Resort | 213 | |
| Sol Duc Hot Springs Resort | 215 | |

## WYOMING

| | Page Number | Map Number |
|---|---|---|
| **Grand Teton National Park/John D.** | | |
| **Rockfeller, Jr., Memorial Parkway** | 217 | 11 |
| Colter Bay Village | 219 | |
| Dornan's Spur Ranch Log Cabins | 221 | |
| Flagg Ranch Resort | 223 | |
| Jackson Lake Lodge | 225 | |
| Jenny Lake Lodge | 228 | |
| Signal Mountain Lodge | 230 | |
| Triangle X Ranch | 232 | |
| **Yellowstone National Park** | 234 | 10 |
| Canyon Lodge and Cabins | 236 | |
| Grant Village | 238 | |
| Lake Lodge Cabins | 240 | |
| Lake Yellowstone Hotel and Cabins | 242 | |
| Mammoth Hot Springs Hotel and Cabins | 244 | |
| Old Faithful Inn | 246 | |
| Old Faithful Lodge Cabins | 248 | |
| Old Faithful Snow Lodge and Cabins | 250 | |
| Roosevelt Lodge Cabins | 252 | |

# ALPHABETICAL LIST OF LODGES

Ahwahnee, 59
Apgar Village Lodge, 109
Big Meadows Lodge, 185
Big Spring Lodge, 105
Bluffs Lodge, 139
Bright Angel Lodge, 17
Bryce Canyon Lodge, 177
Bullfrog Resort, 12
Canyon Lodge and Cabins, 236
Cedar Grove Lodge, 48
Cedar Pass Lodge, 164
Chisos Mountains Lodge, 167
Cinnamon Bay Campground, 173
Colter Bay Village, 219
Cottonwood Cove Resort, 128
Crater Lake Lodge, 153
Curry Village, 61
Dornan's Spur Ranch Log Cabins, 221
Drakesbad Guest Ranch, 42
Echo Bay Resort, 129
El Tovar Hotel, 19
Far View Lodge, 74
Flagg Ranch Resort, 223
Flamingo Lodge, Marina, and
    Outpost Resort, 78
Furnace Creek Inn, 33
Furnace Creek Ranch, 35
Glacier Bay Lodge, 3
Glacier Park Lodge, 111
Grand Canyon Lodge, 27
Grant Grove Village, 49
Grant Village, 238
Greyfield Inn, 83
Halls Crossing, 13
Hite Marina, 13
Housekeeping Camp, 63
The Inn at Brandywine Falls, 149
Jackson Lake Lodge, 225
Jenny Lake Lodge, 228
Kachina Lodge, 21
Kalaloch Lodge, 205
Kettle Falls Hotel, 100
Lake Crescent Lodge, 208
Lake Lodge Cabins, 240
Lake McDonald Lodge, 113
Lake Mead Resort, 131
Lake Mohave Resort at Katherine Landing, 133

Lake Quinault Lodge, 210
Lake Yellowstone Hotel and Cabins, 242
Lewis Mountain Cabins, 187
Log Cabin Resort, 213
Mammoth Cave Hotel, 90
Mammoth Hot Springs Hotel and Cabins, 244
Many Glacier Hotel, 115
Maswik Lodge, 22
Mazama Village Motor Inn, 155
Moqui Lodge, 24
National Park Inn, 193
North Cascades Stehekin Lodge, 199
Old Faithful Inn, 246
Old Faithful Lodge Cabins, 248
Old Faithful Snow Lodge and Cabins, 250
Oregon Caves Lodge, 157
Panamint Springs Resort, 38
Paradise Inn, 195
Peaks of Otter Lodge, 141
The Pisgah Inn, 143
Prince of Wales Hotel, 117
Rising Sun Motor Inn, 120
Rock Harbor Lodge, 96
Rocky Knob Cabins, 145
Roosevelt Lodge Cabins, 252
Signal Mountain Lodge, 230
Skyland, 189
Sol Duc Hot Springs Resort, 215
Stehekin Valley Ranch, 201
Stony Creek Lodge, 52
Stovepipe Wells Village, 39
Swiftcurrent Motor Inn, 122
Temple Bar Resort, 134
Thunderbird Lodge (Canyon de Chelly), 7
Thunderbird Lodge (Grand Canyon), 21
Triangle X Ranch, 232
Tuolumne Meadows Lodge, 69
Village Inn, 124
Volcano House, 87
Wahweap Lodge, 9
Wawona Hotel, 66
White Wolf Lodge, 71
Wuksachi Village and Lodge, 54
Yavapai Lodge, 25
Yosemite Lodge, 64
Zion Lodge, 180

# INTRODUCTION

Have you ever thought about waking up, looking out your window, and viewing the morning sun shining on the north face of the Grand Canyon? How about a walk down a dirt road from the historic hotel where you just had a dinner of walleye pike, and standing where French fur trappers portaged their canoes around a waterfall? Maybe you would enjoy sitting on a wooden deck outside your room, listening to the roar of a mountain stream. Perhaps you are a closet cowboy who has always wanted to spend a week riding horses at a dude ranch. Maybe you would like to walk outside your lodge and view a dormant volcano. These are just a few of the dreams that can be brought to life by staying at a national park lodging facility.

We have spent a good part of our lives in America's national park areas. Most of our visits have occurred during the twenty-five summers we crisscrossed the United States in a series of four Volkswagen campers. We have driven several hundred thousand miles and visited nearly every one of the areas managed by the National Park Service. During the trips we have spent nights in many of the lodges. Even on trips spent mostly in national park campgrounds, we often explored the wonderful buildings described in this book.

Most national park lodges are in the well-known and heavily visited parks, such as Grand Canyon, Death Valley, Everglades, Yosemite, Yellowstone, Olympic, and Glacier. However, some lesser-known park areas, including Oregon Caves National Monument, Isle Royale National Park, Big Bend National Park, and Lassen Volcanic National Park, each offer comfortable and interesting lodge facilities. Some of the biggest and busiest parks do not have lodges. For example, Great Smoky Mountains National Park, Rocky Mountain National Park, and Acadia National Park do not offer conventional lodging inside the park boundaries, although accommodations are available directly outside each of these parks.

Not all areas managed by the National Park Service are classified as national parks. In fact, only about 15 percent of the areas officially carry the title "national park." The National Park Service also manages many national monuments, national lakeshores, national historic sites, national recreation areas, national memorials, and several other types of facilities. Each of these areas has something unique to offer or it wouldn't be included in the system. Some of them even have lodging. We mentioned Oregon Caves National Monument, in which a classic old lodge awaits you. Lodging is also available at Canyon de Chelly National Monument, Blue Ridge Parkway, Cumberland Island National Seashore, Ozark National Scenic Riverways, and Glacier Bay National Monument.

Staying in a park lodge during your trip to a national park area will almost surely enhance your park experience. It certainly did ours. Spend some time talking to the employees and learning about the history of the building where you are staying. Most of all, travel and enjoy.

## Considerations in Planning a Stay at a National Park Lodge

National park lodges provide a different kind of vacation experience. Most of the lodges are in close proximity to the things you want to see, the places you want to visit, and the facilities you will want to use when you visit a park. At Crater Lake Lodge, you can sleep in a room with windows that overlook the crater rim. In Yellowstone's Old Faithful Inn, you can walk out the entrance and view an eruption of Old Faithful. At the Grand Canyon's El Tovar, you can walk a few steps outside the hotel and look down into the canyon. Many park lodges have large rustic lobby areas where you can relax with other guests in front of a blazing fireplace. The lodges are often near National Park Service visitor centers or campgrounds where guided walks originate and natural history programs are presented. Evening programs or other entertainment can be enjoyed in many of the lodges.

Most lodge facilities in national park areas are owned by the government but managed by private concerns subject to oversight by the park in which they are located. Managements of these lodges operate as concessionaires and are required to obtain the approval of the National Park Service for room rates, improvements, and the prices charged for everything from food to gasoline. Some lodges remain under private ownership on private property within a park. In general, lodges under private ownership were in operation prior to the establishment of a park or prior to an expansion of the park boundaries. Lodges on private property are subject to fewer restrictions regarding what they can offer and the prices they can charge.

Some basic information regarding reservations, facilities, and policies can be helpful if you have never stayed in a national park facility or have stayed in only one or two lodges. Most national park lodges experience large public demand for a limited number of rooms, especially during peak season, when you are most likely to want a room. Thus, you should make a reservation as early as possible, especially if your planned vacation coincides with the park's busiest period. Try to book rooms at a popular lodge at least six months before your expected arrival. Several lodges in very busy locations such as Yosemite Valley should, if possible, be booked nearly a year in advance. Choosing to vacation in off-peak periods, normally spring and fall, will make it much more likely that you are able to obtain a reservation on the dates you desire. Other important factors regarding national park lodges are discussed below.

**FACILITIES.** National park lodges range from luxurious and expensive facilities, such as Yosemite National Park's Ahwahnee and Death Valley National Park's Furnace Creek Inn, to very rustic cabins without bathrooms, such as those at Grant Grove in Kings Canyon National Park. Some facilities call themselves lodges but are not what most of us picture when we think of a lodge. For example, Old Faithful Lodge Cabins (not the more famous Old Faithful Inn, which sits nearby) offers only cabins as overnight accommodations. Likewise, Signal Mountain Lodge in Grand Teton National Park does not have a main lodge building with overnight accommodations; rather, it has several types of cabins that rent at a fairly wide range of prices. The variation in facilities between and within parks makes it important that you understand exactly what types of accommodations are being discussed when you are making a reservation.

Most national park lodging facilities don't have amenities such as spas, swimming pools, game rooms, and some of the other niceties you may expect to find at commercial facilities outside the parks. In fact, most park lodges don't have telephones or televisions in the rooms, although public telephones are nearly always available somewhere in the facility. Several older lodges, including Old Faithful Inn and Lake Crescent Lodge, offer some rooms without a private bathroom. Community bathrooms and shower rooms are available for occupants of these rooms. Some cabins do not have private bathrooms.

**ROOMS.** Rooms in a lodge often vary considerably with regard to size, bedding, view, and rate. Likewise, a single lodging facility may offer rooms in the main lodge building, rooms in motel-type buildings, and a variety of cabin rooms. This is the case with Lake Crescent Lodge in Olympic National Park and with Big Meadows in Shenandoah National Park, for example. Potential differences in rooms mean that it is worthwhile to learn what options are available at a particular location where you plan to stay. If you wait to make a reservation near your planned arrival date, you are likely to find a limited variety of accommodations. For example, you may find that all the rooms with private bathrooms are already taken. On the other hand, call early and you are likely to have a wide choice of rooms that are offered at a wide range of rates. Ask about a view room, for example. Sometimes rooms with an excellent view are more expensive, and sometimes they are not. Some buildings do not have elevators, so the floor you are assigned may be important. Higher floors tend to offer better views but require more climbing. Rooms near the lobby may be noisy. Some lodges allow you to reserve a particular room, but most lodges guarantee only a particular type of room. Even when a particular room won't be guaranteed, a lodge will often make note of your preferences and attempt to satisfy the request when room assignments are made.

**RESERVATIONS.** Reservations can generally be made by either telephone or mail, and sometimes by fax or the Internet. The disadvantage of using the mail is the uncertainty that a room will be available on the dates you request. If rooms are unavailable on the specified dates, you must wait for a reply and then start over again, but at a much later date, when even fewer rooms are available. This can sometimes be avoided by listing alternative dates that you find acceptable.

Choosing to make a reservation by telephone allows you to immediately determine room availability and, if necessary, choose alternative dates. Using the telephone will also allow you to discuss with the reservation agent the types of facilities that are available. The best bet is to write early for literature so that you have a basic understanding of the facilities and rates prior to calling. This will allow you to know which type of room and building to ask for and what to expect regarding rates. Be aware that it is often difficult to get through to a reservation agent via telephone, especially if you call late in the spring, when everyone else in the country seems to be trying the same number. Try calling at odd hours, such as weekend mornings.

Most lodges require a deposit of at least one night's lodging soon after making a reservation. Some lodges allow you to charge the deposit to a credit card, while other lodges will require that you send a check or money order. A few lodges permit you to guarantee the reservation with a credit card and to pay for the entire stay when you check out. When sending a deposit check or giving a credit card number, always ask for a deposit receipt to take on your vacation. In a couple of cases, our reservations have gotten lost. In the event your plans change, refund of a deposit requires advance notice, usually forty-eight hours, but this varies by lodge.

**RATES.** In general, accommodations in the national parks aren't cheap. You can expect to pay $80 and up for most double rooms, although some rustic cabins are much cheaper, while a room at one of the nicer facilities can run $150 and up. In addition, discounts for seniors, AAA members, and so on, that you expect at most commercial facilities are generally unavailable at national park lodges. Most lodges quote rates for two adults, which means that you must pay a double rate even if you travel alone. Additional adults pay extra, although children are generally free when staying with adults. Some lodges allow children twelve years and under to stay free, while other facilities limit free stays to children three and under. Lodges sometimes offer reduced rates during their off-seasons or have special packages that include meals or a lower rate for multiday stays. Ask about specials when you book a reservation, but don't get your hopes too high. The dollar cost of rooms and meals for summer 2001 is used in this book. Expect somewhat higher prices in subsequent years.

**PAYMENT, CHECK-IN, AND CHECKOUT.** Most lodges accept major credit cards, but you should determine acceptable methods of payment when a reservation is made. For example, you may end up at a lodge that will not accept any credit cards (unusual), will accept only a few major cards, or will not accept a personal check. A lodge that requires a personal check for a deposit may accept a credit card to satisfy the balance of your bill.

Most lodges specify an 11:00 A.M. checkout and a 4:00 P.M. check-in, but the times can be different depending on which lodge you will be using. For example, some lodges specify a 2:00 or 3:00 P.M. check-in, while some don't require a checkout until noon. The checkout time can generally be postponed by at least an hour with a request to the front desk the prior night or the morning of your planned departure. You may be able to check in prior to the specified time, but don't count on it. If you arrive early in the morning, you are likely to roam around without a room until late afternoon. Lodges that assign a particular room to each guest are less flexible in getting guests into rooms before the scheduled check-in time.

**OBTAINING A ROOM WITHOUT A RESERVATION.** Some national park lodges have space available, especially during off-peak periods. Even busy lodges experience cancellations or early departures that free up rooms. Thus, you may be able to obtain a room without an advance reservation. For example, you may locate a room in a busy park like Yellowstone during peak summer months just by dropping in at one of the nine lodges and asking about a vacancy. If rooms are available, they are unlikely to be the exact configuration, location, or price category you would choose. For example, you may have to accept a room without a private bathroom or a room that is more expensive than you would ordinarily reserve. In a large park like Yellowstone or Glacier, the only available rooms may be in a different facility that is many miles from the lodge where you are making the request. Taking a chance on a vacancy is a risky strategy. Being unsuccessful may result in a long drive to a distant location where you are likely to overpay for an inferior room. Hedge your bets by calling ahead.

**PETS.** National park lodges generally prohibit pets of all kinds except for seeing-eye dogs. There are exceptions, but not many. Some of the larger lodges such as those at Mammoth Caves National Park, the South Rim of Grand Canyon National Park, and Yosemite National Park have kennels available, but don't count on this convenience at the park you plan to visit. Ask about the policy regarding pets at the time you make a reservation. Each of the national parks requires that pets be kept on a leash at all times. In addition, pets are normally prohibited from park trails. The bottom line is that pets should be left at home if you are making a trip to a national park, especially if you plan to visit several parks during the same trip.

**REDUCING EXPENSES.** Most national park lodges are pricey. If you are on a limited budget but want to experience a stay at one or more of the lodges, it is possible to take steps to reduce your expenditures. Accepting a room without a private bathroom (if available) can often cost $20 per night less than comparable rooms with a private bath. These rooms also tend to be easier to reserve, because many individuals demand a private bath.

Another money-saving strategy is to spend every second or third night camping. Most parks with lodges also have campgrounds that charge $10 to $14 per night. Arrange the campground stays into your schedule when reservations are being made. For example, spend two nights in a lodge, then move to a campground for the third night. Keep in mind that some national park campgrounds operate under a reservation system.

Another strategy is to spend the night prior to arrival at an inexpensive commercial facility that is within an hour or two of the park. Staying in close proximity permits you to enjoy most of a full day in the park before checking in at the lodge. Likewise, obtain a reservation at a motel a couple of hours outside the park on your departure date so that you can spend most of an extra day finishing your park sightseeing.

Take along a cooler with some food and drink, including snacks such as pretzels, candy, soft drinks, and fruit. Most lodges have ice machines that can be used to resupply a cooler. Buy groceries outside the park, where they are likely to be cheaper. Eat a breakfast of fruit and cereal in your room, and have a picnic lunch or supper. If you take the trouble to visit a national park, you may as well enjoy nature. If you choose to eat in a lodge restaurant, keep in mind that lunch can be quite a bit less expensive than dinner. In parks that offer several restaurant facilities, examine the menus before choosing a place to eat, since prices can vary a great deal from one restaurant to another. In general, cafeterias are considerably less expensive places to eat than dining rooms.

Play it safe by establishing a budget for your trip before you leave. Estimate how much you are going to spend for lodging, food, transportation, and incidentals, then make a real effort to stay within your budget. You might find that some things are more expensive than planned. You may be able to substitute a couple of picnic lunches for restaurant meals and save enough for a guided park tour. Using a budget may keep you from buying all the T-shirts during the first visit to a gift shop.

Take advantage of the many free things that are offered at virtually all the park areas. National Park Service personnel offer guided walks and programs, generally at no charge. These are fun and informative. Parks with campgrounds typically have evening history and nature programs that are offered without charge. Park visitor centers have exhibits and audio-visual programs to help you understand the park. Some of the lodges even offer free lodge tours. Many parks offer Junior Ranger programs for children. It is best to stop at the park visitor center and obtain a list of daily activities.

**PARK FEES.** Many areas operated by the National Park Service charge an entrance fee. Visitors, including those staying in a lodge within a park, are required to pay the park entrance fee. Most parks charge a vehicle entry fee that covers everyone inside the vehicle. Hikers, motorcyclists, bicyclists, and visitors entering in commercial vehicles pay a separate fee applicable to individual entry. Entrance fees range from $5.00 to $20.00 per private vehicle, with the higher price charged at large national parks, including Yellowstone, Yosemite, and Grand Canyon. The park fee generally provides exit and entrance for three to seven days, depending on the park. Inquire about this at the entrance station if you may need to go outside the park during a stay of several days. The National Park Service sells four types of passes that provide free entrance at all national parks. The National Parks Pass ($50) allows unlimited entry to any and all areas operated by the National Park Service for one year from the month of purchase. For an extra $15 a hologram is attached and converts this pass to a Golden Eagle Passport that provides entrance to additional areas operated by the Bureau of Land Management, the National Forest Service, and the Corps of Engineers. For seniors (age sixty-two and over), the Golden Age Passport provides lifetime free entrance for a one-time fee of $10. The Golden Access Passport (no charge) is available to individuals who are disabled. Both the Golden Age and Golden Access passports, which must be purchased in person, also allow a 50 percent reduction in fees for parking, boat launching, and most tours. All four passes may be purchased at most National Park Service entrance stations and visitor centers. The National Park Pass is available by phone (call 1–888–GOPARKS), on the Internet (www.nationalparks.org), or via mail by sending a check or money order to National Parks Pass, 27540 Avenue Mentry, Valencia, CA 91355. A shipping charge of $3.95 applies to passes purchased by mail, phone, or via the Internet.

The dollar cost of rooms and meals is for summer 2001.
Taxes are not included.

---

*The prices and rates listed in this guidebook were confirmed at press time. We recommend, however, that you call establishments before traveling to obtain current information.*

*Maps provided are for reference only and should be used in conjunction with a road map. Distances suggested are approximate.*

---

# ALASKA

**STATE TOURIST INFORMATION**
(907) 929–2200
www.travelalaska.com

## GLACIER BAY NATIONAL PARK AND PRESERVE

Glacier Bay National Park and Preserve
Gustavus, AK 99826
(907) 697–2230
www.nps.gov/glba

Glacier Bay National Park and Preserve comprises approximately 3.3 million acres that include some of the world's most impressive examples of tidewater glaciers, rivers of ice that flow to the sea. The park is rich in plant and animal life and is the home to brown and black bears, mountain goats, seals, humpback whales, and porpoises. A short road links the small town of Gustavus and its airport with the lodge, but most of the natural features of the park can be seen only by boat or airplane. Park headquarters is at Bartlett Cove, 7 miles north of the mouth of Glacier Bay. The park is located in southeastern Alaska, approximately 65 miles northwest of Juneau. No roads lead to the park, and access is via plane or boat.

**PARK ENTRANCE FEE:** No charge.

### Lodging in Glacier Bay National Park

Glacier Bay Lodge offers the only overnight accommodations in Glacier Bay National Park. The rustic fifty-six-room lodge is located in the southeastern section of the park near the mouth of Glacier Bay, about 9 miles from the small town of Gustavus. There are several bed-and-breakfasts in Gustavus.

# GLACIER BAY NATIONAL PARK AND PRESERVE

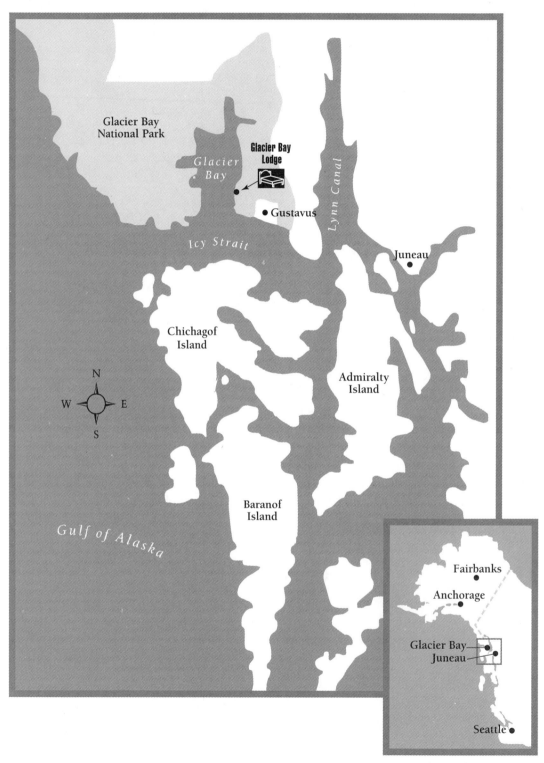

# GLACIER BAY LODGE

199 Barlett Cove Road • Gustavus, AK 99826 • (907) 697–2225
www.glacierbaytours.com

Glacier Bay Lodge is a wilderness resort situated among Sitka spruce in a rainforest. The complex includes a two-story wooden chalet-type lodge building that houses a lobby, registration desk, restaurant, theater, gift shop, and cocktail lounge, connected by boardwalk to sixteen nearby one-story wooden buildings that provide guest accommodations. The lodge is located on Bartlett Cove, 9 miles from the town of Gustavus in the southeastern corner of the park. A road connects the lodge with the town of Gustavus and its small airport, but no roads lead from the mainland into the park. Access is via boat or airplane.

The lodge offers fifty-six rooms in sixteen one-story wooden buildings that are close to but separate from the main lodge building. These buildings each have from two to six rooms. The rooms have radiant heat, telephone, and a private bathroom with either a shower or a combination shower-tub. All the rooms are the same size, and most have two double beds or two twin beds, although two rooms have a queen-size bed. The rooms have wood paneling and a vaulted ceiling. The lodge also offers two less-expensive dormitories, each with three bunk beds. The dorms have a community shower and bathroom and are a low-cost alternative for budget-conscious travelers.

Glacier Bay Lodge is certainly a place to get away from it all. It is in a very remote location that offers spectacular scenery, abundant wildlife, and a wild and unique environment. A deck attached to the main lodge allows guests to sit and watch the sun set over Bartlett Cove. A variety of activities are available, including guided nature walks, kayaking, hiking, and whale watching. Whale-watching excursions, overnight wilderness cruises, and sport-fishing charters depart from a nearby dock. Films and slide programs about Glacier Bay are presented by National Park Service rangers each evening in the lodge auditorium.

- **ROOMS:** Singles, doubles, triples, and quads. All rooms in the lodge have private baths. Dormitories have community shower and rest room facilities. Handicap-accessible rooms are available in the lodge.

- **RESERVATIONS:** Glacier Bay Park Concessions, Inc., 226 2nd Avenue West, Seattle, WA 98119. Phone (800) 451–5952; fax (206) 623–7809. Cancellation is required 91 days prior to first day of arrival.

- **RATES:** Lodge rooms ($82.50); dormitory rooms ($28). Rates for lodge rooms are per person, double occupancy. The rate for dormitory rooms is per person. Children under two stay free with adults.

- **LOCATION:** Approximately 9 miles northwest of Gustavus, on the shore of Bartlett Cove.

- **SEASON:** Early May through mid- to late September.

- **FOOD:** A dining room specializing in fresh Alaskan seafood serves three meals daily (dinner $12–$25). Lighter meals, including sandwiches, nachos, and halibut tacos, are served on the deck. A small grocery is in the town of Gustavus.

*Glacier Bay Lodge*

- **TRANSPORTATION:** Daily passenger ferry service operates between Juneau and the community of Gustavus. A small airport is in nearby Gustavus. A lodge shuttle that operates between the lodge and Gustavus is available for a fee.

- **FACILITIES:** Restaurant, cocktail service, auditorium, gift shop. A ranger station and boat dock are nearby.

- **ACTIVITIES:** Hiking, fishing, guided walks, fishing charters, wildlife and whale-watching cruises, and day cruises to the glaciers.

The glaciers here remain from the Little Ice Age that began about 4,000 years ago. Glaciers form when mountain snowfall exceeds snow melt. Accumulating weight of the snow presses lower layers into solid ice that eventually flows slowly downslope. Glacier Bay National Park includes sixteen glaciers that terminate at the sea's edge. The most spectacular are the twelve glaciers that actively calve icebergs into the bay.

# ARIZONA

**STATE TOURIST INFORMATION**
(888) 520–3434
www.arizonaguide.com

## CANYON DE CHELLY NATIONAL MONUMENT

P.O. Box 588
Chinle, AZ 86503
(928) 674–5500
www.nps.gov/cach/

Canyon de Chelly (pronounced "d' SHAY") National Monument comprises nearly 84,000 acres of Navajo land that include ruins of Indian villages built between A.D. 350 and 1300 in steep-walled canyons. The visitor center is located near the park entrance. The canyon can be seen from scenic overlooks along North Rim Drive (36 miles round-trip) and South Rim Drive (34 miles round-trip). White House Ruin is accessible via a 2.5-mile (round-trip) trail that begins at a trailhead on South Rim Drive. All other trails and all four-wheel-drive travel within the park require a park ranger or authorized guide. Information is available at the visitor center. Canyon de Chelly is in northeastern Arizona, approximately 85 miles northwest of Gallup, New Mexico, near the town of Chinle, Arizona.

**MONUMENT ENTRANCE FEE:** No charge.

### Lodging in Canyon de Chelly National Monument

Thunderbird Lodge, near the monument entrance, is the only lodging facility in Canyon de Chelly National Monument. The lodge includes a cafeteria and gift shop. Guided tours leave from the lodge. A Best Western and a Holiday Inn are in the town of Chinle and a short distance outside the monument entrance.

# CANYON DE CHELLY NATIONAL MONUMENT

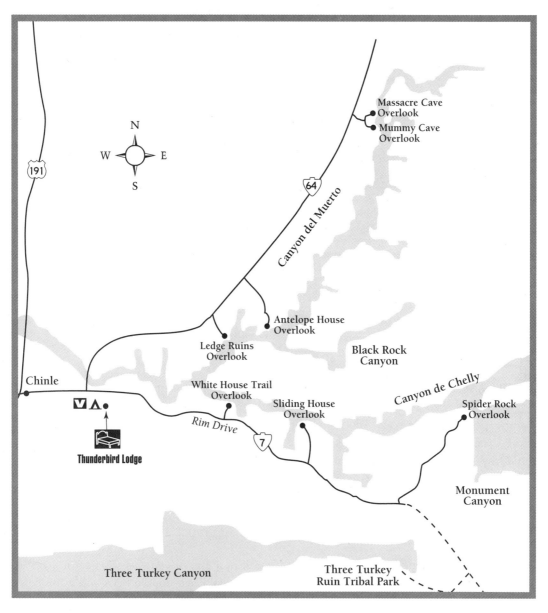

# THUNDERBIRD LODGE

P.O. Box 548 • Chinle, AZ 86503 • (520) 674–5841

tbirddechelly@juno.com

*De Chelly Units at Thunderbird Lodge*

Thunderbird Lodge is an attractive, well-maintained motor lodge, offering seventy-two rooms just inside the entrance to Canyon de Chelly National Monument. The lodge, situated in a grove of cottonwood trees, comprises a complex of several adobe and stone buildings, including three adobe units that contain most of the lodging rooms. The adobe registration building is separate but adjacent to the buildings containing the rooms. Separate stone buildings house a small number of rooms, a gift shop, and a cafeteria. Thunderbird Lodge is on Navajo Route 7, 3 miles east of the intersection with Highway 191 in the town of Chinle.

The lodge offers several types of rooms, although the majority are very similar. All rooms have televisions, air-conditioning, heat, and telephones, and several ice machines are in the lodge complex. The interiors are decorated in an attractive Southwest style. Forty-one "Adobe" motel-type rooms have two queen-size beds and a full bath. These rooms are housed in a single long building built into the back of a hill. Adequate parking is in front of the building. Twenty-four "De Chelly" rooms each contain two double beds and a full bath, all but two of which are in two buildings constructed around a grassy courtyard with cottonwood trees. Rooms in these buildings back up to one another, with half facing the courtyard and half facing the parking lot. Four of the De Chelly rooms are fully handicap accessible. One suite in a separate stone building in the center of the complex has one king-size bed, a queen-size sofa bed, and a refrigerator. Six smaller rooms in stone buildings each have two double beds and are rented only on-site. We recommend you choose from De Chelly rooms 14 through 18 or 24 through 29, which face the courtyard. These are quieter and front on a nice yard.

Thunderbird Lodge is a handy accommodation for visitors who wish to tour Canyon de Chelly National Monument. The lodge is a half-mile walk from the National Park Service visitor center, which has a variety of exhibits, including a Navajo home called a hogan.

Interpretive programs at the visitor center include talks by rangers and guided walks. Evening campfire programs are offered at the monument's campground, a short walk from the lodge. Half- and full-day guided tours into the canyon in four- and six-wheel-drive vehicles begin at the lodge, where tickets may be purchased at the gift shop. Half-day tours only are offered in winter months. All-day and overnight horseback trail rides are also available. The lodge cafeteria offers food service from early morning to evening, and fast-food restaurants are a short distance away in the town of Chinle. The lodge gift shop features a Navajo rug room with a large selection of handwoven Navajo rugs.

- **ROOMS:** Doubles, triples, and quads. All rooms offer a full private bath. Four rooms are handicap accessible.

- **RESERVATIONS:** Thunderbird Lodge, P.O. Box 548, Chinle, AZ 86503. Phone (800) 679–2473; fax (928) 674–5844. Reservations may be made up to a year in advance. Cancellation must be made twenty-four hours in advance for a full refund.

- **RATES:** Summer rates for one person from April 1 to November 15: Adobe units ($111); De Chelly units ($106); Suite ($145 for two persons). Each additional person is $6.50 per night. Winter rate for two persons from November 16 to March 31: Adobe or De Chelly ($65). Rollaway or crib is $6.50. Special packages are offered during winter months. Call for information on winter specials. Senior discounts and government rates are offered.

- **LOCATION:** The lodge is a short distance inside the park entrance.

- **SEASON:** The lodge is open year-round. Heaviest season is from April through October, when reservations are advised.

- **FOOD:** A lodge cafeteria offers basic food at reasonable prices from 6:30 A.M. to 9:00 P.M. daily. Most meals range from $9.00 to $12.00, with steak dinners from $9.00 to $15.50. Alternative eating facilities are in the town of Chinle.

- **TRANSPORTATION:** No public transportation serves Canyon de Chelly National Monument or the town of Chinle.

- **FACILITIES:** Cafeteria, gift shop, stable, National Park Service visitor center. Three miles west the town of Chinle has fast-food outlets, service stations, grocery stores, laundries, and a bank.

- **ACTIVITIES:** Hiking, half- and full-day guided tours into Canyon de Chelly and Canyon del Muerto, National Park Service interpretive programs, horseback riding.

*Thunderbird Lodge was originally constructed in 1902 as a trading post on the Navajo Reservation. The post served as a store, bank, post office, community meeting place, and courtroom. The owner began offering rooms and food service to accommodate an increasing number of tourists, who came to view the cliff dwellings and spectacular scenery. The present-day cafeteria is in the original trading post, while the building housing the gift shop originally served as home for the trading post's owner.*

# GLEN CANYON NATIONAL RECREATION AREA

P.O. Box 1507
Page, AZ 86040
(520) 608–6200
www.nps.gov/glca/

Glen Canyon National Recreation Area comprises 1.25 million acres of high desert surrounding and including Lake Powell and its nearly 2,000 miles of shoreline. Lake Powell is formed by the Glen Canyon Dam near Page, Arizona, which backs up the Colorado River for nearly 200 miles. Most of the activities here, including boating, fishing, and waterskiing, are water-related. Houseboat rental is available at several locations on Lake Powell. Although nearly all of the recreation area is in southern Utah, the most accessible part is along U.S. Highway 89 near Page, Arizona, where the Glen Canyon Dam is located.

**RECREATION AREA ENTRANCE FEE:** $10.00 per vehicle or $3.00 per person, good for seven days.

## Lodging in Glen Canyon National Recreation Area

Four locations in Glen Canyon National Recreation Area offer overnight lodging facilities. The largest and nicest facility by far is at Wahweap, 6 miles north of Page, Arizona, on Highway 89. Wahweap also has the largest marina on the lake. Smaller and less elaborate facilities are at Bullfrog and Halls Crossing, in the central section of Lake Powell, and Hite, in the northern section. Houseboat rentals are available at all four locations.

### WAHWEAP LODGE

Box 1597 • Page, AZ 86040 • (520) 645–2433
lakepowell@aramark.com • www.visitlakepowell.com

Wahweap Lodge offers 350 rooms as part of a marina resort complex on Lake Powell, just north of Page, Arizona. Wahweap (an Indian term for "bitter water") also offers twenty-five less expensive rooms at Lake Powell Motel, which sits on a bluff overlooking Lake Powell, 2.5 miles west of the lodge. The lodge comprises a separate registration building and eight identical two-story lodging buildings laid out in a V formation along a peninsula on Lake Powell. The landscaped stucco buildings are finished and decorated in a Southwest design. The complex also has two swimming pools, a gas station, a restaurant, snack bar, lounge, and a grocery/gift shop. An RV park and campground are a short distance away. A very large marina complex is beside the lodge, which is situated directly on Lake Powell.

All 350 spacious rooms (other than the two suites) in Wahweap Lodge are identical except for beds and vistas. The majority have two queen-size beds, while forty-three rooms have one king-size bed. All of the rooms have heat, air-conditioning, a television, a telephone, a full bath, a desk, a table, three chairs, a refrigerator, coffeemaker, blow dryer, and an alarm

# GLEN CANYON NATIONAL RECREATION AREA

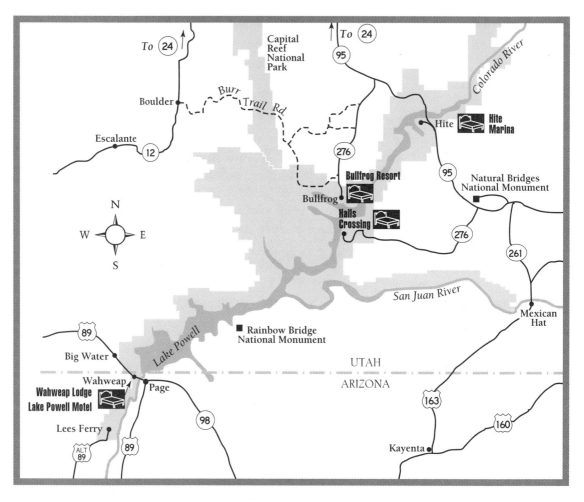

*Wahweap Lodge*

clock. Each room has a private balcony or patio with chairs. Each building is constructed with rooms on both sides and access through an interior corridor that runs the length of the building. Four rooms are fully handicap accessible. Half the rooms face Lake Powell; the other half face the large central parking area. Although the lakeside rooms cost $10 per night extra, you may feel that the lake view is well worth the additional expense. The two suites each have a bedroom with one king-size bed and a living room with a wet bar. An extra-large balcony wraps around the room. Each room in the suites has a television.

The Lake Powell Motel is 2.5 miles west of the lodge complex. The two-story stucco building faces the lake but is some distance from both the lake and any facilities. Twenty-four basic rooms each have two queen-size beds, a television, a telephone, a small table, two chairs, and a full bath. A front sliding glass door provides access to each room. One suite on the first floor has a bedroom with two queen-size beds and a separate living room. It also has a full bathroom, kitchen (with utensils), telephone, television, refrigerator, and microwave. The suite has a private backyard with a grill. No restaurant is at the motel.

Wahweap Lodge offers most of the amenities one expects at a lakeside resort, including conference facilities with meeting and banquet rooms. Two swimming pools, a pool bar, and an outdoor spa are part of the lodge complex. The registration building contains a large gift shop, a tour desk, an attractive full-service restaurant, a lounge, and a special Navajo Room that during summer serves an evening buffet accompanied by Native American entertainment. The Navajo Room is used as a meeting room during the off-season. The lobby area has a stone fireplace and chairs and sofas for relaxing. The main restaurant is a tiered circular dining room with a wall of windows that present a panoramic view of the lake. Various types of boats, from canoes to 59-foot houseboats, can be rented at the marina. A variety of half- and full-day boat tours can be arranged in the lobby of the registration building. Air tours are available at the Page Airport. Special packages that include a boat tour and room at the lodge are available. A gas station and general store are nearby.

- **ROOMS:** Doubles, triples, and quads. All rooms have private baths with a combination shower-tub. Four rooms are handicap accessible.

- **RESERVATIONS:** Lake Powell Resorts & Marinas, P.O. Box 56909, Phoenix, AZ 85079. Phone (800) 528–6154 or, from the greater Phoenix area, (602) 278–8888; fax (602) 331–5258. A deposit of one night's lodging is required. A cancellation notice of twenty-four hours is required for a refund.

- **RATES:** Wahweap Lodge: (high season: January 1 to March 31 and November 1 to December 31/value season April 1 to October 31) standard ($155/$109); lakeview ($165/$116); suite ($275/$275); additional person ($12). Lake Powell Motel: room ($89); suite ($150); additional person ($8.00). Rates quoted are for two adults. Children under eighteen years of age stay free.

- **LOCATION:** Wahweap Lodge is on Highway 89, 6 miles north of Page, Arizona. Lake Powell Motel is 2.5 miles west of the lodge.

- **SEASON:** The lodge is open all year. The heaviest season is during the summer months. The motel is open from April 1 to October 31.

- **FOOD:** A full-service restaurant that overlooks the lake serves breakfast ($4.00–$10.00), lunch ($6.00–$10.00), and dinner ($15–$25). Room service is available. Each evening during the summer season, a dinner buffet is served, along with traditional Native American dance entertainment, in the Navajo Room. Itza Pizza provides indoor/outdoor dining or delivery service to your room during the summer season. From April through October the Canyon King paddlewheeler provides breakfast, lunch, and dinner cruises. Advance reservations are required. No food service is available at Lake Powell Motel.

- **TRANSPORTATION:** Regularly scheduled flights to Page, Arizona, operate from Phoenix. Charter flights are available to other cities within the region. Rental cars are available at the airport. From mid-May through mid-October, Wahweap operates scheduled bus service between the lodge and the airport, as well as other destinations in the town of Page. A courtesy shuttle service to various locations around the Wahweap area is offered year-round to lodge guests.

- **FACILITIES:** A general store (with limited groceries), cocktail lounge, gift shop, gas station, two restaurants, pizza parlor, and marina. Two swimming pools and an outdoor spa are at the lodge. A coin-operated laundry is at the nearby RV park. Postal services and stamps are available at the marina. Fax service is available for a fee.

- **ACTIVITIES:** Swimming (two pools and a beach); various outdoor games, including volleyball, badminton, croquet, shuffleboard, and horseshoes; walking and hiking; boat rentals (all sizes); waterskiing; fishing; float trips, half-day and all-day; many water tours of from one hour to all-day; evening campfire programs at Wahweap campground are presented by the National Park Service.

## Additional Lodging Facilities at Glen Canyon National Recreation Area

lakepowell@aramark.com • www.visitlakepowell.com

Although Wahweap Lodge is the major lodging facility at Glen Canyon National Recreation Area, overnight accommodations are offered by the same concessionaire at three other locations. The three facilities are on a much smaller scale than Wahweap and at relatively remote locations in southern Utah. Reservations are made using the same address and phone number listed for Wahweap. All of the locations permit pets.

## BULLFROG RESORT

Box 4055 • Lake Powell, UT 84533 • (801) 684–3000

Bullfrog Resort offers forty-eight lodge rooms at Defiance House Lodge plus eight housekeeping units. The lodge rooms (standard $110/lakeview $120), April 1 to October 31; ($77/$84) November 1 to March 31 are in a single stucco building that sits atop a high bluff overlooking Bullfrog Bay. Both the building, constructed in the early 1980s, and the rooms within are identical to those in Wahweap Lodge. Eight freestanding prefabricated housekeeping units ($180; value season $125 for one to six persons per unit) each contain three bedrooms, two full baths, a living room, a full kitchen, microwave, dishes and utensils for eight people, linens, and a television but no telephone. Pay phones are available. All of the units have heat and air-conditioning. The interiors are attractive and nicely furnished. One housekeeping unit is handicap accessible.

The resort is located at Bullfrog Basin on Utah Highway 276 on the west side of Lake Powell. A toll ferry at Bullfrog crosses the lake. Bullfrog Resort offers a restaurant, liquor store, cocktail lounge, gift shop, and marina. Like the resort, the restaurant is open year-round. It offers cocktails and three meals a day. A fast-food restaurant at the marina is open from Memorial Day through Labor Day. A marina store sells basic food supplies and beverages. A gas station is located at Bullfrog. Ranger programs and a medical clinic operate during summer months. A National Park Service visitor center adjacent to the resort contains exhibits concerning the Colorado Plateau and the evolution of Glen Canyon plant and animal life. A concessionaire offers half- and full-day boat tours during the summer. Boat rental is available.

Lake Powell was created by the Glen Canyon Dam, which is just south of Wahweap. The dam backs up the Colorado River for 200 miles and supplies water and electricity to California, Arizona, and Nevada. Concrete for the dam and power plant was poured around the clock for more than three years. Dam tours once offered have been discontinued indefinitely.

## HALLS CROSSING

Box 5101 • Lake Powell, UT 84533 • (801) 684–7000

Halls Crossing is located on Utah Highway 276 between Blanding and Hanksville. It offers twenty freestanding housekeeping units identical to those at Bullfrog Resort. One unit is handicap accessible. Halls Crossing has auto service, a marina, and a store with limited supplies. Boat rentals and tours are offered. A toll ferry provides continuation of Highway 276. Transportation is available from a small airport 10 miles from Halls Crossing. Rates are the same as at Bullfrog Resort.

## HITE MARINA

Box 501 • Lake Powell, UT 84533 • (801) 684–2278

Hite Marina is off Utah State Highway 95 on the north end of Lake Powell between Blanding and Hanksville. This is the smallest of the four lodging complexes at Lake Powell, offering only five housekeeping units that are identical to those at Bullfrog and Halls Crossing. One housekeeping unit is totally handicap accessible. Hite offers a gas station, a ranger station, a supply store, and a marina where boats can be rented. Rates for housekeeping units are the same as at Bullfrog Resort.

# GRAND CANYON NATIONAL PARK

P.O. Box 129
Grand Canyon, AZ 86023
(928) 638–7888
www.nps.gov/grca

Grand Canyon National Park, covering 1,904 square miles, is one of the most popular parks operated by the National Park Service, especially the South Rim section. The Grand Canyon itself is so spectacular that first-time visitors are likely to think they are viewing a painting. The canyon has been created by massive uplift and the cutting effect of the Colorado River, which originates in the Rocky Mountains. The river now flows nearly a mile below the South Rim and even farther below the higher North Rim. Although the developed areas of the North Rim and the South Rim are separated by only about 10 miles, the distance by road is 214 miles. An alternative is the 21-mile Kaibab Trail, which leads from Yaki Point on the South Rim to within 2 miles of Grand Canyon Lodge on the North Rim. A daily shuttle service (fee charged) is offered between the South Rim and the North Rim.

North Rim or South Rim? The two sides of the Grand Canyon are so different that they share little other than the same canyon and river. The more popular South Rim is open year-round and has easier canyon access, more facilities, and many more visitors. The South Rim offers more eating facilities, more stores, more places to walk, and more people to bump into. Vehicles and people are in constant motion. Things seem to move much more slowly at the North Rim, where services and visitors are limited. The higher elevation of the North Rim results in cooler temperatures and more trees. Vistas from the North Rim seem more intimate, and fewer people will be standing next to you straining for the same view. The North Rim is closed in winter. If you are lucky, you will be able to sample both rims, perhaps on the same trip.

**PARK ENTRANCE FEE:** $20 per vehicle or $10 per person, good for seven days.

## Lodging in Grand Canyon National Park

Grand Canyon National Park has eight lodges, six at the popular South Rim, one on the floor of the canyon, and one at the North Rim. We have also included Moqui Lodge, which is immediately outside the south entrance to the South Rim. Lodging alternatives range from small lodge rooms without a private bath, to rustic cabins, to rooms in a classic historical hotel building. Rates also vary a great deal depending on where you decide to stay (or are able to locate a room). The wide variation in accommodations means that you should have a basic understanding of the alternatives when you call or write for reservations. All the lodges are operated by one concessioner, and reservations are made using the same address and telephone number. The lodges are all very popular, and reservations should, if possible, be made many months in advance. Keep in mind that several motels are a short distance outside the south entrance, which is only 7 miles from Grand Canyon Village and the South Rim.

# SOUTH RIM (SEVEN LODGES)

www.grandcanyonlodges.com

**M**ost visitors reach the South Rim of the Grand Canyon via Highways 180 and 64 from Flagstaff, Arizona. An alternative route via Highway 89 to Highway 64 and the east entrance is longer and slower but offers numerous views of the canyon. The center of activity for the South Rim is Grand Canyon Village, where you will find lodges, cabins, gift shops, restaurants, a large National Park Service visitor center, and the start of numerous tours. Grand Canyon Village is generally very popular, and thus, crowded, partcularly in summer months. Parking is often difficult to find, so grab the first parking space you see and use the free shuttles to get around the South Rim developed area. Shuttles operate year-round in the Grand Canyon Village area and provide access to the new visitors center at Canyon View Information Plaza. The shuttle to Hermits Rest, west of Grand Canyon Village, operates March through November. All shuttles run every fifteen to thirty minutes.

The seven lodges at the South Rim offer very different accommodations. Some are quite rustic, while others are more luxurious. All have their individual charm and prices. Because the lodges are in close proximity, most of the facilities, activities, and reservation information are described in the following section. All of the restaurants, gift shops, and guided walks are equally accessible no matter where you choose to stay, especially in view of the free shuttle.

- **RESERVATIONS:** Grand Canyon National Park Lodges, Amfac Parks and Resorts, 14001 East Iliff Avenue, Suite 300, Aurora, CO 80014. Phone (303) 297–2757; fax (303) 297–3175; or visit the websites www.amfac.com or www.grandcanyonlodges.com. The cost of the first night's lodging is required as a deposit. Cancellation notice of forty-eight hours is required for a full refund. Reservations may be made up to twenty-three months in advance. Try to make reservations six or more months in advance for the busy summer months. Space is often available on short notice because of cancellations.

- **FOOD:** A variety of restaurants and snack bars are scattered around Grand Canyon Village. Inexpensive cafeterias are at Maswik and Yavapai Lodges, while an elegant and expensive restaurant is at El Tovar. Excellent steaks are served at The Arizona Room. A very nice restaurant is located in Bright Angel Lodge. Make reservations early at El Tovar. The Arizona Room does not take reservations. A full-service grocery store, bank, and post office are located at Market Plaza.

- **TRANSPORTATION:** Commuter air service from Phoenix, Los Angeles, and Las Vegas is available to Grand Canyon Airport at Tusayan, 6 miles south of the park visitor center. Rental cars are at the airport, and hourly shuttles operate between the airport and Grand Canyon Village. Air service from Phoenix is also available on America West or Delta to Flagstaff, where several rental car agencies operate. Train service on Amtrak is available to Flagstaff and Williams.

- **FACILITIES:** Grand Canyon Village *is* truly a village. It includes a full-service grocery store, a post office, a full-service bank, a laundry, gift shops, emergency medical and dental services, bookstores, film processing, an ice cream shop, and an array of restaurants. An auto service garage is available, and gasoline is available in Tusayan and at Desert View, but not in Grand Canyon Village.

# GRAND CANYON NATIONAL PARK

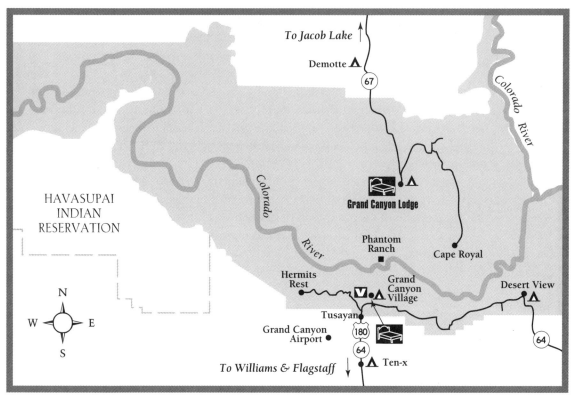

# GRAND CANYON VILLAGE

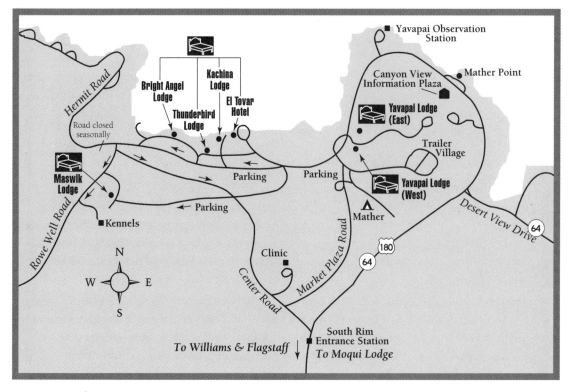

■ **ACTIVITIES:** A variety of activities begin in the village. Shorter narrated motor coach tours of various sites along the South Rim are offered. Additional activities, some of which begin outside the village, include river raft excursions, hiking, mule rides to Plateau Point and to the canyon floor, horseback riding, and helicopter and airplane trips over the canyon. The National Park Service offers programs on the history and geology of the park throughout the day and evening. A fall chamber music festival is offered annually in September. Make the new Canyon View Information Plaza an early stop so you can plan your visit.

## BRIGHT ANGEL LODGE

*Historic Cabin at Bright Angel Lodge*

Bright Angel Lodge is a complex consisting of a main registration building plus eighteen cabins and dormitory-style buildings that provide a total of eighty-nine rooms. The buildings with lodging are separate from but adjacent to the main registration building, which also houses a tour desk, gift shop, lounge, steak house, and restaurant. The complex is at the center of South Rim activity and handy to the other hotels, eating facilities, and gift shops. This area of Grand Canyon Village is very busy with people and traffic, which makes it a hectic setting for individuals and families intent on discovering nature. On the plus side, Bright Angel provides some of the least expensive rooms on the South Rim and the cabins retain a flavor of the South Rim's historic nature.

Bright Angel Lodge provides three types of rooms. All have heat but no air-conditioning, which typically isn't needed. The least expensive "standard," or "lodge," rooms are in Powell Lodge and Bucky Lodge, two dormitory-style buildings. Thirty-eight basic rooms each offer one double bed and a telephone. Some also have a television. Some of the rooms have a full bath, while others have a shower or tub. Likewise, some have a sink and a toilet, while some have only a sink. Common bath and shower facilities are in the hallway. These rooms

> The oldest surviving structure on the South Rim is Bucky O'Neill's cabin, which was constructed in the early 1890s. O'Neill, a prospector-turned-tourism promoter, was killed in Cuba while serving as a member of Theodore Roosevelt's Rough Riders. The cabin was preserved by Mary Colter, architect of Bright Angel Lodge, who incorporated the structure into her design for one of the lodge buildings. Today the cabin is rented to guests as the "Bucky Suite."

are particularly popular with hikers who want a relatively inexpensive place to crash after returning from a trek through the canyon.

One step up are thirty-eight rooms in sixteen wooden or wood-and-stucco buildings called historic cabins. Some of these buildings have a single cabin, while others have two, three, or four cabin-style rooms. Although the exteriors are very rustic, the interiors are nicely furnished and comfortable. Each of the cabins has a television and telephone. Some have a full bath, while others have a shower only. The most expensive rooms in Bright Angel are fifteen rim cabins that offer a view of the Grand Canyon. These rooms are situated in several buildings beside a paved walking trail along the rim. Rim cabins each have one queen-size bed, a full bath, a refrigerator, a telephone, and a television. Some also have a fireplace. A single "Bucky Suite" has two rooms with a king-size bed, a refrigerator, a wet bar, a television, and a telephone. The suite rents for three to four times the cost of other lodging at Bright Angel.

Bright Angel Lodge is a handy location for all the activities and facilities the South Rim offers. The main registration building, which is a short walk from all of the Bright Angel lodging buildings, has a gift shop, lounge, fountain ice cream shop, and restaurant. A wooden thunderbird hangs above a giant stone fireplace in the lobby. Although none of the rooms are directly on the rim and most don't offer a view of it, spectacular vistas of the canyon are only a few steps from any of the buildings. Other dining facilities, including a cafeteria, a steak house, and the most elegant dining room on the South Rim, are a reasonable walk from any of the rooms at Bright Angel. Parking can be a problem in the busy season, when a relatively large parking lot directly in front of the lodge is packed. Parking spaces scattered among the cabins can generally be counted on to yield a few empty slots, although they may not be directly outside your room.

> The original Bright Angel Hotel was constructed in 1895 to serve stagecoach passengers passing through this area. In 1905 the hotel became Bright Angel Camp, which eventually included cabins and an adjoining tent village to serve tourists who were attracted by the canyon's spectacular scenery. In 1935 the Fred Harvey Company replaced the camp with today's Bright Angel Lodge.

- **ROOMS:** Singles and doubles. Rollaways are available. All but rooms in the two lodge buildings have full private baths. The two lodge buildings with standard cabins have common baths and showers. There are no handicap-accessible rooms at Bright Angel Lodge.

- **RATES:** Standard rooms ($60); historic cabins ($70); rim cabins ($100–$121); suite ($235). Each additional person is $7.00 per night.

- **LOCATION:** On the South Rim at the center of activity in Grand Canyon Village.

- **SEASON:** Rooms at Bright Angel Lodge are open year-round.

■ **FOOD:** A full-service restaurant is inside the main registration building and convenient to all the rooms (dinner $4.00–$15.00). The restaurant is open daily from 6:30 A.M. to 10:00 P.M., and alcoholic beverages are served. The Bright Angel Fountain, open May through September, directly outside the registration building, offers hot dogs, soft drinks, and ice cream. A fine steak house offering steaks, poultry, and seafood is attached to the east end of the Bright Angel registration building (dinner $12–$25). Open only for dinner, this restaurant serves great steaks.

## EL TOVAR HOTEL

*El Tovar Hotel*

El Tovar is the regal hotel of the Grand Canyon's South Rim. Constructed in 1905 by the Santa Fe Railroad to promote the firm's transportation services, the hotel was named after Spanish explorer Pedro de Tovar, who led a 1540 expedition to this area. El Tovar is the type of hotel most people envision when they think about a national park lodge. It is a single large wood-and-stone four-story structure that commands a hilltop vista on the canyon rim. The two-story lobby area is complete with log beams, a large stone fireplace, and comfortable sofas and chairs for chatting with other guests. Several verandas and a large covered front porch have rocking chairs for relaxing in the early morning or after dinner or an evening walk. A nice mezzanine with an overlook of the lobby area has tables, stuffed chairs, a television, and a fireplace. Complimentary coffee and tea are served here each morning.

El Tovar offers four classes of accommodations in a total of seventy-eight rooms, all of which are more expensive than any of the other lodging facilities at the South Rim. An extensive renovation of the rooms, dining room, and kitchen was completed in 1998. All the rooms have a full bath with a hairdryer, heat, a telephone, and a television. This is the only hotel in Grand Canyon Village that has cooling units in each room. Although a number of rooms provide good window views, the siting of the hotel results in only a few rooms having an excellent view of the Grand Canyon. The least expensive lodging at El Tovar is a standard double with one double bed in a relatively small room. Standard queen rooms are also small, but the bed type may vary from one queen to one king to two queens. Deluxe rooms are larger and offer either a king- or two queen-size beds with a living area. Eight nonview suites each have one king- or two queen-size beds in one room, plus a separate living room with a couch (some make into a bed), chairs, a refrigerator, and a second television. Some of these suites have a balcony. Four view suites, two on the second floor and two on the third floor, each offer the same accommodations as the nonview suites. The view suites, which should be reserved at least a year in advance, each have a balcony that faces the canyon.

El Tovar provides most of the things you will want or need during a trip to the Grand Canyon. The ground floor has a gift shop, a newsstand, a lounge, and the elegant El Tovar dining room (reservations recommended), which offers an extensive menu in a formal setting. The dining room looks like it belongs in a national park. Murals on the walls reflect customs of different Indian tribes, and a number of tables offer diners a view of the rim. A small private dining room that holds up to ten persons is available at no charge with a forty-eight-hour advance reservation. The lounge has a bar and windows that overlook the canyon. Travel information is available, and tours can be booked at a small tour desk in the lobby across from the registration desk. Service at El Tovar is a cut above that found at other lodging facilities at the Grand Canyon. For example, room service is available from the El Tovar dining room, and mints are placed on your bed each evening. No elevators are in the building, but bellhops are stationed near the registration desk to assist with baggage. A circular drive in front of the hotel is available for registration and baggage drop-off, but parking near the hotel is very limited.

- **ROOMS:** Singles, doubles, triples, and quads. Some suites can sleep up to six, and rollaways are available. All rooms have full baths. There are no handicap-accessible rooms.

- **RATES:** Standard double ($116); standard queen ($130); deluxe ($174); suites (nonview $199–$279); (view $274–$284). Rates quoted are for two adults. Each additional person is $11 per night.

- **LOCATION:** Center of Grand Canyon Village, directly east of Kachina Lodge and just up the hill from the historic train depot.

- **SEASON:** El Tovar Hotel is open year-round.

- **FOOD:** A first-class dining room off the hotel's lobby serves breakfast ($7.00–$10.00), lunch ($7.00–$15.00), and dinner ($20–$25). Alcoholic beverages are available, and reservations are recommended. A lounge is in the lobby area. Other, less expensive food service, is within easy walking distance.

El Tovar Hotel was built to be a first-rate lodging facility, and at its completion, in 1905, many considered it to be the most elegant hotel west of the Mississippi. Designed as a cross between a Swiss chalet and a Norwegian villa, the hotel was constructed of stone and Oregon pine. The building was equipped with a coal-fired steam generator to provide electric lighting, and Santa Fe railroad tank cars brought fresh water from a distance of 120 miles. Hens raised here supplied fresh eggs, and a dairy herd provided milk. Fresh fruit and vegetables were grown in greenhouses on the premises.

# KACHINA LODGE/THUNDERBIRD LODGE

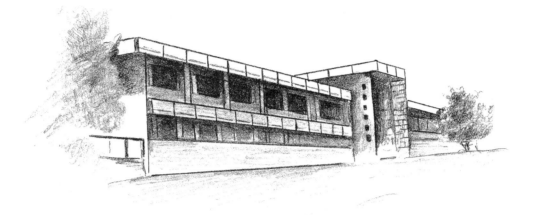

*Kachina Lodge*

Kachina Lodge and Thunderbird Lodge are two virtually identical facilities that sit side by side on the South Rim of Grand Canyon Village between El Tovar Hotel and Bright Angel Lodge. The two-story stone buildings house a total of 104 rooms that, other than the view they provide, are identical. Approximately half the rooms, on the north side, face the rim, while the remainder, on the south side, face the road and parking lot. No registration facilities are in either of the lodges. Registration for Kachina Lodge is at the registration desk of El Tovar Hotel, and registration for Thunderbird Lodge is at the registration desk in the main building of Bright Angel Lodge.

Of all the lodging on the South Rim, Thunderbird and Kachina most resemble what one expects in a standard hotel. In fact, perhaps a better description is that these buildings have the appearance, both inside and outside, of up-scale college dormitories. All rooms in both lodges have heat, a telephone, a television, and two queen-size beds. Rollaways are available but result in a crowded room. All rooms have a full bath with a hairdryer. Thunderbird has only a single row of rooms on the second floor, and all have a window that faces the canyon. Kachina has two rows of rooms on the second floor, and only half face the canyon. Rim-view rooms in both buildings rent for $10 per day extra. Two medium-size conference rooms in Thunderbird can be reserved. Some rooms on the first floor of both buildings are handicap accessible.

Thunderbird and Kachina Lodges are in a convenient location at the center of South Rim activity. On the other hand, the rooms don't have

The Colorado River carved the Grand Canyon over a period of 4 to 6 million years to expose nearly half of the earth's 4.6-billion-year history. The Glen Canyon Dam, constructed in 1964, reduced much of the river's erosive power. Although the Grand Canyon area is now a high-desert plateau, this region once contained numerous seas and mountains as high as the Himalayas. The geologic history of this region lies exposed in the walls of the canyon.

much of the ambience that some people may desire in a national park visit. Once inside a room, you may as well be in Flagstaff or Phoenix. Also, the central location results in insufficient parking during the busy summer season. No information desk or commercial facilities are in either building, but food service, gift shops, and anything else offered at the South Rim is just a short walk from any of the rooms at these two lodges.

- ■ **ROOMS:** Singles, doubles, triples, and quads. All rooms have full baths. There are handicap-accessible rooms at both Kachina and Thunderbird.

- ■ **RATES:** Nonview rooms ($114); view rooms ($124). There's an extra charge of $9.00 per person per night for more than two persons.

- ■ **LOCATION:** On the Rim between El Tovar Hotel and Bright Angel Lodge.

- ■ **SEASON:** All rooms are available year-round.

- ■ **FOOD:** No eating facilities are available in either building. Restaurants and cafeterias are within easy walking distance.

## MASWIK LODGE

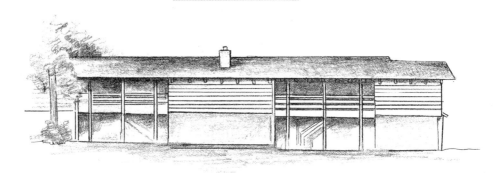

*Maswik North at Maswik Lodge*

Maswik Lodge (named for a Hopi kachina who guards the Grand Canyon) is a complex of modern apartment-type buildings and older cabins that provide 278 rooms in two large areas on each side of a centrally located registration building. All of the buildings with rooms are separate from the main lodge building, which houses registration and eating facilities. All of the rooms and the cabins have two queen-size beds, heat, a telephone, and a television but no air-conditioning. The rooms have a full bath, while the cabins have a bath with shower but no tub. Some rooms in the North Unit are handicap accessible.

The North Unit, nearest the canyon rim, underwent an extensive renovation in 1999/2000. These units, which have ceiling fans, offer the newer and more expensive rooms in a cluster of twelve buildings. Most of the structures in this section are ten- and twelve-unit two-story buildings that resemble small apartments or college housing. Each room runs the depth of the building, with a front window and either a window or a sliding glass door in back. Those with sliding doors have either a patio or a balcony. Two one-story buildings in the North Unit have four and six rooms, respectively. The South Unit comprises six two-story motel-type buildings with smaller rooms that back up to one another. These rooms have no balcony or rear window and rent for about $40 per night less than rooms in the North Unit. Seven rustic quad-style cabin buildings house a total of twenty-eight rooms. These are nice rooms and rent for about half the price of rooms in the North Unit.

The lodge's location on the west side of the village, across the main road from the rim, is relatively peaceful. Staying in Maswik allows you to avoid the hustle and bustle of vehicles and crowds that roam over the rim area and yet remain within easy walking distance of the rim and most facilities in Grand Canyon Village, including hotels, gift shops, and restaurants. Of course, you are unable to view the Grand Canyon from the window of your room, but the same disadvantage exists with many rooms in other complexes closer to the rim. Maswik offers plentiful parking, a considerable advantage if you are driving, because other areas of the village are often very crowded.

The only eating facility at Maswik is a cafeteria in the main lodge building. It offers an extensive menu, and you can also purchase sandwiches, fruit, and snacks when the facility is open, from 6:00 A.M. to 10:00 P.M. Seating is plentiful, and customers move through the food and checkout lines rapidly. The food is typical cafeteria fare and relatively inexpensive, so this is a good place to eat when you are in a hurry. Maswik also offers a full-service sports lounge with a big-screen TV and a tour desk. Other services and food establishments are within easy walking distance of any of the rooms at Maswik.

*Grand Canyon Railway operates a vintage train that offers daily service between Williams, Arizona, and Grand Canyon Village year-round. The 62-mile trip (one-way) from Williams to the canyon takes two and a quarter hours, with departure in the morning. Live entertainment is provided on board. Tours from Grand Canyon Village allow visitors to travel one way in a motorcoach and return on the train. Three classes of service, from coach to a parlor car, are available. The railway offers package plans that include overnight accommodations and meals in the park and in Williams. For information or reservations, call (800) 843–8724.*

- **ROOMS:** Singles, doubles, triples, and quads. All rooms have private baths, most with a combination tub-shower. Maswik North has handicap-accessible rooms.

- **RATES:** Rustic cabins ($63); South Unit ($75); North Unit ($118). Additional person: cabin, $7.00; North and South Units, $9.00.

- **LOCATION:** West side of Grand Canyon Village, approximately a quarter-mile from the canyon rim.

- **SEASON:** All rooms except for cabins (closed in winter) are open year-round.

- **FOOD:** A full-service cafeteria within walking distance of all the rooms offers full meals and snacks from 6:00 A.M. to 10:00 P.M. Additional dining facilities of all types are within walking distance.

## MOQUI LODGE

**M**oqui Lodge (*Moqui* is an Indian term for "vanishing" that was applied to a group of Hopi who fled the tribe and settled this area) provides 136 rooms in a motel-type setting a half mile outside the south entrance to Grand Canyon National Park. The lodge is 3 miles from Grand Canyon Village. We have included Moqui because the facility is managed by the same firm that administers other Grand Canyon lodges and it will be offered as one of the lodging options when you make reservations.

This lodge comprises two large motel-type buildings, one of which is connected to the main A-frame lodge building that faces the highway and houses the registration desk, lobby area, and dining room. The second building has only rooms and is perpendicular to and slightly north of the main lodge building. The two-story wooden buildings that house the rooms in Moqui were built in the 1960s. The main lodge building includes part of the original lodge that was constructed here in the 1920s. The A-frame registration building includes an impressive lobby, highlighted by a massive stone fireplace and huge log ceiling beams. Just off the entrance a nice sitting area is filled with chairs and sofas for relaxing after a day at the canyon. The main lodge building also contains a lounge, a small gift shop, and a unisex hair salon. A gas station is next to the lodge.

Of 136 rooms at Moqui Lodge, 105 have two double beds. The other thirty-one rooms are slightly smaller and contain one double bed. All rooms are decorated in a Southwest motif, with a table, two chairs, a large television, a telephone, and a full bath. All have heat and a large ceiling fan but no air-conditioning. The rooms have an outside entrance with a front window but no back window. There are no balconies or patios. Two rooms on the first floor are fully handicap accessible, including a roll-in shower. Each of the handicap-accessible rooms has a connecting door to an adjoining room. Lodging at Moqui includes a complimentary full breakfast in the lodge dining room. Dinner but not lunch is also served in the dining room. The attractive dining room specializes in Southwestern dishes for dinner, although popular American entrees are also offered. A separate lounge off the lobby area

*Moqui Lodge*

serves beer, wine, and cocktails, beginning at 5:00 P.M.; cocktails are also served in the dining room during dinner. A tour desk in the lobby can provide travel information and book tours.

Moqui Lodge suffers the disadvantage of being 3 miles from the main activity area of the South Rim. Guests with a vehicle must drive to Grand Canyon Village, where parking is at a premium. Alternative transportation is available on a private shuttle (fee charged) that operates between the town of Tusayan (and Grand Canyon Airport) and the South Rim. The shuttle makes stops at Moqui on request. If you consider the location to be a problem, you should attempt to obtain a room at one of the other lodges. On the other hand, the remote location proves to be relatively quiet, especially during the daytime, when most guests are at the canyon. Moqui is also close to the town of Tusayan, which offers restaurants, fast food, a grocery, and a gas station.

*Many visitors to Grand Canyon National Park decide to take an air tour of the canyon. Several airline and helicopter companies in the town of Tusayan and at the Grand Canyon Airport offer scenic flights over the canyon. The helicopter tours are generally shorter and somewhat more expensive than flights in fixed-wing aircraft but add extra excitement to the trip. Most firms offer several types of tours of various lengths. Any of the tours presents a very different perspective of the Grand Canyon. Prices begin at about $75 per person.*

- **ROOMS:** Singles, doubles, triples, and quads. All rooms have a private bath. Two rooms are handicap accessible.

- **RATES:** All rooms ($94), which includes breakfast. Each additional person is $12.

- **LOCATION:** Moqui Lodge is on Highway 64, a half mile south of the south entrance to Grand Canyon National Park.

- **SEASON:** The lodge is open from Presidents' Day through the end of November.

- **FOOD:** A dining room in the main lodge building specializes in Southwestern food but offers a full dinner menu ($7.00–$15.00) from 6:00 to 10:00 P.M. A complimentary full American breakfast is offered each morning for lodge guests. The dining room is closed from 10:00 A.M. to 6:00 P.M. On Friday and Saturday nights, June through August, a Western Cookout is offered for $21.95.

## YAVAPAI LODGE

Yavapai Lodge is a complex of sixteen buildings a short distance from a separate registration building that houses a gift shop and large cafeteria. The sixteen buildings with lodging are in two separate clusters. Yavapai Lodge is located on the east side of Grand Canyon Village near Market Plaza and the new National Park Service Visitor Center, between Yavapai Point and El Tovar. It is a moderate walk from the rim of the Grand Canyon. Although the lodge is not in the center of Grand Canyon Village activity, free shuttle transportation to various points in the village is available.

*Yavapai West at Yavapai Lodge*

Yavapai Lodge, with 358 rooms, is the largest lodging complex in Grand Canyon National Park. The facility is divided into two separate complexes composed of very different styles of buildings. The newest (constructed in the mid-1970s) and more expensive rooms are in Yavapai East. Six two-story wooden buildings each contain thirty-three spacious rooms that have two double beds, a telephone, a television, a full bath, heat, and a fan but no air-conditioning. The buildings have an outside staircase that leads to an inside corridor with access to the rooms. A large window in each room provides a nice view of the pine and juniper woodlands in which the buildings sit. None of the rooms have balconies or patios. The buildings, which sit well back from large parking areas, have the appearance of a nice apartment complex. Handicap-accessible rooms are available both here and in the Yavapai West complex.

At the bottom of Grand Canyon, Phantom Ranch provides food and overnight accommodations for hikers, rafters, and mule riders. Cabin accommodations are included with two-day mule tours, while dormitory-style lodging and a limited number of cabins are available to backpackers. The ranch was originally constructed in 1922, and dormitories were added in 1976. Space is limited, so plan to make reservations (phone 303–297–2757; fax 303–297–3175) well in advance for both lodging and food service. Reservations are accepted up to twenty-three months in advance.

Ten buildings in the slightly less expensive Yavapai West were constructed in the late 1960s and have the appearance of a motel. These one-story brick buildings each contain sixteen rooms with two queen-size beds, a telephone, a television, a daybed, and a full bath. The rooms are quite small compared with rooms in Yavapai East. Plenty of parking is immediately in front of each structure, and the buildings are widely spaced in two large circles and surrounded by woodlands. Rooms are accessed via a front door that faces the parking lot. The rooms have a window but no balcony in the rear. Rooms in buildings 7 to 10 have larger back windows that provide a good outside view.

Yavapai Lodge provides a relatively quiet setting and plenty of parking, two items that are in short supply in most other lodging units in the park. With the free shuttle service throughout the village area, Yavapai's location outside the main activity area isn't a significant disadvantage. Also, Yavapai is convenient to the Canyon View Information Plaza and to Market Plaza, which contains a post office, a bank, a general store with a relatively large grocery selection, and a large cafeteria with reasonable prices. The larger rooms in Yavapai East are worth the extra $15 per day compared with the older rooms in Yavapai West. If you don't mind climbing a few stairs, ask for a second-floor room for more privacy and a better view.

- **ROOMS:** Doubles, triples, and quads. All rooms have a full bath. Handicap-accessible rooms are available at both Yavapai East and Yavapai West.

- **RATES:** Yavapai East ($102); Yavapai West ($88). Rates quoted are for two adults. Each additional person is $9.00 per night.

- **LOCATION:** On the east side of Grand Canyon Village, across from Market Plaza.

- **SEASON:** Yavapai Lodge is open from mid-March through November. Rooms are also available seasonally at Thanksgiving and Christmas.

- **FOOD:** A nice large cafeteria is a moderate walk from both Yavapai East and Yavapai West. A general merchandise store at Market Plaza offers a full line of grocery items, including beer, wine, and other alcoholic beverages.

# NORTH RIM

Visiting the North Rim of Grand Canyon National Park makes you feel you are in an entirely different park compared with a visit to the South Rim, except, of course, for the Grand Canyon itself, which is the common thread dividing these two areas. With fewer visitors, the North Rim provides fewer facilities and is much more relaxing to visit than the South Rim. Also, the North Rim offers only a single lodge in which to stay. The address, phone number, activities, and facilities for Grand Canyon Lodge are different from those for the seven lodges on the South Rim discussed above.

## GRAND CANYON LODGE

North Rim, AZ 86052 • (928) 638–2611

www.grandcanyonnorthrim.com

Grand Canyon Lodge is the only lodging facility at Grand Canyon National Park's North Rim. The lodge consists of a classic main lodge building that houses the registration desk, lobby, and dining room, and more than 200 cabin units scattered along a peninsula of the Kaibab Plateau. The peninsula is surrounded by two spectacular canyons that snake off the Grand Canyon, which can be viewed at the tip of the peninsula. All of the rooms are in buildings that are separate from but within walking distance of the main lodge, which itself has no overnight rooms. The lodge is at the end of Highway 67, which leads into the park from Jacob Lake.

The main lodge building at the North Rim was constructed in 1936, after the original lodge burned. It is what every national park lodge should look like. It was designed by Gilbert

*Western Cabin at Grand Canyon Lodge (North Rim)*

Stanley Underwood, who also served as architect for the Ahwahnee Hotel at Yosemite National Park and the lodge at Bryce Canyon National Park. The U-shaped building is constructed of massive limestone walls and timber beams and is situated on the canyon rim near Bright Angel Point. The spectacular high-ceilinged dining room provides wonderful vistas of the canyon. A large sunroom that provides canyon views through three huge windows is just off the registration area. A veranda off the sunroom provides an area where guests can enjoy equally spectacular views from wooden rocking chairs. The building has two huge stone fireplaces, one in the sunroom and the other outside on the veranda. The lodge also houses a tour desk, snack shop, gift shop, post office, and coffee shop/saloon.

More than a hundred rustic log cabins constructed in the 1920s provide 205 rooms for visitors. Four basic types of rooms are offered. Fifty-one Western Cabins and four Western cabins that face the canyon are constructed either two or four to a building. These are log cabins with finished interiors and vaulted log-beamed ceilings. All have a fireplace and private front porch, two queen-size beds, a full bath, a desk, a table, chairs, heat, and a telephone. These are the largest and nicest units at the North Rim. Two Western Cabins are handicap accessible. Eighty-three small Frontier Cabins are constructed two units to a building. Each unit has one double and one single bed, a private bath with shower, a telephone, heat, and a desk and chair. Two Frontier Cabins with one double bed are handicap accessible. Twenty-seven Pioneer Cabins each have two bedrooms, one on each side of a shared small bath. The Pioneer Cabins have a telephone, heat, and a private bath with a shower but no tub. One bedroom in each cabin has two single beds, and the other bedroom has a double and a single bed. Relatively steep cement walks lead to some of the Pioneer Cabins. Two motel-type wooden buildings provide a total of forty rooms that were remodeled in 1999. All the motel rooms have one queen-size bed, desk, chair, telephone, heat, and private bath with shower but no tub.

We recommend the Western Cabins, which are slightly more expensive but offer more room and a nicer interior. Four of these units sit next to the canyon rim and provide impressive views from the windows and a private front porch. Cabins 301, 305, 306, and 309 are rim-view units that rent for about $10 extra per day. Cabins 310, 320, and 332 also offer a nice view and rent for the regular rate. The Pioneer Cabins farthest from the road (and parking) offer the best views. Choose units 98, 107, 117, 127, 135, or 142 if this is what you are seeking. If you choose the motel, try to obtain a room on the back side, which provides better views. Motel units 415, 416, 432, and 433 are larger than other motel units in the same building but rent for the same price.

Most of the lodging units, especially the cabins, are some distance from parking. In addition, visitors (other than handicapped) are not permitted to drive to the main lodge that houses the registration desk. You should park in any open spot, walk down the road to the main lodge, and check in at the registration desk before removing any luggage from your vehicle. Once you determine the location of your assigned unit (a diagram of the lodging complex is available at the registration desk), you may want to move your vehicle to a different parking place closer to where you will be staying. Porters are available to help with luggage.

Grand Canyon Lodge offers everything you will need for an enjoyable vacation. The main lodge building houses a large gift shop, a coffee shop (morning)/saloon (afternoon and evening), a post office, and a snack shop. The beauty of the dining room is surpassed only by the dining room in Yosemite's Ahwahnee. A gas station and laundry facilities are near the campground, 1 mile north of the lodge. The campground also has a store that sells groceries, camping supplies, and fast food. Several hiking trails originate near the lodge, and guests can enjoy mule rides and evening programs. Guided hikes are provided by the National Park Service.

Construction for the North Rim's original Grand Canyon Lodge was completed in the winter of 1927 and opened for its first guests in 1928. The lodge was constructed by the Union Pacific Railroad, which wanted destinations to compete with hotels constructed by the Santa Fe Railroad on the canyon's South Rim. The Union Pacific bused passengers to lodges in Bryce Canyon, Zion, and the North Rim from the train station at Cedar City. The main lodge building on the North Rim burned to the foundation in 1932. Today's lodge, based on the original, was completed in 1937.

- **ROOMS:** Doubles, triples, and quads in the Western Cabins and the motel units. Doubles and triples in the Frontier Cabins. Pioneer Cabins are priced for four occupants. All rooms have private baths, although only the Western Cabins offer bathtubs. Two Western and two Frontier Cabins are handicap accessible.

- **RESERVATIONS:** Amfac Parks and Resorts, 14001 East Iliff Avenue, Suite 300, Aurora, CO 80014. Phone (303) 297–2757; fax (303) 297–3175; www.grandcanyonnorthrim.com. The cost of the first night's lodging is required as a deposit. Cancellation notice of forty-eight hours is required for a full refund. Reservations may be made up to twenty-three months in advance.

- **RATES:** Western Cabins ($95); Western Cabins with rim view ($105); Frontier Cabins ($80); Pioneer Cabins ($93); motel units ($87). Rates quoted are for two adults. Each additional person is $10 per night. Children sixteen and under stay free. Rollaways in Western Cabins and some motel rooms are $10.

- **LOCATION:** Forty miles south on Highway 67 from the town of Jacob Lake, Arizona.

- **SEASON:** The lodge is open from mid-May to mid-October.

- **FOOD:** An excellent restaurant with spectacular views offers three full meals a day. Breakfast is from 6:30 to 10:00 A.M., lunch from 11:30 A.M. to 2:30 P.M., and dinner ($12–$20) from 5:00 to 9:30 P.M. Reservations are required for dinner and should be made immediately upon arrival or before arrival by calling the lodge. The Cafe on the Rim serves sandwiches, pizza, and beverages, and is open from 7:00 A.M. to 9:00 P.M. The coffee shop/saloon offers gourmet coffee and rolls each morning beginning at 5:30 A.M. Limited groceries and a snack bar are available 1 mile away at the campground.

- **TRANSPORTATION:** Scheduled air service is available to Kanab, Utah, and Page, Arizona, where rental cars are available. A daily shuttle (fee required) is offered between the North Rim and the South Rim.

- **FACILITIES:** A gift shop, information desk, post office, full-service restaurant, coffee shop/saloon, and snack bar are at the main lodge. A cafe, grocery, laundry facilities, and gas station are 1 mile north at the campground.

- **ACTIVITIES:** Hiking, mule rides, horse rides, evening interpretive program, and guided nature walks. Several short- and intermediate-length trails originate near the lodge.

# CALIFORNIA

**STATE TOURIST INFORMATION**
(800) 862–2543
www.gocalif.com

## DEATH VALLEY NATIONAL PARK

Death Valley, CA 92328
(760) 786–2331
www.nps.gov/deva/

Death Valley National Park comprises 3.3 million acres of harsh desert environment that includes the lowest point in the Western Hemisphere. The park features a desert mansion, ruins of old mining towns, abandoned borax works, mountain peaks, volcanic craters, and some of the highest summer temperatures you have ever encountered. The visitor center is at Furnace Creek. The major part of Death Valley National Park is in southeastern California. The main road is California Highway 190, which provides access to many of the major features and activity areas.

**PARK ENTRANCE FEE:** $10.00 per vehicle or $5.00 per person, good for seven days.

### Lodging in Death Valley National Park

Four lodging facilities in Death Valley National Park range from exquisite and expensive to quaint and moderately priced. Furnace Creek Inn, Furnace Creek Ranch, and Stovepipe Wells Village are each operated by Amfac Parks & Resorts. The first two are near one another and

## Death Valley Temperature Extremes (°Fahrenheit)

|  | Jan. | Feb. | March | April | May | June | July | Aug. | Sept. | Oct. | Nov. | Dec. |
|---|---|---|---|---|---|---|---|---|---|---|---|---|
| *Record high* | 87 | 97 | 102 | 111 | 120 | 128 | 134 | 127 | 129 | 113 | 97 | 88 |
| *Ave. daily high* | 65 | 72 | 80 | 90 | 99 | 109 | 115 | 113 | 106 | 92 | 76 | 65 |
| *Ave. daily low* | 39 | 46 | 53 | 62 | 71 | 80 | 88 | 85 | 75 | 62 | 48 | 39 |
| *Record low* | 15 | 27 | 30 | 35 | 42 | 49 | 52 | 65 | 41 | 32 | 24 | 19 |

# DEATH VALLEY NATIONAL PARK

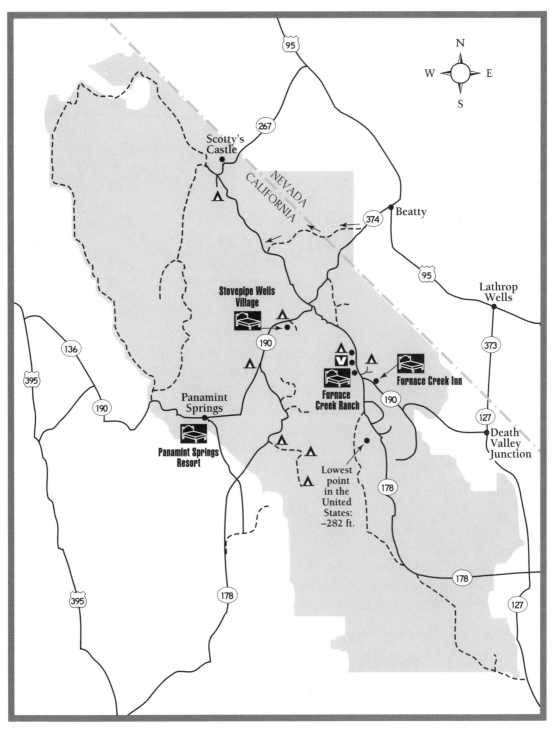

remain under private ownership. Stovepipe Wells Village is owned by the National Park Service and operated as a concesssion. Stovepipe Wells Village is quite isolated, which may make it more or less desirable than the Furnace Creek facilities, depending on your taste. Privately owned Panamint Springs Resort, a small facility near the park's western boundary, only recently became the fourth lodging facility, when Death Valley National Park was expanded.

## FURNACE CREEK INN

P.O. Box 1 • Death Valley, CA 92328 • (760) 786–2361
www.furnacecreekresort.com

*Furnace Creek Inn*

Furnace Creek Inn may be the most elegant hotel located in a National Park Service–administered area, and it is certainly one of the most unique lodging facilities in the United States. Located in the middle of one of the country's most inhospitable environ-ments, the AAA-rated, four-diamond inn has retained its original grandeur. Pacific Coast Borax Company commenced construction of the hotel in the early 1920s to accommodate the increasing number of visitors to Death Valley. Improvements and additions continued into the mid-1930s. Furnace Creek Inn was purchased by Fred Harvey in 1969. The inn is built of stone and adobe in a Mission-style architecture. It sits on a hill overlooking a desolate but starkly beautiful desert that encompasses both the lowest point in the Western Hemisphere (282 feet below sea level) and the Panamint Mountain Range, which soars to more than 11,000 feet. Furnace Creek Inn is situated on the back side of an oasis of green grass and palm trees complete with stone walkways, a stream, and ponds on a terraced hillside. Services include shuttle service to Furnace Creek Ranch or the nearby airstrip, seasonal room service, and seasonal massage therapy. A large conference room with stone walls, beamed ceiling, and large windows that face the swimming pool has stone fireplaces at each end. A bar at the end of the pool serves beverages and snacks in season.

Furnace Creek Inn offers a total of sixty-six rooms, all of which were remodeled in 1998. The rooms are rented in five categories according to size, view, and amenities. Each of the rooms has heat, air-conditioning, a ceiling fan, a refrigerator, telephone, and a television. The least expensive nonview Hillside rooms generally have one king-size bed and no view. Similar rooms with a view rent for about $20 extra. Larger Deluxe view rooms and Luxury view rooms with a spa tub are also available. Two suites each have a living room with a sofa bed and a bedroom with one king-size bed. Second-floor rooms in the north wing have balconies. Rooms in the main building and in one wing are accessed from interior back hallways, so most of the rooms have a view out the front (toward the west) of the building. An elevator for guests is in the main building. Handicap access is available to the hotel and some rooms. One of the unique rooms at Furnace Creek Inn is room 199, which is isolated from other rooms and requires decending several staircases. It is located on the second floor of a separate building with a private outside staircase to the swimming pool. The room has stone walls and a beamed ceiling.

The rumor is that room 199 at Furnace Creek Inn, the Pool Bungalow is haunted by a ghost, most probably the former chef. The inn's maids claim to have made up the room, closed the curtains, and turned off the lights, only to find the curtains open and the lights on again soon after they had left. Despite the ghost story, this room remains much in demand, so you will need to make an early reservation in order to check if the rumor is really fact.

Furnace Creek Inn has about anything you will need for a first-class (and expensive) vacation. The attractive, spring-fed swimming pool offers a respite from the summer heat. Four lighted tennis courts, a nearby eighteen-hole golf course, horseback riding (mid-October through mid-May), and hiking are available for sports-minded visitors. A first-class hotel dining room serves three meals a day. Two other restaurants at nearby Furnace Creek Ranch can be reached by hotel shuttle. A lounge is located off the lobby at the inn. The Death Valley National Park Service visitor center, with exhibits and naturalist talks, is about 2 miles from the inn.

- **ROOMS:** Doubles, plus a limited number of triples and quads. All rooms have a private bath, many with a combination shower-tub. A few of the inn's rooms are handicap-accessible.

- **RESERVATIONS:** Furnace Creek Inn & Ranch Resort, P.O. Box 1, Death Valley, CA 92328. Phone central reservations (800) 236–7916 or on site (760) 786–2345; fax (760) 786–2514; www.furnacecreekresort.com. Cost of the first night's lodging is required as a deposit. Cancellation of forty-eight hours required for full refund.

- **RATES:** High season (mid-October through mid-May, except April and holidays)/low season (remainder of the year, except April and holidays): Hillside ($230/$155); View ($250/$175); Deluxe View ($275/$190); Luxury View ($315/$210), including spa); suites ($330/$225). Holidays and April are higher. Rates are for two persons. Additional person is $20; cribs and rollaways, $20. Children seventeen and under stay free. Senior discounts are available.

- **LOCATION:** Furnace Creek Inn is 120 miles northwest of Las Vegas and 300 miles northeast of Los Angeles.

- **SEASON:** The inn is open all year. The high season is spring until two weeks after Easter. It is also very busy in July, August, and all holidays.

- **FOOD:** Diners are treated to a scenic view of the Panamint Mountains from the elegant Inn Dining Room, which offers a complete menu for breakfast, lunch, and dinner mid-October to mid-May. (Lunch is not served in the summer season.) Entrée prices range from $20 to $30. Two less expensive restaurants at nearby Furnace Creek Ranch are described in the write-up of that facility.

- **TRANSPORTATION:** The nearest major airport is in Las Vegas, where rental cars are available. The resort has a concrete airstrip with lights for private planes. Transportation from the airstrip is available (contact the inn in advance).

- **FACILITIES:** The inn has a large, spring-fed swimming pool (constant 82° Farenheit), a sauna, massage therapy (mid-October through mid-May), four lighted tennis courts, a restaurant, a lobby-lounge, a gift shop, and four meeting rooms, two of which can be used as banquet rooms. A gas station and general store are at Furnace Creek Ranch.

- **ACTIVITIES:** Swimming, tennis, and golf (year-round); horseback riding, group hay rides, and carriage rides (mid-October to mid-May). The National Park Service offers interpretive programs throughout the park.

## FURNACE CREEK RANCH

P.O. Box 1 • Death Valley, CA 92328 • (760) 786–2345
www.furnacecreekresort.com

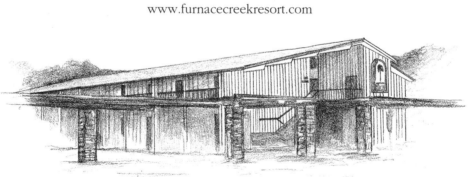

*Deluxe Units at Furnace Creek Ranch*

Furnace Creek Ranch is the family alternative to the more expensive and elegant Furnace Creek Inn. Located in an oasis area of Furnace Creek, about 1.5 miles from the inn, Furnace Creek Ranch offers a total of 224 rooms in three classifications of accommodations. The buildings sit amid tall palm and tamarisk trees, with an eighteen-hole golf course at one end. The ranch offers more activities and eating places than the more famous inn. A small building just to the right of the stone entrance gate houses the registration desk. Inside the gate and to the left in a western-style wooden building are a general store, a saloon, and two restaurants. An ice cream shop is on the right (seasonal). Lodging rooms are in six one- and two-story motel-type buildings behind the restaurant building, plus fourteen freestanding wood cabins beside the registration building. All of the buildings with overnight rooms are within easy walking distance of the registration building and restaurants. Plentiful parking is available near each of the buildings.

All of the rooms at Furnace Creek Ranch have heat, air-conditioning, television, and telephone. One hundred and sixty-four Deluxe rooms are in four two-story wooden buildings constructed in the 1960s. These buildings have an entrance at each end, with access to the rooms through an interior corridor. Second-floor rooms each have a balcony, and rooms on the bottom floor have a patio. Each Deluxe room has two double beds, a refrigerator, a desk, two chairs, a dresser, and a nightstand. Half the 164 rooms face either the golf course or a grassy area surrounding the swimming pool. Rooms on the opposite side of each building face one another. All these rooms rent for the same price, so try for one with a view toward the golf course.

Two one-story wood buildings contain thirty-two Parkside rooms, which each have a sliding glass patio door on the back side that opens to a large grassy area near the swimming pool. These rooms rent for about $20 per night above the rate for rooms in the two-story units. Parkside rooms may be a little bigger but are priced higher because they have recently been refurbished and offer closer access to the swimming area. Parking is immediately outside the front door of these units.

*Furnace Creek Golf Course, at Furnace Creek Ranch, is situated 214 feet below sea level, which qualifies it as the lowest grass golf course in the world. The course was opened in 1931 and, during the early years, closed each summer when it was leased to a cattle rancher. A small flock of sheep kept the course mowed during winter months. The 6,215-foot course was renovated in 1997 by Peter Dye. Even though the course lies in the middle of a desert, nine of its eighteen holes have water hazards.*

Twenty-eight newly remodeled Cabin units are constructed two to a building. Each has two double beds and a bath with a shower but no bathtub. The Cabin units are nicely done but quite a bit smaller than the Deluxe or Parkside rooms.

Furnace Creek Ranch provides all the facilities you will need for a comfortable stay in Death Valley National Park. Best of all, the facilities are near the rooms. The golf course, the Borax Museum with interesting displays, and the National Park Service visitor center are a walk from any of the rooms. If you desire a special dinner, take the free shuttle or drive a little more than a mile to the Furnace Creek Inn. You can play golf in the morning on the newly renovated course, swim in the afternoon in a spring-fed pool, have a beer in the saloon, take a nap, and walk to a restaurant without ever getting in your vehicle. Keep in mind that some of these things are easier to handle in the spring, winter, and fall than in the heat of the summer. On the other hand, this is a great place to spend a spring weekend, when daytime temperatures are more reasonable.

- ■ **ROOMS:** Doubles, triples, and quads. All rooms have a private bath with a combination shower-tub except the cabins, which have only a shower. Handicap-accessible rooms are available in both the Deluxe and Parkside units.

- **RESERVATIONS:** Furnace Creek Inn & Ranch Resort, P.O. Box 1, Death Valley, CA 92328. Phone central reservations (800) 236–7916 or on site (760) 786–2345; fax (760) 786–2514. Cost of the first night's lodging is required as a deposit. Cancellation of forty-eight hours required for full refund.

- **RATES:** High season/low season cabins ($102/$97), Deluxe ($133/$128), and Parkside ($154/$149). Rates quoted are for two adults. Children under eighteen stay free when accompanied by an adult. Each additional person is $20 per night.

- **LOCATION:** Furnace Creek Ranch is 120 miles northwest of Las Vegas and 300 miles northeast of Los Angeles. The ranch is approximately 1.5 miles north of Furnace Creek Inn.

- **SEASON:** The ranch is open all year. The busiest seasons are mid-July through August, spring, and all holidays, when the hotel is frequently full.

> *Water, the lifeblood for development in the Furnace Creek area, flows from two nearby hot water springs. The springs caused the 49ers to camp here during their rush for riches, and even resulted in ranchers giving this area a try. The water now flows from the springs to a holding tank that supplies Furnace Creek Inn, and eventually, Furnace Creek Ranch and the Furnace Creek Golf Course. The National Park Service sells the water to the lodging facilities for irrigation and drinking water, as well as for the two swimming pools. Take a swim and enjoy the warm water.*

- **FOOD:** The Wrangler Steakhouse offers a buffet for breakfast ($9.00) and lunch ($10.00). Dinner is ordered from a menu that includes steaks, seafood, and poultry ($19–$28). The 49er Cafe offers seasonal breakfast, lunch ($7.00–$9.00), and dinner ($11–$17). The Ice Cream Shop has ice cream and yogurt (seasonal). The Saloon offers hot dogs, pizza, and snacks. Beer, wine, other beverages, and limited groceries are sold in the general store.

- **TRANSPORTATION:** The nearest major airport is in Las Vegas, where rental cars are available. The resort has a concrete airstrip with lights for private planes. Transportation from the airstrip is available (contact the ranch in advance).

- **FACILITIES:** The ranch has a large, spring-fed swimming pool (constant 82° Fahrenheit), two lighted tennis courts, a basketball court, a horseshoe area, a volleyball court, an eighteen-hole golf course, the Borax Museum, two restaurants, an ice cream shop, a saloon, a gas station, and a general store.

- **ACTIVITIES:** Swimming, tennis, golf, basketball, volleyball, horseshoes, and hiking. Horseback riding, group hay rides, and carriage rides are offered from mid-October to mid-May. The National Park Service offers interpretive programs throughout the park except during summer.

# PANAMINT SPRINGS RESORT

P.O. Box 395 • Ridgecrest, CA 93556 • (775) 482–7680
panamint@starband.com • www.deathvalley.com

*Panamint Springs Resort*

Panamint Springs Resort is a small facility that, if not for the surrounding landscape, causes you to wonder if you are in Key West, Florida. In fact, walk in the front door of the main building that houses the registration area and dining room and you might expect to see Ernest Hemingway sitting on one of the stools at a bar made from a large slab of walnut supported by redwood roots. Most likely, he would be listening to the imitation Wurlitzer jukebox. A large porch wraps around the building, with one side serving as an outside dining area. A small grassy area on one side has chairs for relaxing. Four wooden buildings directly behind the main building house fourteen motel rooms. All of the buildings are wood shingled.

Panamint Springs offers fourteen motel-type rooms and one two-bedroom cottage. The motel rooms are of varying size, but all are relatively small. Some rooms have one queen-size bed, while others have either two or three double beds. Each room has heat, air-conditioning, and a private bath with shower but no tub. The bathrooms were recently remodeled. No television is available in the motel rooms, and the only pay telephone is a cellular unit in the registration building. The cottage has two bedrooms with a

> The best-known man-made structure in Death Valley National Park is Scotty's Castle, which lies just inside the park's north entrance. This unique rock building, which cost nearly $2 million, was constructed in the 1920s as a vacation retreat for Albert Johnson, a partner and lifelong friend of Walter Scott, alias Death Valley Scotty, for whom the castle is named. Today you can take a fifty-minute tour conducted by Park Service rangers in period clothing. The tours are offered daily from 9:00 A.M. to 5:00 P.M., and waits of an hour or two can be expected during busy times of the year. The castle also includes a bookstore, a gift shop, an exhibit room, and a snack bar.

queen-size bed in one room, and a double bunk bed in the other bedroom. It has one bathroom and a television with a satellite hook-up.

Panamint Springs Resort is a small, quaint motel-type facility in the middle of the desert. The resort generates its own electricity, and water is piped from 5 miles away. Panamint Springs certainly isn't fancy, but it is a fun and unique place that you will remember. The dining room on one side of the main building holds about twenty-five persons and is much nicer than you might expect. The homemade food is very good, and the steaks are exceptional. The bar is terrific, and the atmosphere of the whole place can't be beat. Stay here and you will think you are a thousand miles from civilization.

- **ROOMS:** Two people in one double bed to six people in three double beds. All rooms have private baths with a shower but no tub. There are no handicap-accessible rooms.

- **RESERVATIONS:** Panamint Springs Resort, P.O. Box 395, Ridgecrest, CA 93556. Phone (775) 482–7680; fax (775) 482–7682; www.deathvalley.com; panamint@starband.com. A credit card is required to guarantee a room.

- **RATES:** One bed ($65); two beds ($79); three beds ($94); cottage ($139). Pets are $5.00 per night per pet. A 10% discount is given for AAA and AARP.

- **LOCATION:** The resort is on the western edge of Death Valley on Highway 190, 48 miles east of Lone Pine, California.

- **SEASON:** The resort is open all year. The busiest season is mid-July through August.

- **FOOD:** The attractive dining room serves breakfast ($4.00–$8.00), lunch ($4.00–$9.00), and dinner ($10.00–$20.00) from 6:30 A.M. to 10:00 P.M. Beer, wine, cocktails, and soft drinks are available from the bar or coolers just off the registration area. The bar remains open until the registration desk closes at midnight.

- **TRANSPORTATION:** The nearest airports are in Bakersfield, California (168 miles), and Las Vegas (174 miles), where rental cars are available.

- **FACILITIES:** Dining room, bar, and gift shop area. Gasoline, diesel fuel, and propane are available.

- **ACTIVITIES:** Hiking, four-wheel off-road vehicles, bird-watching, sightseeing.

## STOVEPIPE WELLS VILLAGE

Death Valley, CA 92328 • (760) 786–2387

www.furnacecreekresort.com

S tovepipe Wells Village is a complex of eleven wooden buildings that provide overnight rooms and supporting services. A general store, a small gas station, and a National Park Service ranger station are directly across the road. The village has the appearance of a small western town, which in some respects it is. Six separate one-story buildings each contain from eight to twenty-three rooms. The guest registration area is at the center of the complex in a building that also houses an auditorium, a gift shop, and a small lobby area. Employee housing is scattered around the back of the complex. Stovepipe Wells Village is

*Standard Units at Stovepipe Wells Village*

situated in the middle of Death Valley National Park, on Highway 190, approximately 25 miles northwest of Furnace Creek. It is about 33 miles southwest of Beatty, Nevada.

Stovepipe Wells offers three categories of rooms that range from a limited number of small, inexpensive Patio rooms to Deluxe rooms similar to those at Furnace Creek Ranch. All the rooms have heat, air-conditioning, and a private bath but no telephone. Be aware that only two of the buildings have potable water in the rooms. Guests in other rooms will find drinkable water in several locations outside the buildings. Water at Stovepipe Wells has a high mineral content and is treated for drinking purposes. Forty-nine Deluxe rooms in three separate buildings each have either two double beds or one king-size bed, a full bath, a refrigerator, a table, and a desk. Televisions are in Roadrunner and Tucki. Rooms 212 through 223 in the Roadrunner building face the east and provide the best view. Less expensive and smaller Standard rooms, which were recently renovated, each have two single beds (one has a double bed) and a full bath. Standard rooms rent for about $25 less per night than Deluxe rooms. Eight even smaller Patio rooms constructed in 1927 as part of the original building, were renovated in 1999. Each room has one double bed and a bath with shower but no tub. These rooms are attached to the front of the registration building near the highway. All of the buildings with rooms are a short walk from the registration building.

Stovepipe Wells is particularly appealing to someone seeking the solitude of the desert. Being located on Highway 190, which passes through Death Valley, makes it a convenient stop for travelers crossing the park. Stovepipe Wells Village offers an attractive restaurant and saloon with a real western atmosphere. The dining room and saloon have vaulted ceilings and were built with timbers from an old Death Valley mining operation. In fact, staying at Stovepipe Wells is itself a bit of the Old West, even though the rooms are quite comfortable and modern. A general store across the road offers supplies, souvenirs, limited groceries, soft drinks, beer, and wine. A pool with heated mineral water is available for guests.

■ **ROOMS:** Doubles, triples, and quads. All rooms have private baths, although the Patio rooms have showers but no tubs. Handicap-accessible rooms are available in both the Standard and the Deluxe units.

■ **RESERVATIONS:** Stovepipe Wells Village, Death Valley, CA 92328. Phone (760) 786–2387; fax (760) 786–2307. The first night's lodging is required as a deposit. Cancellation of forty-eight hours is required for full refund.

- **RATES:** Patio ($48), Standard ($67), and Deluxe ($88). Rates quoted are for two adults. Children twelve and under stay free when accompanied by an adult. Each additional person is $10 per night. A crib is $5.00 and a rollaway is $10.00.

- **LOCATION:** Stovepipe Wells Village is on Highway 190, near the middle of Death Valley National Park. It is approximately 25 miles northwest of the Furnace Creek Ranch and about 33 miles southwest of Beatty, Nevada.

- **SEASON:** The facility is open all year. The busiest season is mid-July through August, when it is frequently full.

- **FOOD:** The Toll Road Restaurant offers a buffet for all three meals during summer. From mid-October to mid-May, breakfast ($4.00–$6.00), lunch ($6.00–$8.00), and dinner ($10–$20) are ordered from a complete menu. The Badwater Saloon just off the restaurant offers draft beer, cocktails, and appetizers. Beer, wine, other beverages, and limited groceries are sold in the general store.

- **TRANSPORTATION:** The nearest major airport is in Las Vegas, where rental cars are available. A concrete airstrip with lights for private planes is near Furnace Creek Ranch. Another airstrip is next to Stovepipe Wells.

Although not covered with sand, Death Valley does have a few areas where large amounts of sand have collected to form dunes. The best known and easiest to visit are near Stovepipe Wells. These can be accessed from Highway 190 or from the unpaved Sand Dunes Road. Dunes can also be viewed north of Highway 190 on the west side of the park at Panamint Dunes. Other dunes are in both the extreme north and south ends of the park. Dunes require a source of sand, a wind to move the sand, and a place for the sand to collect. Death Valley has an abundance of the first two but only a few of the latter.

- **FACILITIES:** Stovepipe has a heated swimming pool, restaurant, saloon, gift shop, gas station (regular only), and general store.

- **ACTIVITIES:** Swimming, walking, and hiking. The National Park Service offers interpretive programs throughout the park except during summer.

# LASSEN VOLCANIC NATIONAL PARK

Mineral, CA 96063

(530) 595–4444

www.nps.gov/lavo

Lassen Volcanic National Park comprises 106,000 acres of a beautiful and relatively uncrowded mountainous area centered on Lassen Peak, a 10,457-foot plug-dome volcano that last erupted during a seven-year period beginning in 1914. The park has other evidence of geothermal activity, including boiling springs, mud pots, fumaroles, and sulfurous vents. A paved road connecting the southwest entrance station with the north entrance station provides scenic views and access to many features of this beautiful area. Road guides are sold at the information center. Lassen Volcanic National Park is located in north-central California, 42 miles east of Redding on State Highway 44.

**PARK ENTRANCE FEE:** $10.00 per vehicle or $5.00 per person, good for seven days.

## Lodging in Lassen Volcanic National Park

Lassen Volcanic has only one lodging facility, and it is an out-of-the-way location for most visitors who will drive along the single paved road through the park. Drakesbad Guest Ranch is in the southeast part of the park, 17 miles north of the small town of Chester. Private accommodations are available in Chester, Mineral, Mill Creek, Shingletown, Old Station, and Hat Creek.

## DRAKESBAD GUEST RANCH

End of Warner Valley Road • Lassen Volcanic National Park

Chester, CA 96020 • (See below for phone information)

KrisKoeberer@snowcrest.net • www.drakesbad.com

Drakesbad Guest Ranch provides a total of nineteen rooms in a relatively isolated complex of cabins, bungalows, and a two-story lodge. The ranch also has a central dining hall, a swimming pool, and several service buildings. The complex lies beside a meadow in the southeast portion of Lassen Volcanic National Park. It is surrounded by trees, hills, and mountains. Drakesbad Guest Ranch is reached via a 17-mile road from the town of Chester, California. The first 14 miles are a winding but well-maintained paved road. The last 3 miles, through national park land, are on a relatively rough gravel road. Drakesbad can be called directly by asking for the AT&T long-distance operator to connect you with Drakesbad Toll Station No. 2 at area code 530.

Drakesbad offers four types of room accommodations, all of which are fairly expensive because they include three meals a day. The rooms all have heat but no air-conditioning, telephones, television, or electrical outlets. The two-story wooden lodge building has six rooms, all on the second floor. The three even-numbered rooms have one double bed and one single bed. Odd-numbered rooms are a little smaller and have one double bed. All the

# LASSEN VOLCANIC NATIONAL PARK

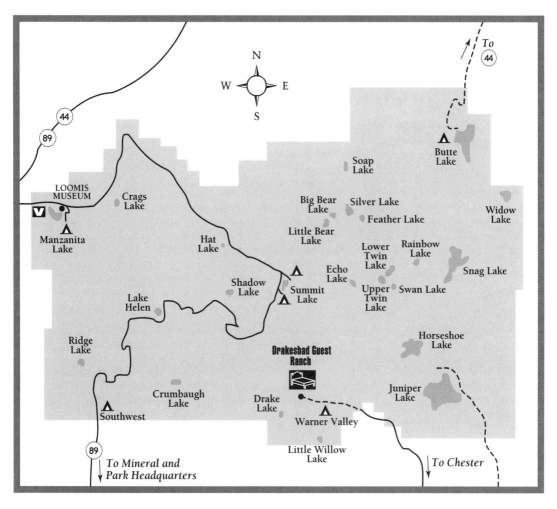

*Lodge Building at Drakesbad Guest Ranch*

lodge rooms have electric lights and a private bath with a sink and toilet but no tub or shower. Four freestanding rustic cabins each have a double and a single bed and the same type of bath as in the lodge. The cabins are paneled and relatively small. No electricity is available in these units, and light is by means of kerosene lanterns. A bathhouse at the swimming pool has showers and bathtubs for lodge and cabin guests. Six bungalows, two to a building, each have two double beds, a full bath with shower, and a back porch that overlooks the meadow. One bungalow is fully handicap accessible with a combination bath-shower. The Northeast Annex behind the dining hall offers two rooms, each with two double beds, electric lights, a bathroom with shower, and a porch that runs across the front of the building. A single wooden duplex has two rooms on each side of a central full bath. One room has two double beds, and the other room has one double and one single bed. The duplex is rented as a single unit to large families. A porch runs across the front of the building.

For most travelers, even frequent visitors to national parks, staying at Drakesbad will be a very different experience. Drakesbad is not for people who expect a fancy lodge with room service; it is a place for individuals who want to get away from it all and experience nature, but without giving up good food and friendship. The facilities at Drakesbad are comfortable but basic. A dinner bell rings three times a day to announce that food is being served in a rustic paneled dining room. The entire bottom floor of the lodge building, filled with chairs, tables, and sofas, serves as a meeting place to read and chat with other guests. A wood stove is near the middle of the room, and a large stone fireplace occupies one end wall. Chairs and sofas are also on the outside porch, which wraps around the lodge. Riding horses are at the nearby stable, and the swimming pool has naturally heated spring water. Equipment is provided for a variety of activities, including table tennis, volleyball, badminton, croquet, and horseshoes. Fly-fishing for trout is excellent for anglers. A fly-fishing instructor is available with advance notice. Several trails, both short and long, lead from the lodge to some of Lassen's best spots. Campfires are held each evening, and programs are presented for both adults and children. Best of all, both employees and guests seem to be family members that have found a good thing few other people have even heard about.

- **ROOMS:** Singles, doubles, triples, and quads. A single duplex holds up to seven individuals. Cabins and lodge rooms have half-baths. Other rooms have a full bath with shower. One bungalow is handicap accessible.

- **RESERVATIONS:** California Guest Services, 2150 North Main Street, Suite 5, Red Bluffs, CA 96080. Phone (530) 529–1512, ext. 120; fax 529–4511. Reservations should be made by the end of February to ensure a choice of rooms and dates. Reservations can be made up to a year in advance. Two nights' deposit is required, and a thirty-day cancellation is required for a full refund, less a 10 percent fee.

- **RATES:** Rates quoted are per person and include three meals per day. Lodge and cabins (single, $128; double, $108; extra adult, $91; child, $70); bungalows and Northeast Annex (single, $153; double, $125; extra adult, $104; child, $70); duplex (double, $133; extra adult, $101; child, $70). Weekly rate is approximately six times the daily rate.

- **LOCATION:** Seventeen miles north of Chester, California, on Warner Valley Road.

- **SEASON:** Open from the first Friday in June to the second Sunday in October, depending on the weather.

- **FOOD:** Three meals are served daily in an attractive dining room that is a short walk from all the lodging units. Breakfast includes fresh fruits, hot and cold cereals, and a hot entree. Lunch is buffet-style (sack lunches are available upon request), while dinner with your choice of two entrees is served at the table. An outdoor cookout is scheduled each Wednseday evening. Beer and wine are available for purchase.

- **TRANSPORTATION:** Scheduled airline service is available to Redding and Chico, California, and Reno, Nevada, where rental cars are available. Private planes may land at a small lighted airport at Chester, where rental cars are available. The lodge will pick up guests at Chester if prior arrangements are made. Amtrak serves Redding and Chico.

- **FACILITIES:** Hot-spring-fed swimming pool, dining hall, and stables.

- **ACTIVITIES:** Horseback riding, fishing, swimming, hiking, canoeing, and a variety of games, including volleyball, croquet, Ping-Pong, horseshoes, and badminton. Fly-fishing lessons are by reservation only.

Drakesbad Guest Ranch is over one hundred years old and predates Lassen Volcanic National Park, which did not achieve national park status until 1916. The ranch was founded and operated by E. R. Drake, who sold it in 1900 to the Sifford family. The Siffords deeded the property to the National Park Service in 1958. The ranch's name is a combination of the original owner's name and the German term for warm-water baths, which at Drakesbad are fed by hot springs. The water is cooled and used in the swimming pool, which is just below a spring. Several of the park's many geothermal areas are a modest hike from the ranch.

# SEQUOIA NATIONAL PARK/KINGS CANYON NATIONAL PARK

Three Rivers, CA 93271

(559) 565–3341

www.nps.gov/seki

Kings Canyon and Sequoia are separate parks that adjoin one another. The parks are administered jointly and nearly always visited together, so they are discussed here as one unit. The two parks have a combined area of 1,300 square miles, including groves of giant sequoias on plateaus surrounded by the scenic High Sierra. The parks are located in central California, between Yosemite National Park and Death Valley National Park. Access from the west is via State Highway 180 from Fresno, which leads through the Grant Grove section of Kings Canyon to Cedar Grove. From the south State Highway 198 leads to the Giant Forest area of Sequoia National Park, then connects with Highway 180 at Grant Grove.

**PARK ENTRANCE FEE:** $10.00 per vehicle or $5.00 per person, good for seven days.

## Lodging in Sequoia and Kings Canyon National Parks

Three locations within Kings Canyon and Sequoia National Parks offer overnight accommodations that range from very rustic cabins to two of the newest lodging facilities of any national park in the country. Wuksachi Village and Lodge is just north of Lodgepole and the only lodging facility in Sequoia National Park. Two lodging facilities in Kings Canyon National Park include rustic cabins and a new lodge building at Grant Grove, as well as a nice motel unit at Cedar Grove. Stony Creek Lodge in Sequoia National Forest between Giant Forest and Grant Grove is included as a fourth lodging alternative, even though it is just outside the northern boundary of Sequoia National Park on Highway 198. Although not included in this book, private lodging facilities are at Mineral King in the southern end of Sequoia National Park and in Sequoia National Forest on the road to Cedar Grove from Grant Grove.

The lodging facilities at Grant Grove and Cedar Grove in Kings Canyon National Park, as well as Stony Creek Lodge in Sequoia National Forest, are operated by Kings Canyon Park Services. The same address, phone number, and deposit and cancellation regulations apply to reservations at each of the three facilities. Wuksachi Village and Lodge is operated by Delaware-North, the same firm that serves as the concessionaire for lodging, food, and gift facilities in Yosemite National Park.

# SEQUOIA NATIONAL PARK/KINGS CANYON NATIONAL PARK

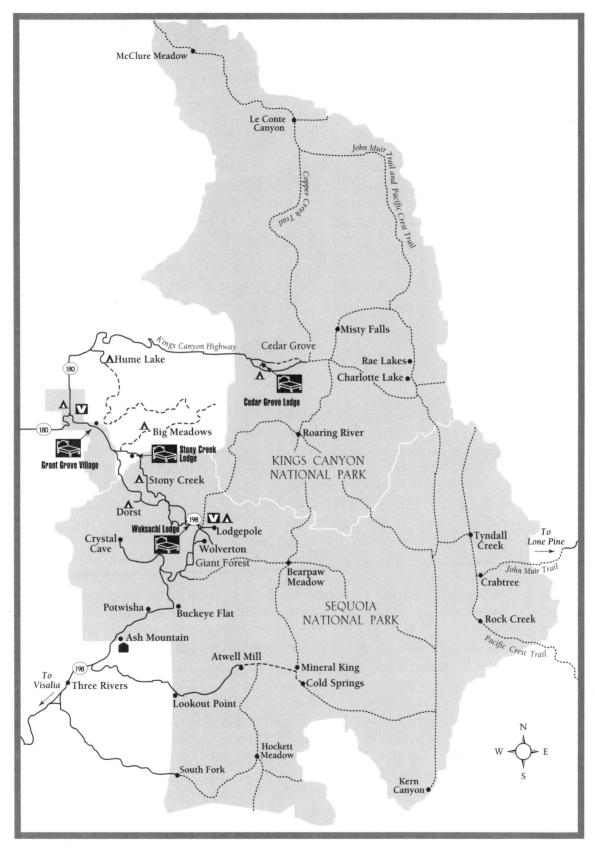

# CEDAR GROVE LODGE

P.O. Box 909 • Kings Canyon National Park, CA 93633 • (559) 565–0100
www.sequoia-kingscanyon.com

*Cedar Grove Lodge*

Cedar Grove Lodge is a modern two-story wooden building in the isolated Cedar Grove area of Kings Canyon National Park. The lodge has the appearance of a ski chalet, with eighteen rooms on the second floor and three rooms on the ground level. The first floor houses a combination market/gift shop, a cafe, and a small guest registration desk just inside the entrance to the market. The lodge sits among giant cedar and pine trees beside the South Fork of the Kings River. Picnic tables are scattered about the grounds, many near the river. A large, covered second-floor balcony provides a restful place to read and relax while viewing the surrounding tree-covered mountains and listening to the river roar. Another large deck area, one floor below on the same side of the building, has picnic tables just outside the snack bar. Cedar Grove Lodge is 31 miles east of Grant Grove Village, 6 miles from the terminus of Kings Canyon Highway. The drive to Cedar Grove is probably the most scenic in either Sequoia or Kings Canyon and worth the time and effort even if you don't plan to stay at the lodge.

All of the rooms at the lodge have heat and air-conditioning but no telephone or television. The second-story rooms are identical in size and furnishings, with two queen-size beds and a private bath that includes a shower but no tub. One handicap-accessible room has a bathtub. Each room has a modest back window but no balcony. The rooms have plenty of space for two people and adequate room for a family of four. The rooms on the second floor are entered through a relatively narrow inside corridor that runs the length of the building between a ramp at one end and a wide stairway at the opposite end. The three ground-level rooms are smaller, with one queen-size bed, a full bath, and a kitchen area with a two-burner stove and a small refrigerator. These rooms offer an excellent view but are directly below the kitchen, so that early morning noise may be a problem. Plentiful parking is in front and beside the lodge.

Cedar Grove is a very pleasant place to spend several days. The lodge is 2,000 feet lower and about twenty degrees warmer than Wuksachi and Grant Grove. It's also somewhat out of the way, near the end of a 30-mile road that leads into Cedar Grove. The remoteness reduces visitation to this area of the park so that Cedar Grove is not nearly as crowded as other, more popular locations. The cafe serves the usual sandwiches, fries, and soft drinks. It also offers other selections, including breakfast items, fried chicken, trout, steak, and pasta at fairly inexpensive prices. The market has a modest selection of essentials, such as milk, ice cream treats, beer, wine, fresh vegetables and fruits, and drugstore items. A small National Park Service visitor center is a short walk down the road and across the bridge. Park rangers conduct evening programs at the campground amphitheater.

- **ROOMS:** Doubles, triples, and quads. All rooms have private baths with showers. One handicap-accessible room has a bathtub.

- **RESERVATIONS:** Kings Canyon Park Services Company, P.O. Box 909, Kings Canyon National Park, CA 93633. Telephone toll free (866) 522–6966; (559) 335–5500; fax (559) 335–2498; www.sequoia-kingscanyon.com.

- **RATES:** Doubles ($90). Rates quoted are for two adults. Children twelve and under stay free unless an extra bed is requested. Each additional person is $10.00 per night.

- **LOCATION:** Cedar Grove Lodge is located just beyond the terminus of Highway 180, Kings Canyon Highway. It is 31 miles east of Grant Grove Village.

- **SEASON:** The lodge is open from mid-May through mid-October, depending on the weather.

- **FOOD:** The cafe serves breakfast ($3.00–$5.00), lunch ($6.00), and dinner ($12), from 7:00 A.M. to 9:00 P.M. Limited food items can be purchased in the market.

- **TRANSPORTATION:** Scheduled air, bus, and train service are available to Fresno, where rental cars are available.

- **FACILITIES:** Laundry. Gift items are available in the market. A small National Park Service visitor center is a quarter mile away.

- **ACTIVITIES:** Hiking, fishing, evening campfire programs, horseback riding.

## GRANT GROVE VILLAGE

P.O. Box 909 • Kings Canyon National Park, CA 93633 • (559) 335–5505, ext. 1603
www.sequoia-kingscanyon.com

Grant Grove Village, one of two major lodging facilities in Kings Canyon Park, includes fifty-two older wood cabins and a new two-story cedar lodge building. Both the cabins and the lodge are located behind a small commercial center that houses the registration desk, restaurant, market, gift shop, and a National Park Service visitor center. No guest rooms are in the registration building, although the lodge and all of the cabins are nearby. Guests for both the cabins and lodge register in the same location. Most of the cabins are situated

*John Muir Lodge at Grant Grove Village*

on a hillside overlooking the meadow. Some of the cabins are surrounded by trees, while others are near the meadow. The lodge is on a hillside a short distance behind and above the cabins. A nice National Park Service visitor center is across the road from the commercial center. The Grant Grove area can be quite busy in summer, so expect heavy traffic. Most parking is close, but not always directly beside the cabins. Parking for the lodge is directly beside the building. Grant Grove Village is 3 miles from the Kings Canyon entrance on Highway 180 from Fresno, California. It is 24 miles north of Lodgepole on a small peninsula of Kings Canyon National Park that juts from the northwest corner of Sequoia National Park.

Grant Grove offers four types of cabin accommodations and two types of lodge rooms. Nine cabins have a private bathroom, while occupants of the other forty-three cabins must use one of two central bathhouses. All cabins have sheets, towels, and daily maid service. The least expensive rooms are nineteen Tent Cabins with wooden sides and canvas roof. These units, which are closed during winter months, offer wooden floors and two double beds in a stark, bare interior without electricity. They have a propane heater, battery operated lamps for light, and an outside picnic table. One step up and about $7.00 per night extra are twelve somewhat larger Rustic Cabins without bath. The Rustic units have two double beds, propane heat, and electricity. Each Rustic Cabin has a covered patio area with a picnic table and an outside wood stove for cooking. Grant Grove also offers twelve Deluxe Rustic Cabins that are similar to the Rustic Cabins, but have carpeting and paneling. These cabins, which cost about $10 more than the Rustics, have interiors that are considerably nicer than cabins in the first two categories. Deluxe Rustic Cabin 510 is a good choice because trees provide a degree of privacy and it is very close to the bathhouse.

The top cabin accommodations at Grant Grove are nine cabins with bath that are much nicer than cabins in the three previous categories. These cabins, which cost about twice as much as the Rustic Cabins, have two double beds, nice furniture, a finished interior, carpeting, and electricity. They are constructed two to a building, with a porch that spans the front of the building. Cabin 9 is a freestanding unit with one queen-size bed, a sofa bed, a coffeemaker, and a refrigerator. We consider this cabin superior to even the more expensive lodge rooms, but it can be difficult to reserve.

John Muir Lodge, which opened in May 1999, offers thirty rooms in an attractive two-story cedar building. Each floor has a large balcony with chairs on the west end of the building. The lodge contains an impressive lobby area with a vaulted beamed ceiling and a large stone fireplace. Furnishings were especially created for the lodge. Twenty-four regular rooms have heat, two queen-size beds, a full bath, a coffeemaker, and a telephone. No television or air-conditioning is in any of the rooms. Six suites are comprised of two rooms, each identical in size to a regular room. One room in each suite has two queen-size beds, and the other has a queen-size bed and sofa bed. The suites have two full bathrooms. The even-numbered rooms, which are on the south side of the building, offer a better view and less noise because they are on the opposite side of the building from the parking lot.

Grant Grove has a wide range of accommodations at different prices. Staying here offers a convenient location for day trips to both Cedar Grove and Giant Forest. You will also find horseback riding, guided hikes, and evening programs. Winter activities include cross-country skiing and snowshoeing. Equipment is available for rental at the market.

■ **ROOMS:** Doubles, triples, and quads. Six to eight people will fit in a lodge suite. Only nine of the cabins have a private bathroom. The John Muir Lodge has handicap-accessible rooms.

■ **RESERVATIONS:** Kings Canyon Park Services Company, P.O. Box 909, Kings Canyon National Park, CA 93633. Telephone toll free (866) 522–6966; (559) 335–5500; fax (559) 335–2498; www.sequoia-kingscanyon.com.

■ **RATES:** Tent Cabin ($38); Rustic Cabin ($45); Deluxe Rustic Cabin ($55); Cabin with Private Bath ($88); lodge rooms ($128); suites ($215). Rates quoted are for two adults. Children twelve and under stay free. Each additional person is $10.00 per night. Rollaways are $7.50. A deposit of two nights' lodging is required. Cancellation of forty-eight hours is required for a refund. Rates are lowered from January to May.

*If you want something to tax your brain, think about this: The complex at Grant Grove spans two California counties. Tulare County on the south side levies a 10 percent hotel/motel tax, while Fresno County on the north side does not. Stay in a cabin on the south side of the complex and you will be charged the tax. Stay in an identical cabin on the north side of the complex and you will not be required to pay it. Occupants of the lodge are fortunate because the building sits in Fresno County, which does not levy the tax. Even the concessionaire was confused by this bizarre situation and was at one time charging tax on all the rooms. Guests in both the cabins and the lodge are charged a National Park Service impact fee of $2.50 per night. How can life on vacation become so complicated?*

■ **LOCATION:** Three miles inside the entrance to Kings Canyon National Park on Highway 180 from Fresno.

■ **SEASON:** Grant Grove Village is open all year. Only the Tent Cabins close for winter.

■ **FOOD:** An attractive coffee shop offers family dining with breakfast ($4.00–$7.00), lunch ($5.00–$17.00), and dinner ($5.00–$17.00). An upscale dining room ($16–$24) is open for dinner only. Both are within easy walking distance of the cabins and lodge. A market offers groceries.

- ■ **TRANSPORTATION:** Scheduled air, bus, and train service from Fresno, California, where rental cars are available.
- ■ **FACILITIES:** Coffee shop, dining room, market, gift shop, post office, and National Park Service visitor center.
- ■ **ACTIVITIES:** Horseback riding, hiking, and interpretive programs. During winter months snowshoeing and cross-country skiing are popular.

## STONY CREEK LODGE

P.O. Box 909 • Kings Canyon National Park, CA 93633 • (559) 565–3909
www.sequoia-kingscanyon.com

*Stony Creek Lodge*

Stony Creek Lodge is a cozy two-story river rock and wood building that offers only eleven guest rooms, all on the second floor. The first floor contains a registration desk, market and gift shop, restaurant, and attractive lobby area with a huge stone fireplace. The lodge is likely to remind world travelers of an intimate European hotel. Stony Creek Lodge is located just off Generals Highway, 15 miles north of Giant Forest. It is in Sequoia National Forest between Sequoia National Park and Kings Canyon National Park. Even though Stony Creek Lodge isn't within the park boundary, it is certainly a viable option for visitors to the parks. The lodge doesn't always fill, so you may be able to obtain a room without a reservation.

The eleven rooms in Stony Creek Lodge are of different sizes and offer different bedding configurations. Some rooms have one queen-size bed or one double bed. Others have either a queen-size or a double bed and a single bed. Two rooms have two single beds. All of the rooms have heat and a private bath but no air-conditioning, telephone, or television. All but one of the rooms have a shower but no tub, while room 11 has two single beds and a tub. The second floor is accessed via either of two stairways, one in the lobby and the other at the opposite end of the building. Rooms are at both the front and the back of the building, with entrance through an interior hallway. No handicap access is available to the second floor, where all the rooms are located. Rooms on the parking side of the building can be noisy, so it is best to choose a room on the highway side. Plentiful parking is directly outside the building.

Surrounded by big pine, fir, and cedar trees, Stony Creek Lodge is a pleasant place to get away from the hustle and bustle common at other busy locations in Sequoia and Kings Canyon National Parks. You can spend the day driving through the park or roaming through the busy areas, then spend a quiet, restful night at this secluded spot. The location is especially convenient if you plan to spend one day in Sequoia and the next day in Kings Canyon. An attractive restaurant with two walls of windows and a vaulted ceiling serves three meals a day. A small market offers supplies, including a large selection of beer and wine, and some groceries. Nearby Stony Creek (the stream after which the lodge is named), a short downhill walk from the lodge, offers several small swimming holes to beat the summer heat. Many trailheads are near the lodge, including one that provides access to the Jenny Lake Wilderness Area.

- **ROOMS:** Doubles, triples, and one quad. All rooms have a private bath with a shower, but only one room has a bathtub. Handicap-accessible rooms are not available.

- **RESERVATIONS:** Kings Canyon Park Services Company, P.O. Box 909, Kings Canyon National Park, CA 93633. Telephone toll free (866) 522–6966; (559) 335–5500; fax (559) 335–2498; www.sequoia-kingscanyon.com.

- **RATES:** All rooms ($96.50), which includes a continental breakfast. Rates quoted are for two adults. Children twelve and under stay free unless an extra bed is required. Extra adults and children over twelve are charged $10.00 each per night.

- **LOCATION:** In Sequoia National Forest, 15 miles north of Giant Forest on Generals Highway. The lodge is just outside the northern boundary of Sequoia National Park.

- **SEASON:** Stony Creek Lodge is open May through Labor Day, depending on weather.

- **FOOD:** A continental breakfast is included with the room rental. An attractive restaurant serves breakfast from 7:00 to 10:00 A.M., lunch from 11:00 A.M. to 4:00 P.M., and dinner ($9.00–$15.00) from 5:00 to 9:00 P.M. Limited groceries, beer, and wine are available in the market.

- **TRANSPORTATION:** Scheduled airlines serve Fresno, California, where rental cars are available.

- **FACILITIES:** Restaurant, laundry facilities, and a market with gifts, supplies, and groceries.

- **ACTIVITIES:** Fishing and hiking.

# WUKSACHI VILLAGE AND LODGE

P.O. Box 89 • Sequoia National Park, CA 93262 • (559) 565–4070
www.visitsequoia.com

*Lodge Rooms, Wuksachi Village and Lodge*

**W**uksachi Village and Lodge, named for a Native American tribe that once lived in Sequoia, is comprised of an attractive registration/dining building and three nearby buildings that provide a total of 102 overnight rooms. The four cedar buildings of the lodge first opened in May 1999, and plans call for several additional lodging units and an expansion of the registration/dining building. The complex is on a hillside amid large cedar and fir trees. Excellent mountain views are available from the windows of many of the rooms. Parking is down a hill from the buildings, and transporting luggage may require more exercise than you desire. Luggage carts are in each of the lodge buildings, and bellboys are at the registration building to assist with luggage.

The registration building has a beamed vaulted ceiling and a handsome lobby area that includes comfortable chairs and a couch in front of a wood-burning stove. A small gift shop just off the registration area sells the usual assortment of T-shirts, sweatshirts, jewelry, and souvenirs, along with some fine pieces of pottery. The dining room around the corner from the registration area has a large stone fireplace and features a wall of windows that provide an outstanding view of this beautiful area of the park. A lounge is situated just outside the dining room. Public telephones and conference rooms are downstairs. The entire complex is attractively done with first-class furnishings.

Each of the three lodge buildings is virtually identical, with a split-level design and two floors on a side. Rooms are accessed from a central corridor that can be entered from either end of each building. The top floor of each lodging unit is designated for smoking rooms. No elevators are in any of the three buildings. All of the 102 rooms have heat, a full bathroom with combination shower-tub, telephone with data port, coffeemaker, and very attractive furnishings. No air-conditioning or television is available in any of the rooms. In addition, none of the rooms has a balcony. Each building offers rooms in three classifications. Twenty-four standard rooms, the lowest classification, and sixty deluxe rooms are quite similar except for a difference in beds and about a 3-foot difference in room depth. Standard rooms are offered with either one or two queen-size beds. Deluxe rooms have either one king- or two queen-size beds. Eighteen Superior rooms with either two queen-size beds or one-king-size bed and a sofa bed also have a side room with a sofa bed and chair. The extra room can be closed off with two sliding wood doors. Handicap-accessible rooms are available in each category. We suggest you choose a standard room with a mountain view. Rooms within each classification rent for the same price, so obtaining a room with a view doesn't cost extra. The standard room is at least as large, if not larger, than most nice motel rooms.

Wuksachi Village and Lodge is a great place to spend a restful weekend or to serve as a base to explore the Kings Canyon/Sequoia area. The location makes it convenient to visit most of the park's features. Lodgepole, a major activity area with a large visitor center, market, laundry facilities, mountain shop, deli, and nature center, is only 2 miles away. Giant Forest, with trails and access to the park's namesake sequoias, is 4 miles south of Lodgepole. A free shuttle service from Wuksachi to Lodgepole, Wolverton, General Sherman Tree, Moro Rock, and Crescent Meadow operates from mid-June to early September.

*Although Wuksachi Village and Lodge opened in May 1999, the planning for this facility had been in the works for well over a decade. The major activity and lodging center of Sequoia National Park was for many years at Giant Forest, 6 miles south of Wuksachi. Here there were cabins, motel-type units, and two two-story lodge buildings. The area also had a restaurant, market, gift shop, and pizza pub. For a variety of reasons, including an antiquated sewage system, danger from falling trees, high maintenance costs, and harm to reproduction of the area's sequoias, the National Park Service closed all commercial activities here in October 1998 and subsequently began removing most of the structures.*

- **ROOMS:** Doubles, triples, and quads. Superior rooms can sleep up to six. All rooms have private baths with shower-tub combination. Handicap-accessible rooms are available.

- **RESERVATIONS:** Delaware North Park Services, 5410 East Home Avenue, Fresno, CA 93727. Phone (888) 252–5757; fax (559) 456–0542; Web site www.visitsequoia.com. One night's deposit required. Cancellation requires forty-eight hours' notice.

- **RATES:** Peak season rates apply from mid-May to mid-October and during holidays. Off-season rates are applicable the remainder of the year: standard (peak $130/off-peak $80); deluxe ($155/$95); superior ($185/$115). Rates quoted are for two adults. Each additional person is $10 per night. Children twelve and under stay free unless an extra bed is required. Rollaways and cribs are $10 per night.

- **LOCATION:** Wuksachi Village and Lodge is just off Generals Highway in the northern section of Sequoia National Park. The lodge is approximately 2 miles west of Lodgepole.

- **SEASON:** The lodge is open all year.

- **FOOD:** The restaurant serves breakfast ($6.50–$9.00), lunch ($6.50–$12.50), and dinner ($9–$24) daily. Two miles away, Lodgepole has a market and deli, as well as a snack bar that serves breakfast, sandwiches, and pizza.

- **TRANSPORTATION:** Scheduled air service is available to Fresno, California, where cars may be rented.

- **FACILITIES:** Restaurant, lounge, gift shop, conference rooms. Two miles away, Lodgepole offers a mountain shop, post office, laundry facilities, deli, market, snack bar, and a National Park Service visitor center.

- **ACTIVITIES:** Hiking and fishing. Horseback riding offered at a stable near Wolverton. Cave tours are at Crystal Cave, about 20 miles from Wuksachi. Buy tickets at Lodgepole or Foothills visitor center. Winter activities include cross-country skiing, snowshoeing, and guided walks.

# YOSEMITE NATIONAL PARK

P.O. Box 577
Yosemite National Park, CA 95389
(209) 372–0200
www.nps.gov/yose

Yosemite National Park comprises 761,000 acres of scenic valleys, high-country meadows, and granite peaks and domes in one of America's most spectacular and popular national parks. The three major features of the park are beautiful Yosemite Valley, groves of giant sequoias at Crane Flat and Mariposa Grove, and the alpine wilderness reached via Tioga Road. The park's main activity area is in Yosemite Valley. Tioga Road is a beautiful paved road that cuts through the High Sierra and connects on the east side of the park with U.S. Highway 395 at Lee Vining, California. Yosemite National Park is in east-central California, approximately 190 miles due east of San Francisco. The southern edge of the park is approximately 60 miles north of Fresno via Highway 41.

**PARK ENTRANCE FEE:** $20 per vehicle or $10 per person, good for seven days.

## Lodging in Yosemite National Park

Yosemite has seven lodging facilities, four of which are in Yosemite Valley. These include the Ahwahnee, Yosemite Lodge, Curry Village, and Housekeeping Camp. Accommodations in the valley range from the upscale and expensive Ahwahnee to downscale and relatively inexpensive tent cabins. Outside the valley the Wawona Hotel is a wonderful old hotel near the park's south entrance. Two separate facilities, Tuolumne Meadows Lodge and White Wolf Lodge, offer canvas tent cabins and a few wood cabins on Tioga Pass. Yosemite is very popular during summer months, so make reservations at the earliest possible date. Accommodations with private bath are often booked ten to twelve months in advance.

- **RESERVATIONS:** A central reservation office services all the lodging facilities in Yosemite National Park. For reservations write or call Yosemite Reservations, 5410 East Home Avenue, Fresno, CA 93727. Phone (559) 252–4848; or fax (559) 456–0542. Reservations can be made online at www.yosemite.com/html/accom_reservation.html. Reservations may be made up to a year and a day in advance. Cancellation with a full refund requires a seventy-two-hour notice.

- **TRANSPORTATION:** Scheduled air service is available to Fresno, where rental cars are available. Amtrak serves Yosemite Valley through a combination train-bus service. A free shuttle bus system within Yosemite Valley serves all the lodges and other popular points of interest.

# YOSEMITE NATIONAL PARK

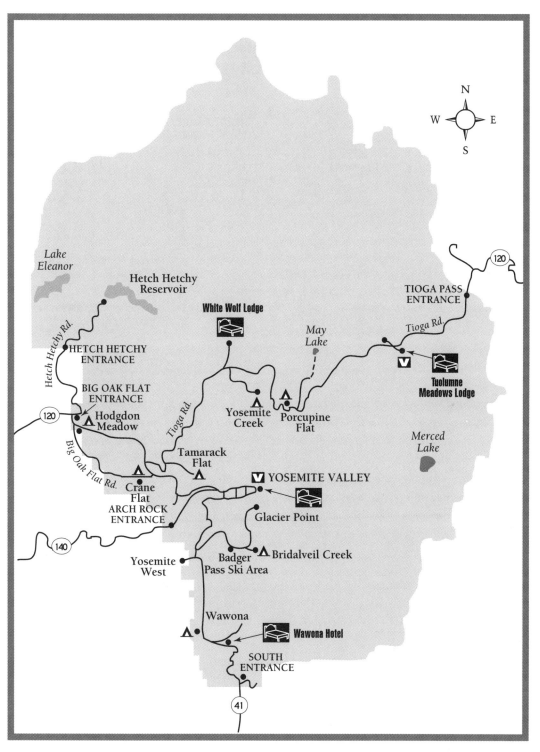

*Lake Eleanor*

Hetch Hetchy Reservoir

**White Wolf Lodge**

*May Lake*

**TIOGA PASS ENTRANCE**

Tioga Rd.

Hetch Hetchy Rd.

**HETCH HETCHY ENTRANCE**

**BIG OAK FLAT ENTRANCE**

Tuolumne Meadows Lodge

Hodgdon Meadow

Tioga Rd.

Yosemite Creek

Porcupine Flat

*Merced Lake*

Big Oak Flat Rd.

Tamarack Flat

Crane Flat

**YOSEMITE VALLEY**

**ARCH ROCK ENTRANCE**

Glacier Point

Yosemite West

Badger Pass Ski Area

Bridalveil Creek

Wawona

Wawona Hotel

**SOUTH ENTRANCE**

120

120

140

41

N
W E
S

# YOSEMITE NATIONAL PARK — YOSEMITE VALLEY

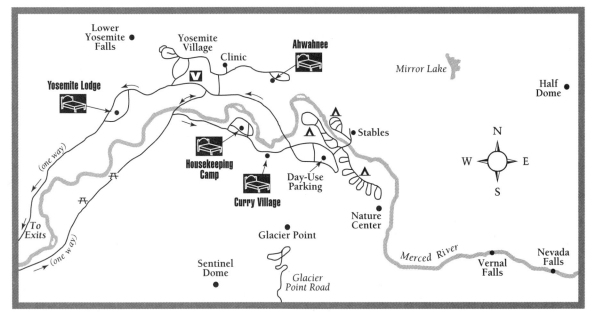

R eservations for all Yosemite lodging can be made up to 366 days prior to your intended arrival date. For a summer stay in the Ahwahnee, Yosemite Lodge, or Wawona Hotel, it is not a bad idea to make reservations on the first possible day—that is, a year and a day before your stay will begin. If this isn't possible and the hotels are fully booked when you call, call again thirty, fifteen, or seven days prior to your arrival, when previous reservations by others are most likely to be canceled. Another possibility is to take a chance and stop by the front desk at any of the seven hotels and place your name on a waiting list for canceled rooms. Keep in mind that the tent cabins at Curry Village can often be reserved with only a couple of weeks' notice.

## Yosemite Valley Lodging

www.yosemitepark.com

Yosemite Valley has four very different lodging facilities that range from tents to what is probably the most elegant hotel in any national park. A free shuttle stops at each facility as well as other major points of interest in the valley. The valley can be congested in the summer, so plan on parking your vehicle and using the shuttle.

# AHWAHNEE

Yosemite National Park, CA 95389 • (209) 372–1407

Many travelers claim that the Ahwahnee in Yosemite Valley is the finest lodging facility at any national park. This is difficult to dispute. The Ahwahnee, built in the late 1920s with a name that Native Americans gave to what is now Yosemite Valley, is both a National Historic Landmark and a world-class facility. Everything about this six-story hotel makes you want to stay, except perhaps the cost, which is rivaled only by Death Valley's Furnace Creek Inn and Grand Teton's Jenny Lake Lodge. The Great Lounge, with a 24-foot-high beamed ceiling, stained glass windows, and two of the largest stone fireplaces you will ever see, is a jewel. The spectacular dining room, with its 34-foot-high vaulted beamed ceiling and floor-to-ceiling windows, is one of the most beautiful you will ever enter. Native American baskets, paintings, and rugs are placed throughout the public rooms. The Ahwahnee offers a total of 123 rooms in both the main hotel building and several nearby secluded cottages. The Ahwahnee is located in the northeast section of Yosemite Valley, at the base of the Royal Arches. The location is remote enough to avoid most of the congestion that typifies much of the valley. Adequate parking is nearby, and valet parking is available. Bellhops will assist with luggage.

*The Ahwahnee is famous for the Bracebridge Dinner, a three-hour Christmas pageant and feast that is presented five times each season, on December 22, Christmas Eve, and Christmas Day. The pageant, which is adapted from Washington Irving's "Sketch Book" of a Christmas Day in 1718 at Squire Bracebridge's Old English Manor, is held in the main dining room. The event is so popular—60,000 requests are made for a total of 1,675 seats—that seats are allocated by lottery. Applications for the lottery can be obtained by writing Yosemite Concession Services Corporation, 5410 East Home Avenue, Fresno, CA 93727. Applications are accepted from December 1 through January 15 for the following year's dinner.*

The Ahwahnee offers two types of lodging. The main hotel has ninety-nine rooms on six floors. Most rooms have one king-size bed, while a few have two double beds. The rooms are nicely furnished, with matching chair and love seat, television, telephone, guest bathrobes, iron and ironing board, hairdryer, and full bath. Four elegant parlor rooms that provide spectacular views of the valley are available for guests who wish to convert their adjoining room into a suite. One or more large windows in each hotel room offer differing views depending on room location; the best views are from corner rooms that have windows on two sides. The Ahwahnee has eight separate but nearby buildings that house a total of twenty-four cottages that were redecorated in 1996. Most cottages have one king-size bed, while five have two double beds, and the same amenities as the hotel rooms plus a small refrigerator. The single-story cottages are in a secluded and quiet wooded area near the hotel but away from the hotel traffic. Though air-conditioning is not available in the cottages, the trees and ceiling fans keep the cottages comfortable. The interiors, which are larger than the hotel rooms, are beautifully decorated to highlight Yosemite's Native American heritage. While many frequent Ahwahnee guests request the cottages, first-time visitors should probably

*Ahwahnee*

choose a room in the main hotel in order to fully appreciate the delight of staying overnight in this outstanding facility.

The Ahwahnee offers fine lodging in a beautiful setting. If you can afford it, it is a wonderful place to spend a week while exploring the beauty and enjoying the many activities offered by Yosemite National Park. If you can't, try to schedule at least one night's lodging in this unique hotel. Walk through the lobby into the Great Lounge, where afternoon tea accompanied by background piano music is an Ahwahnee tradition for its guests. On through the lounge past the second fireplace provides entry to the Solarium, whose massive windows furnish a sweeping view of a grassy area surrounded by trees with a background of granite cliffs. The hotel also offers a cocktail lounge, a sweetshop, a swimming pool, tennis courts, and a very nice gift shop. A free shuttle bus operates throughout Yosemite Valley, so that activities and facilities in other locations are only a few minutes away.

- ■ **ROOMS:** Singles, doubles, triples, and quads. All rooms have a full bath. Two cottage rooms are handicap accessible.

- ■ **RATES:** Hotel rooms and cottages ($318.75). Some hotel rooms have connecting parlors at an extra charge. Children twelve and under

Yosemite National Park is open all year, and many people prefer to visit in winter. Yosemite Valley generally experiences moderate winter weather while the park's Badger Pass Ski Area receives an average snowfall of 180 inches. Winter activities include ice skating, (outdoor rink at Curry Village) and cross-country skiing (ski rental at Curry Village). A sightseeing tour of Yosemite Valley is also available in winter months. Badger Pass, located 23 miles from Yosemite Valley, has four chair lifts and one cable tow to serve nine ski runs. Ninety miles of marked cross-country ski trails begin here.

stay free in the same room with an adult. Each additional person is $20 per night. A variety of packages are offered.

- ▨ **LOCATION:** North section of Yosemite Valley, at the end of a dead-end road.
- ▨ **SEASON:** The Ahwahnee is open year-round. It is often fully booked a year ahead for busy periods such as holidays and summer months.
- ▨ **FOOD:** An elegant dining room serves breakfast ($5.00–$14.00), lunch ($7.00–$14.00), and dinner ($18–$30) until 10:00 P.M. Dinner requires reservations and appropriate attire; athletic clothing is not allowed. A Sunday buffet is served from 7:00 A.M. to 3:00 P.M. The cocktail lounge serves light meals from 11:00 A.M. to 10:00 P.M. Room service is available.
- ▨ **FACILITIES:** Swimming pool, tennis courts, gift shop, tour desk, cocktail lounge, sweet-shop, and full-time concierge service.
- ▨ **ACTIVITIES:** Hiking, swimming, tennis, evening programs, guided hotel tours.

## CURRY VILLAGE

Yosemite National Park, CA 45389 • (209) 372–8333

*Cabins without Baths at Curry Village*

Curry Village is the largest lodging complex in Yosemite Valley, with a total of 628 rooms, mostly in canvas tents. The term *village* is certainly appropriate for this facility, because Curry is much like a small town, with tents, cabins, cafeteria, fast-food restaurants, camp store, "sitting lodge building" (a cabin used as a lounge), post office (summer only), shower building, and rest rooms. The location, in the southeast section of Yosemite Valley, is near several campgrounds and a convenient place for campers to roam and eat.

Curry Village offers four types of accommodations. The least expensive lodging is 427 canvas tent cabins with a wooden platform and canvas walls and roof. These units are available in different sizes, with a variety of bedding options that range from two singles to a double and three singles. The bedding consists of metal cots, with linens, towels, soap, and maid service provided for a nominal extra charge. A padlock is available for the front door. A light is in each tent, although there are no electrical outlets, heat, or plumbing. Rest room and shower facilities are centrally located. A few heated tent cabins are available in the winter.

Curry Village also has 183 wooden cabins, 103 of which have private baths, mostly with showers but no tubs. The remaining cabins have no bath or running water. Cabins with a bath are older and have electric heat and a porch. Some units have one double bed, while others have a double and single or two doubles. Units 61A and 61B are the nicest of these units, and both are handicap accessible. Cabins without a bath all have propane heat and two double beds. These cabins have interior paneling and are nicer than the more expensive cabins with a bath. Curry Village also has three deluxe cabins, which have a living room, a bathroom, and one or two bedrooms. Two also have fireplaces. These deluxe cabins sleep from two to four persons; they are by far the nicest lodging facilities at Curry Village. A single motel-type building, Stoneman House, has eighteen standard rooms with private bath and shower but no tub. These units have heat and a ceiling fan. Beds range from one to three doubles; the three double beds are in units with a loft.

*One of Yosemite's best-known activities was the evening Firefall, during which a massive pile of glowing red fir bark embers was pushed over the cliff at Glacier Point near Camp Curry. The practice was begun in the 1870s, abandoned several years later, then revived in 1899 by David Curry, proprietor of Camp Curry. The evening activity became so popular that everything in the valley would come to a halt when the time came for embers to be pushed over the side. The Firefall continued until 1968, when it was permanently halted by park management.*

Lodging facilities at Curry Village are tightly packed. Basically, this is a low-cost alternative to the Ahwahnee and Yosemite Lodge. The many tent cabins are the cheapest of Yosemite's overnight offerings outside the campgrounds. That Curry includes a variety of eating facilities makes it a handy center of operations. Food options include a dining pavilion that serves an all-you-can-eat-style buffet for breakfast and dinner, a sandwich shop, a pizza patio, a coffee corner, and an ice cream shop. Evening programs are presented at an outside amphitheater. A free shuttle service can transport you to other areas of the valley. The decision on whether to stay here depends on how much you are willing to spend, what lodging facilities are available when your reservation is made, and because this area can be very busy in the summer, how well you tolerate crowds.

■ **ROOMS:** Doubles, triples, and quads; a few units will hold five or six persons. Most rooms, including all the tent cabins, do not have private baths. Two cabins with bath are handicap accessible. The central bathhouses are handicap accessible, although there are no paved walkways from the cabins to the bathhouses.

- **RATES:** Canvas tent cabins ($44); cabins without bath ($57); cabins with bath ($75); deluxe cabins ($110–$150); standard motel-type rooms ($103). Children twelve and under stay free except in the tent cabins, where an additional child is $4.00 per night. Rates for an additional person are from $7.00 to $10.00. Prices are slightly lower from November through March, excluding holidays. Further reductions are available for midweek stays from November through March.

- **LOCATION:** Southeast side of Yosemite Valley.

- **SEASON:** All of the lodging facilities in Curry Village are open spring through fall. Some of them are also open during the winter.

- **FOOD:** A dining pavilion serves a buffet breakfast and a buffet dinner from spring through fall. Pizza, hamburgers, and ice cream are available from 8:00 A.M. to 8:00 P.M. at small fast-food stands. A bar is open from noon to 10:00 P.M.

- **FACILITIES:** Gift shop, mountain shop, bicycle rental and river raft rental stands, camp store, outdoor swimming pool, and post office (summer only). In winter an outside ice-skating rink is available and equipment for cross-country skiing can be rented.

- **ACTIVITIES:** River rafting, hiking, bicycling, swimming, and evening programs. Cross-country skiing and ice skating in winter.

## HOUSEKEEPING CAMP

Yosemite National Park, CA 95389 • (209) 372–8338

*Housekeeping Camp*

Housekeeping Camp is a complex of 226 concrete and canvas guest rooms surrounding several larger wooden structures that provide support facilities, such as a registration desk, a laundry faciltity, and common bathrooms and showers. Rooms are built two to a unit, with the back of each room sharing a concrete wall with another identical room. The rooms are constructed of cement on three sides (each two-room unit has concrete walls constructed in an H pattern), with a canvas entry and a canvas roof that extends over a concrete floor and a front concrete patio area that has a food storage locker, a picnic table, and a cooking shelf. A metal grill for charbroiling is on the ground outside each patio area. A privacy fence constructed of branches surrounds the front of each room. The canvas entry door cannot be secured, which means that you must leave valuables locked in your vehicle.

Each room has one double bed or two single cots, and a single, fold-down bunk bed. The interior also has a mirror, an electric light, and electrical outlets. None of the rooms have a private bathroom, so guests are required to use centrally located bathhouses. Guests must supply their own sheets, blankets, and pillows, although blankets and pillows can be rented at the registration building. Soap and towels for bathing are supplied without charge in the common bathhouses. The dozen or so housekeeping units on the bank of the Merced River are the best choice. Other units have little in the way of privacy or a view.

Housekeeping Camp rooms represent national park lodging at its most basic. These relatively inexpensive rooms are preferable in Yosemite Valley only to the tightly packed tent cabins in Curry Village. No eating facilities are available here, although a camp store is near the registration building. Housekeeping Camp does have showers and a laundry facility. This is a stop on the free shuttle so that guests can ride to other valley locations for food and frolic.

- **ROOMS:** The rooms are identical, with beds for four persons. Two additional cots can be rented. None of the rooms have a private bath. One section has handicap-accessible units.

- **RATES:** One to four persons pay the same price ($48); each additional person is $4.00 per night.

- **LOCATION:** On the bank of the Merced River in the southeast section of Yosemite Valley, a short distance west of Curry Village.

- **SEASON:** Spring to mid-October.

- **FOOD:** No restaurant or snack bar is at Housekeeping Camp. A small market has limited groceries. A variety of restaurants and snack facilities can be reached via the free valley shuttle.

- **FACILITIES:** Small market, shower, and laundry.

- **ACTIVITIES:** River rafting, swimming, and hiking.

## YOSEMITE LODGE

Yosemite National Park, CA 95389 • (209) 372–1274

Yosemite Lodge is a large complex of wooden buildings with two categories of overnight guest facilities, including one two-story motel unit and several one- and two-story lodge units. In all, Yosemite Lodge provides a total of 248 rooms. The units are scattered about a service area that includes the registration building, located just north of the main road. A variety of other stores and restaurants are near the registration building and within easy walking distance of any of the guest rooms. Registration parking is directly in front of the registration building, but overnight guest parking is a distance from some of the rooms.

*Lodge Rooms at Yosemite Lodge*

Bellhops are available to assist with luggage. None of the rooms at Yosemite Lodge have television or air-conditioning. Other amenities vary. Yosemite Lodge is located in the northwest section of Yosemite Valley, near the foot of Yosemite Falls.

Nineteen standard rooms located in Cedar were constructed in the late 1950s. All have a private bath, most with a shower-tub combination. Beds in these rooms vary from one double bed to two queen-size beds. These motel-type rooms each have heat and telephones but no balconies or patios. Although the buildings are situated in a shady area, the views are minimal. This group includes eight extra-large "family" rooms that each contain one double bed and four single beds and rent for the same price as other standard rooms.

Twelve newer one- and two-story buildings constructed in the mid- to late 1960s contain 229 lodge rooms that each have a dressing area, a balcony or patio, a telephone, and additional furniture including a desk, a table, three chairs, and a nightstand. Two chairs and a table are on the patio. These units each have a full bath. The three newest of the lodge buildings are Aspen, Dogwood, and Tamarack. Rooms 621–624 offer a fairly good view of Upper Yosemite Falls; most of the other rooms have views obstructed by trees and bushes.

Yosemite Lodge is located in the center of facilities and activities. The complex is in front of scenic Yosemite Falls. Food service, with a food court and two

**A** variety of tours are offered to Yosemite visitors. These include the two-hour Valley Floor Tour, the four-hour Glacier Point Tour, the Mariposa Grove Tour, the Big Trees Tram Tour, the Tuolumne Meadows Hikers' Bus, and the full-day Grand Tour, which combines the Glacier Point and Mariposa Grove Tours with a lunch at the Wawona Hotel. Most tours depart from Yosemite Lodge. Tickets can be purchased at several locations in the valley. Call (209) 372–1240 for information.

restaurants, is more varied than other locations in Yosemite Valley. You will also find an ice cream stand, an Environmental shop, a gift shop, and a cocktail lounge with a large-screen TV. A tour desk is inside the registration building. The free shuttle stops across the street from the registration building and provides access to all the facilities and activities in the valley.

- ■ **ROOMS:** Doubles, triples, and quads, with six persons in a limited number of rooms. All rooms have private baths. At least one handicap-accessible room is available.

- ■ **RATES:** Peak/value rates. Value season is November through March, excluding holidays. Standard rooms ($103/$91); lodge rooms ($130/$106). Rates quoted are for two adults. Additional discounts available during midweek stays in value season. Each additional person is $10 per night for standard rooms, $12 for lodge rooms. Children twelve and under stay free.

- ■ **LOCATION:** In the northwest section of Yosemite Valley, near the double waterfall.

- ■ **SEASON:** Yosemite Lodge is open year-round.

- ■ **FOOD:** A food court is open for breakfast and lunch, coffee/snacks, and dinner ($4.00–$12.00). The Garden Terrace offers a moderately priced buffet for dinner ($3.00–$14.00). The Mountain Room Restaurant serves upscale dinners ($8.00–$30.00) with an excellent view of Yosemite Falls. The ice cream stand is open from noon until 5:00 P.M.

- ■ **FACILITIES:** Gift shops, food court, restaurants, cocktail lounge, branch post office, bicycle rental, tour desk, swimming pool, outdoor amphitheater.

- ■ **ACTIVITIES:** Evening programs, swimming, biking, hiking.

## Lodging Outside Yosemite Valley

Three very different Yosemite National Park lodging facilities are outside Yosemite Valley. Probably the oldest lodging facility in any national park, the Wawona Hotel comprises six white frame buildings situated in a peaceful setting a few miles inside the park's south entrance. Tuolumne Meadows Lodge and White Wolf Lodge offer mostly tent cabins for an entirely different lodging experience in Yosemite's high country. Although in the same park, these two locations seem worlds apart from one another as well as from lodging facilities in Yosemite Valley.

### WAWONA HOTEL

P.O. Box 2005 • Wawona, CA 95389 • (209) 375–6556

The Wawona (an Indian term meaning "big tree") Hotel is the grande dame of the national parks. While some would argue that Death Valley's Furnace Creek Inn and Yosemite's own Ahwahnee are more elegant, the Wawona is without doubt one of the grandest. The Wawona Hotel is a complex of six white frame buildings, the oldest of which was constructed in 1876. The newest of the buildings was built in 1918. The complex is similar in appearance

*Main Hotel Building at Wawona*

to a late-1800s western military post. The Wawona Hotel is 4 miles inside the south entrance to Yosemite National Park and 25 miles south of popular Yosemite Valley. No public transportation operates between the hotel and Yosemite Valley.

The six buildings at Wawona offer a total of 104 rooms. Each of the buildings contains overnight lodging rooms, although the size of the buildings and the rooms within them vary considerably. The main building, which houses registration, a large dining room, and an attractive lounge area, has twenty-eight rooms, all on the second floor. Both floors of this large, two-story building have an impressive wraparound veranda with white railings and posts. Wicker benches, chairs, and tables on the lower veranda offer a place for guests to relax while viewing the grassy front lawn that surrounds a stone fountain. Beverages are served here during the late afternoon and early evening. The other five buildings are smaller but have a similar architectural style, including verandas with tables and chairs.

Although rooms vary by size, view, and building, only two price categories are used: with or without private bath. Fifty of the 104 rooms have a private bath and rent for about $50 per night more than rooms without a private bath. Guests in rooms without private bath must use community shower and bathroom facilities located in three of the buildings. Community bathrooms, accessed from the outside porches, are a distance from some of the rooms. Nearly all the rooms in the

The Wawona Hotel has been in continuous operation for more than 120 years, longer than any other lodging unit in the national park system. The Wawona had already served travelers for more than a decade before Yosemite National Park was established. In the early days guests enjoyed meals featuring vegetables gathered from a local garden and freshly prepared fish and venison from the nearby streams and woods. The hotel even had its own dairy so guests could enjoy fresh milk and cream. The Wawona, a National Historic Landmark, has its own golf course, which opened for business in June 1918 as the first course in the Sierra Nevada.

main building are relatively small and without a private bathroom. Views vary, with some rooms providing a scenic view toward the front lawn and others in an inside hallway having no view at all. Since the view is not considered in the rate, request a room in the front with a view of the lawn.

If staying in the main building isn't important, request a room in one-story Clark Cottage or Washburn Cottage, but be aware that both cottages have a limit of two persons per room. Clark Cottage is directly beside the main building and has some of the nicest rooms at Wawona. All rooms have a ceiling fan and private bath. Two-story Washburn Cottage, which was renovated in 1999, has a total of sixteen rooms, all with private baths. The upstairs rooms with one queen-size bed, have an interior hallway that causes them to be somewhat smaller than downstairs rooms. These rooms do not have a veranda. The larger first-floor rooms have a king-size bed. Moore Cottage, with nine rooms, sits on a hill directly behind the main hotel building, with private parking next to the building. Two of these rooms have private baths. The upstairs rooms are smaller and do not have a veranda. This is the only building in which children are not allowed. White Cottage has only three rooms, two with private baths. The third room, room 51, must use bathrooms in the Annex. The two-story Annex has thirty-nine rooms, all of which enjoy a veranda. Two handicap-accessible rooms are in this building. All of the buildings are clustered closely together, so there should be no concern about the walking distance to the restaurant or lounge.

The Wawona Hotel is a peaceful alternative to lodging facilities in busy Yosemite Valley. The dining room retains its Victorian flavor, with tall windows offering views out the front and side of the main building. Outside tables are also available. Although named a hotel, the Wawona is actually more of a resort. The hotel has a swimming pool, a tennis court, and a nine-hole golf course. A practice putting green is on the hotel's front lawn. The hotel is adjacent to Pioneer Village, a collection of historic buildings that introduce visitors to some of the events shaping Yosemite's history. Included are a covered bridge, horse-drawn coaches, a homestead, and numerous other historic buildings. A free shuttle bus operates between the hotel and Mariposa Grove, the site of many giant sequoia trees.

> President Teddy Roosevelt came to the Wawona Hotel on May 3, 1903. Assigned to room 215, the president dropped off his bags and went off to the Big Trees area to meet with conservationist John Muir. This meeting gave Muir an opportunity to convince Roosevelt to expand the park to include Yosemite Valley. Mariposa Grove and Yosemite Valley were at the time owned by the state of California.

- **ROOMS:** Mostly doubles, with a few triples and quads. About half the rooms have private baths. Rooms with private bath are often fully booked a year ahead during peak season. Previous guests often request particular rooms, so be as specific as possible about the type and location of the room you want. Limited handicap-accessible rooms are in the Annex.

- **RATES:** Rooms with private bath ($147); rooms without private bath ($96). Rates reduced $8.00 to $20.00 per night from November 30 to mid-March. Rates quoted are for two adults. Each additional person is $16 per night. Children twelve and under stay free. Several packages are offered for fall and winter.

- **LOCATION:** Twenty miles north of the town of Oakhurst and 4 miles north of the south entrance to Yosemite National Park. The hotel is approximately 25 miles from Yosemite Valley.

- **SEASON:** The hotel is open all year.

- **FOOD:** A beautiful dining room in the main building serves breakfast ($4.00–$8.00), lunch ($5.00–$8.00), and dinner ($11–$20). During the summer months an old-fashioned barbecue is served on Saturday night. A snack shop at the golf shop in the Annex offers sandwiches and beverages from spring to fall. A market with limited groceries is a short walk from the hotel.

- **FACILITIES:** Swimming pool, tennis court, nine-hole golf course, putting green, market, gift shop, post office, gas station, historic Pioneer Village.

- **ACTIVITIES:** Golf, tennis, horse rides, stagecoach rides, swimming, fishing, and hiking.

## TUOLUMNE MEADOWS LODGE

Yosemite National Park, CA 95389 • (209) 372–8413

Tuolumne Meadows Lodge is a group of sixty-nine canvas tent cabins situated high in the Sierras. The lodge offers stays of up to seven days and is an attractive location for visitors who plan to hike to other camps in the High Sierra Loop. Tuolumne Meadows also attracts people who enjoy the crisp air of an alpine environment. The tents are on a hill to the east of a canvas lodge that houses the registration area and a dining room. The lodge is located about a mile off Tioga Road, 9 miles from the Tioga Pass Entrance on the east side of Yosemite National Park. It is 52 miles from Yosemite Valley.

The sixty-nine tents at Tuolumne Meadows are virtually identical to those at Curry Village in the valley. Tents are on a cement slab, and each unit has an inside wood stove for heat. Each canvas tent is equipped with either four single beds or one double bed plus two single beds. Sheets, pillows, and blankets are provided. The lodge also has maid service. The tents have no electricity or plumbing, so guests must use a common bathhouse with showers. Guests are also provided with candles for light, wood for the stove, and towels for the bathhouse. A large central parking lot is a moderate walk from many of the tent cabins.

*At an elevation of 8,600 feet, Tuolumne Meadows is a center of summer activity in Yosemite National Park. It is also the main access point for the High Sierra camps—Merced Lake, Vogelsang, Glen Aulin, May Lake, and Sunrise Camp—that offer dormitory-style accommodations. These hike-in camps offer canvas cabins with concrete floors and single and double beds. Linens and blankets are provided. Breakfast and dinner at each camp are served in a central dining tent. The High Sierra camps are very popular, and reservations are made by lottery applications available by writing Yosemite Reservations, 5410 East Home Avenue, Fresno, CA 93727. Applications are accepted October 15 to November 30, with the drawing held in mid-December.*

*Tent Cabin at Tuolumne Meadows Lodge*

Tuolumne Meadows Lodge is in a lovely area of Yosemite National Park and is appropriate for those who don't mind roughing it a little. The tent cabins are near the Tuolumne River's Dana Fork, which runs through the largest subalpine meadow in the Sierra Nevada. No cooking or picnicking is permitted in or near the tent cabins. The nearby restaurant serves regular breakfast items and five or six dinner entrees at reasonable prices. Beer and wine are also available. Other facilities are available at Tuolumne Meadows Store, about 2 miles away on Tioga Road.

*Conservationist John Muir first visited Yosemite in 1868. Muir recruited Robert Underwood Johnson, editor of Century magazine, to use Johnson's influence to protect this area, especially in the high meadows that were being used to graze sheep. Muir and Johnson camped together in Tuolumne Meadows as they planned a strategy to gain national park status for the high county around Yosemite Valley.*

- **ROOMS:** Doubles, triples, and quads. No rooms have private baths. There are no handicap-accessible cabins.

- **RATES:** All tent cabins ($56). Rate quoted is for two adults. Each additional adult is $8.00; each additional child, $4.00.

- **LOCATION:** One mile south of Tioga Road, 9 miles west of the Tioga Pass entrance.

- **SEASON:** Late spring to early fall. Season depends on the weather.

- **FOOD:** A dining room in the registration/dining tent serves breakfast ($8.00) and dinner ($15). Reservations are required for dinner. Box lunches ($6.17) are available when ordered by 8:00 the previous evening. Fast food is available at Tuolumne Meadows Grill from 7:30 A.M. to 6:00 P.M. The grill is 2 miles away on Tioga Road.

- **TRANSPORTATION:** No public transportation is available to the lodge. A free shuttle operates between the lodge and the store.

- **FACILITIES:** Minimal gifts and necessities are sold near the registration desk. Tuolumne Meadows Store has a post office, market, gas station, climbing school, and stable.

- **ACTIVITIES:** Hiking, fishing, horseback riding, and rock climbing.

## WHITE WOLF LODGE

Yosemite National Park 95389 • (209) 372–8416

White Wolf Lodge comprises a wooden registration/dining building, four wood cabins, and twenty-four canvas tent cabins. A central bathhouse with showers is located near the tent cabins. The lodge appeals primarily to people who want to get away from it all, especially the congestion of Yosemite Valley. White Wolf Lodge, at an altitude of 8,000 feet, is in an isolated part of the High Sierra just off Tioga Road. The lodge is approximately 30 miles east of Yosemite Valley.

The lodge has four wood cabins, each with two double beds, propane heat, electricity, and a full bath. The cabins have a small front porch and are built as duplexes. Parking is directly in front of the buildings, and the dining room is next door. The tent cabins at White Wolf

> Yosemite's mountain meadows were once used for sheep grazing. According to legend, a sheepherder in this area claimed he had seen a "white wolf"—thus, the name for this area. It's not certain that wolves ever inhabited this area of the Sierra Nevada, so the sheepherder may actually have spotted a coyote.

Lodge are identical to the cabins described for Tuolumne Meadows Lodge. Each tent has a wood stove, with wood provided, candles for light, and either four single beds or one double and two single beds. Linens with maid service are provided. The tents have no electtricity or plumbing. This area is known to have bears, so food must be stored in metal "bear boxes" located behind the tent cabins.

White Wolf Lodge provides solitude in an attractive outdoor environment. This is a good place to meet other guests, because there are not many activities to divert their attention. The cozy restaurant has a stone fireplace and serves breakfast and dinner in small inside and outside dining areas.

- **ROOMS:** Doubles, triples, and quads. Full bathrooms are only in the four wood cabins. A community bathhouse is available for guests in the tent cabins. No handicap-accessible rooms are available.

*Wooden Cabins at White Wolf Lodge*

- **RATES:** Tent cabins ($52). Rate quoted is for two adults. Each additional adult is $8.00 per night; each additional child, $4.00. Wood cabins with private bath ($71). Rate quoted is for one to four persons.

- **LOCATION:** Just north of Tioga Road, 30 miles east of Yosemite Valley.

- **SEASON:** Late spring to early fall, depending on the weather.

- **FOOD:** A small dining room serves regular breakfast items ($4.00–$6.50) and four to five dinner entrees ($11–$20). Reservations are required for dinner.

- **TRANSPORTATION:** No public transportation is provided to White Wolf Lodge.

- **FACILITIES:** Small store and restaurant. Central bathhouse with showers.

- **ACTIVITIES:** Hiking.

Tioga Road (Highway 120), which accesses both White Wolf Lodge and Tuolumne Meadows Lodge, was originally built as a mining road in 1882–1883. It was modernized in 1961. The two-lane paved road climbs to an elevation of 9,945 feet as it winds 75 miles across the Sierra high country from Yosemite Valley to Lee Vining, California. The road closes in winter and, depending on the weather, generally reopens in May. Road and weather information is available from a National Park Service recording at (209) 372–0200.

# COLORADO

**STATE TOURIST INFORMATION**

(800) 265–6723

www.colorado.com

## MESA VERDE NATIONAL PARK

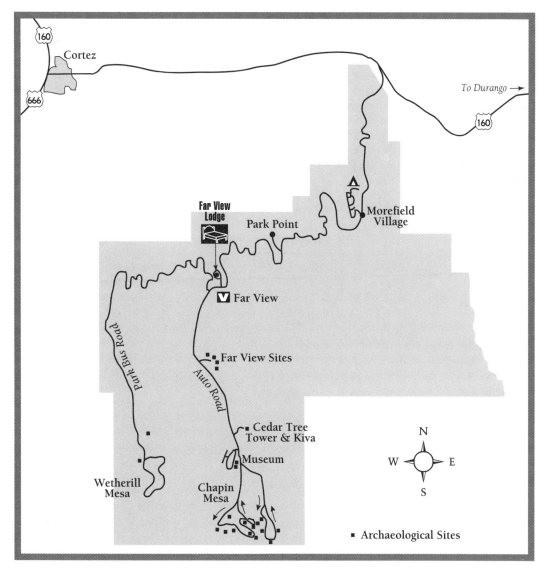

# MESA VERDE NATIONAL PARK

Mesa Verde National Park, CO 81330
(970) 529–4461 or 529–4475
www.nps.gov/meve

**M**esa Verde National Park, stretching over 52,000 acres, has some of the best-preserved pre-Columbian cliff dwellings in the United States. Native tribes lived here for more than 700 years before abandoning their homes in the late 1200s. There are a variety of visitor activities, including guided tours of the ruins and evening programs. Exhibits of prehistoric and historic Indian arts and crafts are at the Far View Visitor Center and the museum at Chapin Mesa. The 12-mile mountain road to Wetherill Mesa is open only during summer months. Vehicles that are more than 8,000 pounds GVW and/or longer than 25 feet are prohibited on this road. Mesa Verde National Park is in the southwestern corner of Colorado, 36 miles west of Durango on U.S. Highway 160. The park's entrance road from U.S. Highway 160 has steep grades and sharp curves. Trailers must be dropped off 4 miles inside the entrance, near the campground.

**PARK ENTRANCE FEE:** $10.00 per vehicle or $5.00 per person, good for seven days.

## Lodging in Mesa Verde National Park

Mesa Verde has only a single lodging facility, which provides a total of 150 rooms in seventeen motel-style buildings. Far View Lodge is 15 miles from the park entrance station, near Far View Visitor Center and Far View Terrace. None of the park ruins are within walking distance of the lodge.

### FAR VIEW LODGE

P.O. Box 277 • Mancos, CO 81328 • (970) 529–4421
www.visitmesaverde.com

**F**ar View Lodge features an attractive adobe building housing the registration desk, a dining room, a gift shop, and a cocktail lounge, with seventeen separate but nearby motel-type wooden buildings, each with from four to twenty rooms that generally offer exceptional views. The lodge is 15 miles inside the park entrance, near the Far View Visitor Center. Paved roads near the lodge lead to the park ruins.

Far View Lodge is situated at 8,250 feet on a shoulder of the Mesa Verde. It provides an outstanding view of up to 100 miles and three states, Colorado, New Mexico, and Arizona (hence the name). The lodge offers 150 rooms. Guests have a choice of one queen-size, one queen and one double, or two double beds, and each room has a bath with shower but no tub, heat, and a clock radio but no telephone, television, or air-conditioning. Forty of the rooms have been upgraded to a Deluxe classification, because they have been recently refurbished and have mini-refrigerators, coffeepots, hair dryers, and iron and ironing board.

*A Four-Unit Building at Far View Lodge*

All of the seventeen lodge buildings are one-level except for two that are two-story. Each room has a large window and a private balcony with two chairs. The buildings are situated on a hillside so that all the rooms offer a view of mesas and canyons. All rooms have at least a good view, but some are better than others. The best views are in rooms 131 through 140 and 111 through 120. All these rooms are on the second floor of a two-story building. Adequate parking is available directly outside each building. A number of rooms are handicap accessible. Small pets are permitted, but a deposit is required.

Far View Lodge is ideally situated for visitors to Mesa Verde National Park. It is a short distance off the main road to Wetherill and Chapin Mesas, a quiet but handy location because most guests plan to visit both these areas. A quarter-mile paved trail from the lodge leads to the park's main visitor center, which has exhibits of both prehistoric and historic tribes of the region, including native jewelry and pottery. Tickets for ranger-guided tours of Cliff Palace, Balcony House, Long House, and other guided tours can be purchased in the visitor center. Another quarter mile along the same trail brings visitors to the Far View Terrace, which offers a cafeteria and a large gift shop. Guided half-day and full-day bus tours of the park begin at the lodge, where reservations can be made and tickets purchased. A small gift shop, a very nice restaurant (dinner only), and a lounge are located in the main registration building.

■ **ROOMS:** Doubles, triples, and quads. Rates quoted are for two adults. All rooms have private baths with shower but no bathtub. Several rooms are handicap accessible.

■ **RESERVATIONS:** Far View Lodge, P.O. Box 277, Mancos, CO 81328. Phone (800) 449–2288; fax (970) 533–7831. Deposit required for one night's lodging. Cancellation notice of twenty-four hours is required for refund of deposit.

■ **RATES:** High-season from mid-June to early October ($99–$110); off-season from late April to mid-June and from early October to mid-October ($90–$97). Rates quoted are for two adults. Each additional person is $8.00 per night. Children twelve and under stay free with adults. Special packages (tours and rooms) are available. AAA and AARP discounts are offered, based on availability.

■ **LOCATION:** Fifteen miles inside the entrance to Mesa Verde National Park. The nearest major town is Cortez, Colorado, 10 miles west of the park entrance.

■ **SEASON:** Far View Lodge is open from mid-April to late October.

■ **FOOD:** The registration building houses the attractively decorated Metate Room, which serves excellent dinners ($12–$26). Many of the tables are situated to take advantage of the great view. Alcoholic beverages are served in the dining room and at a lounge on the second floor. A quarter mile away Far View Terrace, open 6:30 A.M. to 9:00 P.M., offers three meals a day in a nice cafeteria. A small cafeteria offers breakfast and lunch at Spruce Tree Terrace, and the Knife Edge Cafe offers snacks all day at Morefield Village.

■ **TRANSPORTATION:** Scheduled air service serves Cortez and Durango, where rental cars are available. The nearest train service is in Grand Junction, Colorado.

■ **FACILITIES:** Dining room, gift shop, cocktail lounge. Eleven miles away Morefield Village has laundry facilities, a gift shop, snack bar, gas station, and store with groceries, beer, wine, and camping supplies. A gift shop and cafeteria are at Far View Terrace.

■ **ACTIVITIES:** Full- and half-day guided tours of Mesa Verde Indian ruins originate from Far View Lodge. Ranger-guided tours of Cliff Palace, Balcony House, and Long House require tickets, which can be purchased at the visitor center. Chapin Mesa Museum has exhibits on native tribes. Evening campground programs are presented at Morefield Campground. A multimedia tour of Mesa Verde (fee charged) is offered four times each evening at Far View Lodge. Brochures for self-guided tours of the Ruins Road can be purchased at the visitor center. Trails of from 1.5 to nearly 8 miles are available for hikers. Special events, such as Hopi dances and pottery demonstrations, are scheduled from May through October.

The Durango & Silverton Narrow Gauge Railroad offers scenic full-day train trips from Durango, Colorado, to the historic mining town of Silverton and back on tracks originally laid in the early 1880s. The authentic coal-burning, steam-powered locomotives were manufactured in the early 1920s for the Durango and Rio Grande Railroad. This is one of the finest historic train trips in the United States. Reservations are recommended. Write Durango & Silverton Narrow Gauge Railroad Company, 479 Main Avenue, Durango, CO 81301, or phone (970) 247-2733.

# FLORIDA

**STATE TOURIST INFORMATION**

(888) 246–8728

www.flausa.com

## EVERGLADES NATIONAL PARK

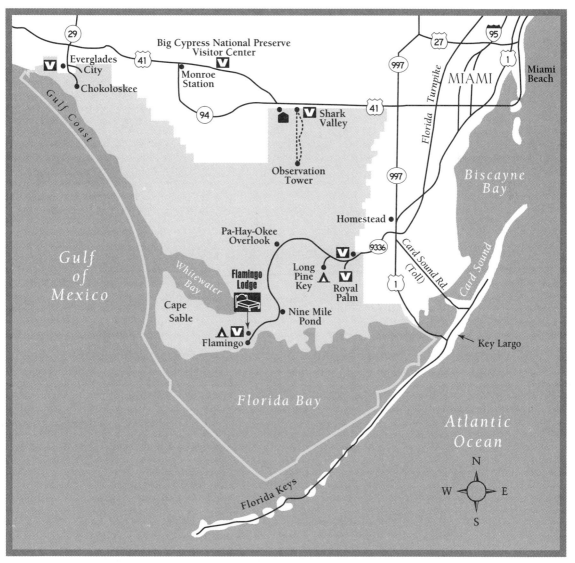

# EVERGLADES NATIONAL PARK

40001 State Road 9336
Homestead, FL 33034
(305) 242–7700
www.nps.gov/ever

Everglades National Park comprises more than 1.5 million acres of subtropical wilderness, including extensive freshwater and saltwater areas, open prairies, and mangrove forests. A large portion of the park is covered by a giant river only a few inches deep and 50 miles wide. The park's main visitor center is near the main entrance, west of Florida City. A 38-mile paved road that leads from the visitor center to Flamingo provides access to many trails, both long and short, through the park. These trails offer the best chance to see wildlife close-up. Many of the trails are only one-fourth- to one-half-mile long. Longer trails near Flamingo lead deeper into the Everglades. The park also has many miles of canoe trails. The park is located across the southern tip of Florida, with main access from State Highway 9336. The entrance is 11 miles south of Florida City.

**PARK ENTRANCE FEE:** $10.00 per vehicle or $5.00 per person, good for seven days.

## Lodging in Everglades National Park

The park's lodging consists of a single motel-style facility and cottages at Flamingo, near the terminus of the main park road. A restaurant and marina are nearby. No other accommodations or eating facilities are in the park. A variety of lodging and eating establishments are outside the park at Florida City and Homestead. Flamingo is approximately 83 miles southwest of Miami International Airport.

### FLAMINGO LODGE, MARINA, AND OUTPOST RESORT

1 Flamingo Lodge Highway • Flamingo, FL 33034 • (941) 695–3101
info@flamingolodge.com • www.flamingolodge.com

Flamingo Lodge is part of a resort complex consisting of motel buildings, multiple cottage units, a full-service marina with a store, the National Park visitor center, and a main building with a restaurant, bar, cafe, and gift shop. The lodge provides a total of 127 rooms, most of which are in the motel buildings. The motel buildings and the cottages are separate from but only a short walk to the restaurant and marina. The resort is on Florida Bay at the southern tip of Everglades National Park.

Accommodations at the lodge consist of 103 rooms in six cement motel buildings and twenty-four rooms in twelve wood duplex cottages. Rooms in the four one-story and two two-story motel buildings each have a telephone, heat, air-conditioning, and television. The rooms are carpeted and have two double beds and a private bathroom with a combination shower-tub. The forty-two rooms in the one-story buildings each have a back sliding-glass

*Flamingo Lodge*

door. Sixty rooms in the two-story buildings have a large back window. One suite has one bedroom with two double beds, two baths, a kitchen, and a sitting/dining area with a sofa bed. Most of the motel rooms offer a view.

Twelve cottage buildings are constructed as duplex units to offer twenty-four rooms, each with a fully equipped kitchenette and one bedroom with two double beds. These units do not have television. The kitchenette is fully equipped for cooking, and an attached sitting area has a sofa bed. All but the bathroom and kitchen are carpeted. The cottages have a private bath with a shower but no bathtub. One cottage is handicap accessible with a combination shower-tub and one double bed. Adequate parking is available for both the motel units and the cottages.

Flamingo Lodge is a good place to stay while you explore one of America's most unique national parks. The lodge enjoys a scenic location on Florida Bay and is close to a restaurant, cafe, and cocktail lounge, although these facilities are limited April through October. A National Park Service visitor center is also nearby. This is a pleasant place to walk, jog, or bike. A screened pool that overlooks the bay is available for guests of both the motel units and the cottages. Houseboats, motorboats, kayaks, canoes, and bicycles are available for rent at the marina. Narrated boat tours are available at the marina. Be warned that mosquitoes can get nasty in the wet season, which begins in late spring and continues through summer. The best time to visit is in winter, when the weather is mild and mosquitoes are less numerous.

- ■ **ROOMS:** Doubles, triples, and quads. The suite and cottages can hold up to six. All rooms have a private bathroom. One cottage is handicap accessible.

- ■ **RESERVATIONS:** Flamingo Lodge, 1 Flamingo Lodge Highway, Flamingo, FL 33034. Phone (800) 600–3813; fax (941) 695–3921. One night's deposit is required within two weeks of making a reservation. Cancellation requires at least forty-eight hours' notice for refund of deposit.

- **RATES:** High season (December 15–March 31); swing season (April 1–April 30 and November 1–December 14); low season (May 1–October 31). Lodge room ($95/$79/$65); Cottage ($135/$99/$89); Lodge suite ($145/$110/$99). Rates quoted are for two adults in lodge units and for four adults in suites and cottages. Children under seventeen stay free with an adult.

- **LOCATION:** Directly on Florida Bay at the southern tip of Everglades National Park. Flamingo is 38 miles southwest of the park's main visitor center.

- **SEASON:** Flamingo Lodge is open year-round. Services offered vary seasonally and are limited during the summer. Peak season is during winter.

- **FOOD:** A full-service restaurant serves three meals a day during winter months but may be closed in spring, summer, and fall. A cafe in the same building is open seasonally. Food service April through October is limited. Limited groceries are sold at the marina year-round.

- **TRANSPORTATION:** Scheduled air, train, and bus service is available at Miami, about 85 miles northeast of Flamingo and 45 miles northeast of the park's main visitor center. *Note:* No public transportation to the park.

- **FACILITIES:** Restaurant, cocktail lounge, cafe, store, rentals of canoes, kayaks, boats, and bicycles, gift shop, full-service marina.

- **ACTIVITIES:** Swimming, fishing, bird-watching, hiking, biking, boating, charter fishing, sightseeing boat tours, guided hikes.

*Flamingo Lodge derives its name from several hundred flamingos that once wintered in Florida Bay following migration from their summer breeding grounds in the Bahamas. In the late 1800s a small fishing village here selected the name for its post office. Habitat destruction and the killing of the birds for their meat caused an end of the migration around the turn of the century. Although it is uncertain where the birds come from, flamingos are still occasionally sighted in the Florida Bay area.*

# GEORGIA

**STATE TOURIST INFORMATION**
(800) 847–4842
www.georgia.org

## CUMBERLAND ISLAND NATIONAL SEASHORE

P.O. Box 806
St. Marys, GA 31558-0806
(912) 882–4335
www.nps.gov/cuis

Cumberland Island National Seashore comprises more than 36,000 acres of freshwater lakes, magnificent beaches and dunes, and saltwater marshes on Georgia's southernmost coastal barrier island. The island is 18 miles long and, at its widest, 3 miles wide. The National Park Service limit of 300 visitors per day results in a visit to Cumberland Island National Seashore being one of life's great pleasures. The seashore is in southeast Georgia, approximately 30 miles north of Jacksonville, Florida, via Interstate 95 and Georgia Highway 40. Main access to the national seashore is only by a concessioner-operated boat (fee charged) from the small coastal town of St. Marys, Georgia. Access to the island's only public lodging facility is via an inn-operated boat from Fernandina Beach, Florida. No bridges provide vehicular access from the mainland to the island.

## Lodging on Cumberland Island National Seashore

The only public accommodations on Cumberland Island National Seashore are at Greyfield Inn, a privately owned and operated, turn-of-the-century mansion situated in the southern portion of the island. Access to the inn is via a private ferry that makes three trips daily from Dock D at the waterfront in Fernandina Beach, Florida. Fernandina Beach is on Amelia Island, situated at the extreme northeast corner of Florida. No vehicular access is available to the island or the inn.

# CUMBERLAND ISLAND NATIONAL SEASHORE

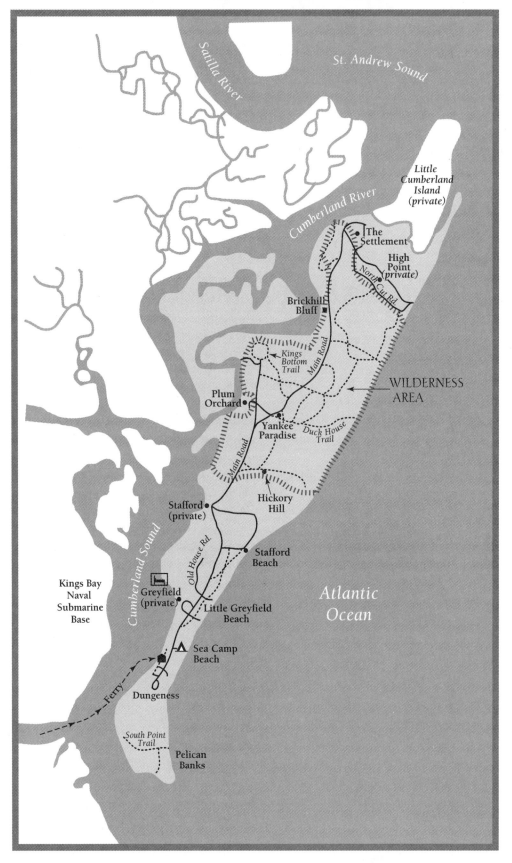

# THE GREYFIELD INN

8 North Second Street • P.O. Box 900 • Fernandina Beach, Florida 32035-6408
(904) 261–6408
seashore@greyfieldinn.com • www.greyfieldinn.com

*Greyfield Inn*

Greyfield Inn is a turn-of-the century, four-story wooden mansion, constructed in 1901, for Margaret Ricketson, daughter of business tycoon Thomas Carnegie (brother to steel magnate Andrew). Margaret Ricketson's daughter, Lucy Ferguson, and her family opened the home to the public in 1962 as an inn. The inn provides eleven rooms in the main house and six rooms in two, separate but nearby cottage buildings. Both the main house and the two cottages are on the western side of the island near the dock area, where employees meet the ferry from Fernandina Beach. Other nearby buildings include a maintenance barn, where bicycles are stored, a bathhouse, and several private homes. The inn and its surrounding buildings sit in a large, cleared area surrounded by forests on three sides and the Intercoastal Waterway on the western side. The Greyfield Inn is accessible only via the inn's private boat that leaves from Fernandina Beach, Florida, and docks adjacent to the inn. Guests of the inn who arrive by private boat may also utilize the dock. Greyfield Inn offers day trips for $75 per person that include boat transportation, a picnic lunch, and use of the inn's facilities.

Greyfield Inn is entered via stairs on the south side that lead to a impressive second-floor veranda with rocking chairs and a large porch swing. The second floor of the house contains a large living room with fireplace, library, self-serve bar, and one bedroom. The dining room, kitchen, breakfast room, offices, and a small gift shop are on the first floor. Bedrooms and bathrooms occupy all of the third and fourth floors. No elevator is available.

Eleven of the seventeen rooms available at the Greyfield Inn are in the main house. Of these, only one bedroom, the Library Suite, is on the second floor of the house. Eight rooms are on the third floor, and two newly remodeled suites are on the fourth floor. The rooms differ in price, size, furniture, and bath facilities, but all of the bedrooms have one bed, either a double, a queen, or a king, depending on the size of the room. Price is determined by the size of the room and its accompanying bath facilities. All of the rooms have heating and air-conditioning, but not all rooms have a private bathroom. All eight bedrooms on the third floor have either an adjoining bathroom (one bathroom separating two bedrooms) or a shared bathroom (a bathroom in the hallway). The third floor has three bathrooms for eight bedrooms. The Stafford and Dungeness Suites on the fourth floor, and the Library Suite on the second floor, each have a private bathroom. All bedrooms in the two one-story cottage units have private bathrooms. The larger cottage building has four bedrooms that share a common living area and a covered porch. The smaller cottage building has two bedrooms, with a common living area and a small, covered front porch. All the bedrooms are comfortable and nicely decorated with family heirlooms and antiques. Our choice would be the Stafford Suite on the fourth floor of the main house, if you don't mind climbing stairs. If stairs are a problem, choose the Library Suite on the second floor. The inn accepts reservations for a particular room.

Greyfield Inn is a perfect place to relax and get away from it all. You don't need to cook, make the bed, or worry about meeting a deadline. There are no televisions to watch, cars to drive, or telephones to answer. In fact, the inn has just one telephone that it reserves for emergency use only. As a guest you will be treated to a full Southern breakfast, with fresh baked rolls, and a gourmet dinner at which guests are expected to dress appropriately (dinner jackets are available for those who left theirs behind). Your stay will include a half-day naturalist-guided tour to the north end of the island and the church where John Kennedy, Jr., was married in 1996 to Carolyn Bessette. One of the country's most beautiful and uncrowded beaches is a short hike from the inn. Here you can jump in the waves, fish in the surf, or just stroll the pristine beach as far as you like. Perhaps you would like to hop on a bicycle and peddle down the dirt road to view the remains of Dungeness, Thomas Carnegie's burned mansion. A National Park Service visitor center is nearby. Stay alert and you may see some of the island wildlife, including the famous wild horses. Maybe you would prefer to curl up by the living room fireplace and read a book or sit in the porch swing on the veranda. Regardless, you should return home rested and ready for battle.

Pittsburgh residents Thomas and Lucy Carnegie first came to Cumberland Island in 1881. After purchasing 4,000 acres on the island, the couple set about building an impressive plantation home, which they named Dungeness, that would rival homes constructed by other millionaires on neighboring Jekyll Island. Thomas died in 1886, prior to completion of the home. Widow Lucy stayed on and expanded the family holdings until she had acquired nearly 90 percent of the island. The mansion that is now Greyfield Inn, given as a wedding gift to daughter Margaret and her husband Oliver Ricketson, is one of four homes that Lucy Carnegie had built on Cumberland Island for her children. The uninhabited Dungeness was destroyed by fire in 1959. The ruins at the south end of the island continue to attract tourists.

- **RESERVATIONS:** The Greyfield Inn, 8 North 2nd Street, P.O. Box 900, Fernandina Beach, Florida 32035-0900. Phone (888) 357–7617 or (904) 261–6408. Two- and three-night minimum stays apply to weekends and holidays, respectively. A deposit equal to half the stay is required. A full refund requires thirty days' notice except for holidays, when no refunds are granted. Check-in is 1:00 P.M. and checkout is 11:00 A.M.

- **RATES:** Rates range from $290 (North Porch, without private bath) to $450 (Stafford Suite and Library Suite, each with private bath) per room per night. Most rooms are $375 or $395 per night. Taxes and gratuities add approximately 25 percent to the quoted room charge. Rates are for single or double occupancy and include three meals per day. Also included in the rates are unlimited snacks and nonalcoholic beverages, canapés at the evening cocktail hour, a three- to four-hour guided nature tour, the boat trip to and from Fernandina Beach, and use of bicycles, beach equipment, and fishing gear.

- **LOCATION:** The inn is located on Cumberland Island, the southernmost barrier island off the coast of Georgia. Access is from the boat dock in downtown Fernandina Beach, north of Jacksonville.

- **SEASON:** Greyfield Inn is open all year.

- **FOOD:** Three meals a day are included in the price of the room. Meals include a full breakfast, a picnic lunch, and a gourmet dinner of regional specialties. Canapés are served during the cocktail hour. Complimentary coffee, tea, soft drinks, and snacks are available throughout the day. A full self-service bar is available to guests on an honor system.

- **TRANSPORTATION:** Scheduled airlines and Amtrak serve Jacksonville, Florida, where rental vehicles are available. The inn offers free boat transportation from Dock D in downtown Fernandina Beach to the inn, three times a day, at 9:30 A.M., 12:15 P.M., and 5:30 P.M. The boat leaves Cumberland Island for Fernandina Beach at 8:00 A.M., 10:45 A.M., and 3:30 P.M. The boat ride takes about 45 minutes.

- **FACILITIES:** Dining room, bar, and gift shop.

- **ACTIVITIES:** Guided nature tour, beach walking, hiking, swimming in the ocean, birdwatching, bicycling, and fishing.

# HAWAII

**STATE TOURIST INFORMATION**
(808) 423–1811
www.visit.hawaii.org

## HAWAII VOLCANOES NATIONAL PARK

Hawaii Volcanoes National Park, HI 96718
(808) 967–7311
www.nps.gov/havo

Hawaii Volcanoes National Park comprises 220,000 acres of active volcanism, including 13,676-foot Mauna Loa and famous Kīlauea, near where most of the park's activity is centered. An 11-mile paved road that circles the Kīlauea Caldera provides access to scenic stops and nature walks. Hawaii Volcanoes National Park is located in the southeastern corner of the island of Hawaii. The visitor center is approximately 29 miles southwest of Hilo, on Hawaii Highway 11, which bisects the park.

**PARK ENTRANCE FEE:** $10.00 per vehicle or $5.00 per person, good for seven days.

### Lodging in Hawaii Volcanoes National Park

Volcano House, with forty-two rooms, is the only hotel facility in the park. It is located just off Highway 11 on the north end of Crater Rim Drive, which circles Kīlauea Crater. Ten camper cabins operated by the same firm are at Namakani Paio Campground, 3 miles west of the park entrance, on Highway 11. Additional lodging is available in nearby communities and in Hilo. Members of the military may find accommodations at Kīlauea Military Camp, 1 mile west of Park Headquarters. Phone (800) 438–6707 from Oahu and (808) 967–8333 from out of state.

# HAWAII VOLCANOES NATIONAL PARK

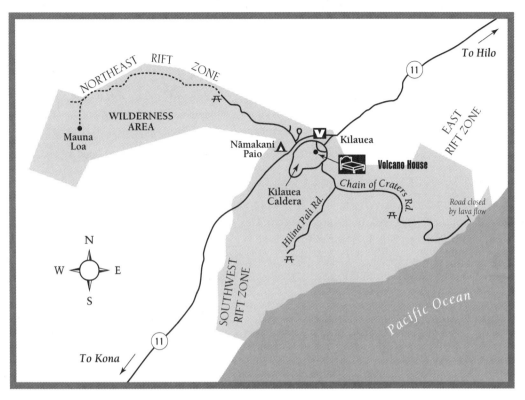

## VOLCANO HOUSE

P.O. Box 53 • Hawaii Volcanoes National Park, HI 96718 • (808) 967–7321

Volcano House is a rustic, two-story wood-and-stone hotel constructed in 1941 and expanded in 1962. The hotel has since been completely renovated. It is the oldest continuously operated hotel in Hawaii. The dining room, gift shops, cocktail lounge, snack bar, lobby, and most of the accommodations are all in a single building on the edge of Kīlauea Crater. A separate two-story building with a small lobby houses ten garden-view rooms. Ten less expensive wood cabins without private bath are 3 miles from the hotel, in the Namakani Paio Campground. Volcano House is located just off Highway 11, on Crater Rim Drive, which circles Kīlauea Caldera.

The hotel has a total of forty-two rooms, twenty of which offer a crater view. Twelve rooms without a crater view rent for about $30–$50 less than rooms with the view. All of these rooms are approximately the same size. Ten somewhat smaller garden-view rooms in a separate building (the Ohia Wing) rent for approximately $80–$90 less than crater-view rooms. Bedding varies from one king, to two doubles, to two twins. Three rooms have a queen plus two twin beds. All rooms are carpeted, are furnished with koa wood furniture, and include heat, telephone, and private bath with shower. Two handicap-accessible rooms have a tub.

The ten single-room wood cabins at Namakani Paio Campground, 3 miles from Volcano House, each have one double bed and two single bunk beds. The cabins also have an electric light (no outlets) and an outdoor grill and picnic table. Linens, pillows, and one blanket are provided when you check in at the Volcano House registration desk. You may wish to bring additional blankets. Cabin guests must use community bathroom facilities, which are situated among the cluster of cabins.

Volcano House is a convenient and interesting place to stay when you will be spending several days touring the Big Island, including a day in this unique national park. The location on the edge of the huge caldera is spectacular. The large lobby includes a famous fireplace that has been burning continuously for many years. The first-class restaurant serves three meals a day, including breakfast and lunch buffets.

*The original Volcano House was constructed in 1866 of grass and ohia poles. The first wooden hotel was built here eleven years later. This structure is across the road from the hotel and now serves as the Volcano Art Center. The main building of the hotel burned in 1940 and was replaced by the current Volcano House, which opened in November 1941.*

- **ROOMS:** Doubles, triples, and quads. All forty-two rooms in the hotel have a private bath. Cabins at Namakani Paio do not have private baths. Two rooms are handicap accessible.

- **RESERVATIONS:** Volcano House, P.O. Box 53, Hawaii Volcanoes National Park, HI 96718. Phone (808) 967–7321; fax (808) 967–8429. One night's deposit required within ten days of confirmation. Cancellation required seventy-two hours ahead of scheduled arrival.

- **RATES:** Crater view ($165–$185); no crater view ($135); Ohia Wing of Volcano House ($85–$95); Namakani Paio cabins ($40). Rates quoted are for two adults. Each additional person is $15.00 per night in Volcano House and $8.00 in the cabins. Children twelve and under stay free with adults.

*Volcano House*

- **LOCATION:** Just off Highway 11 on the north section of Crater Rim Drive. Volcano House is 30 miles from Hilo.

- **SEASON:** Both Volcano House and Namakani Paio cabins are open year-round.

- **FOOD:** Ka Ohelo Dining Room serves daily breakfast ($9.50) and lunch buffets ($12.50). Dinner ($12–$22) is ordered from a menu. A less expensive snack bar serves chili, salads, sandwiches, and beverages. Limited groceries are available in nearby Volcano Village.

- **TRANSPORTATION:** The nearest scheduled airline service is in Hilo, where rental cars are available. A city bus operates between Hilo and the park's visitor center, which is across the road from the hotel.

- **FACILITIES:** Restaurant, snack bar, cocktail lounge, gift shops, National Park Service visitor center, art center, golf course (1 mile away).

- **ACTIVITIES:** Hiking, interpretive programs, golf.

# KENTUCKY

**STATE TOURIST INFORMATION**

(800) 225–8747

Kentuckytourism.com

## MAMMOTH CAVE NATIONAL PARK

P.O. Box 7

Mammoth Cave, KY 42259

(270) 758–2328

www.nps.gov/maca

Mammoth Cave National Park covers 52,830 acres, including the longest recorded cave system in the world. The park features rugged hillsides and beautiful rivers. A variety of guided cave tours are offered throughout the day. The park also has 70 miles of hiking trails, a gravel bicycle trail, and scenic boat rides. Mammoth Cave National Park is located in central Kentucky, approximately 90 miles south of Louisville via I–65.

**PARK ENTRANCE FEE:** No charge.

## Lodging in Mammoth Cave National Park

A single lodging complex in the park, managed by Forever Resorts, offers a wide variety of accommodations that are all close to the visitor center and ticket sales area for cave tours. Buses near the visitor center provide transportation to the cave entrance.

### MAMMOTH CAVE HOTEL

P.O. Box 27 • Mammoth Cave, KY 42259-0027 • (270) 758–2225

www.mammothcavehotel.com

Mammoth Cave Hotel is a lodging complex consisting of a two-story brick hotel, four one-story motel buildings, and thirty cottages; it provides ninety-two total lodging units. Registration for all the lodging is just inside the front entrance to the hotel, which

# MAMMOTH CAVE NATIONAL PARK

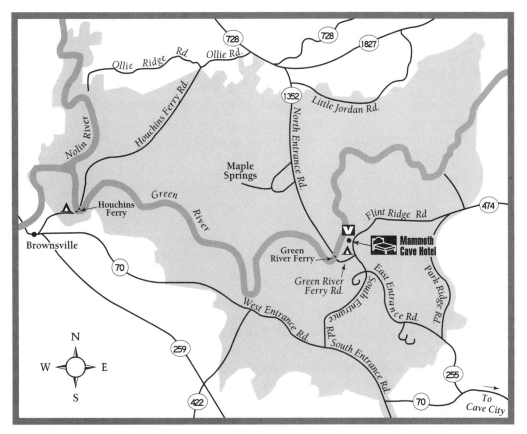

also has a gift shop, a lower lobby, a craft store, a meeting room, and three places to dine. The hotel, motel units, and cottages are all in an expansive grassy area near the National Park Service visitor center, where tickets are sold for tours to this famous cave. Tours leave from just behind the visitor center, which is an easy walk from any of the rooms at the hotel. A big parking area is in front of the hotel. Mammoth Cave Hotel is located just off Highway 70, in the southeastern section of Mammoth Cave National Park. The park is just off I–65 at either the Park City or the Cave City exit.

Four types of accommodations are available at Mammoth Cave Hotel. The least expensive lodging is the twenty Woodland Cottages, clustered on the north side of the visitor center. These rustic wooden structures were constructed in the 1930s and are available in one-, two-, three-, and four-bedroom units. Beds in each bedroom range from a double bed to a double and a twin bed. Only one each of the three- and four-bedroom units is available. Each of these two large buildings has two bathrooms with showers but no tubs. The predominant units are two-bedroom, constructed with one bedroom on each side of a central bathroom. Each of these units has a ceiling fan but no air-conditioning, telephone, or television. Keep this in mind if you will be staying during a period that is likely to be hot and humid.

Ten Hotel Cottages are located across the parking lot from the main hotel. The small wood cabins, also constructed in the 1930s, are in a semicircle along the top of a wooded hillside. Each cabin has air-conditioning, a television, electric heat, carpeting, and a private

*Mammoth Cave Hotel*

bath with shower but no tub. The cottages have a small stone porch. The Hotel Cottages are worth the $10 extra per night compared with the rates for Woodland Cottages because the interior is that much nicer, they have air-conditioning, and the location is less crowded.

The main hotel, constructed in the 1960s, has thirty-eight Heritage Trail rooms in a two-story brick building immediately next to the lobby/registration building. Four handicap-accessible rooms are near the lobby. Although separate, the two buildings are so close together that they are essentially a single structure. The rooms all have a full bath with a combination shower-tub, and most have a private balcony or patio with chairs and a small table. These rooms have heat, air-conditioning, telephone, and television and are nicely furnished. Beds range from one double bed to one king-size bed; a queen-size bed and a double plus a single are also available. Rooms on both floors are entered through an interior corridor that runs the length of the building. This building is the most convenient to the lobby and the dining facilities. Choose a back room on the second floor, with a balcony overlooking a wooded ravine. The handicap-accessible rooms can be entered at ground level from the parking lot.

The four Sunset Point Motor Lodge units are single-story buildings constructed in the 1960s. These units each have heat, air-conditioning, a telephone, a television, and a full bath with a combination shower-tub. All the units have two double beds and are generally recommended for families. A grassy area in front of the units is a good place for kids to play.

Mammoth Cave National Park offers more than the cave tours for which it is so famous. In fact, this is one of our favorite parks. The area in which the lodging facilities are located is very pleasant, with lots of trees and open grassy spaces. Most park visitors have completed their cave tours by the late afternoon so that evenings are perfect for a quiet walk. Inexpensive scenic boat rides on the Green River are operated several times each day. Hiking trails and ranger-led walks are also available. If you plan to take a ranger-led cave tour, be certain to check in at the visitor center behind the hotel as soon as possible after your arrival so that you can reserve a tour time. In fact, you may want to make a reservation (800–967–2283) prior to your arrival.

■ **ROOMS:** Singles, doubles, triples, and quads. Only a couple of buildings will handle more than four. All rooms and cabins have private baths. Four rooms in the hotel are handicap accessible.

- **RESERVATIONS:** Mammoth Cave Hotel, P.O. Box 27, Mammoth Cave, KY 42259-0027. Phone (270) 758–2225; fax (270) 758–2301. One night's deposit required. Refund of deposit requires forty-eight-hour cancellation notice. Pets are allowed only in the Woodland Cottages. A kennel is available without charge for pets brought by room guests.

- **RATES:** Woodland Cottages ($48); Hotel Cottages ($52); Heritage Trail rooms ($68); Sunset Point Motor Lodge ($72). Rates quoted are for two people in the hotel cottages and the Heritage Trail rooms and for four people in the Woodland Cottages and the Sunset Point Motor Lodge. Each additional person is $7.00 per night. Children under sixteen stay free when extra bedding is not required.

- **LOCATION:** The lodging complex at Mammoth Cave is located near the visitor center in the eastern section of the park. From I–65, take exit 53 when traveling south and exit 48 when traveling north.

- **SEASON:** The hotel and motel units are open all year. The Hotel Cottages are open from March to November, and the Woodland Cottages are open from May to October.

- **FOOD:** A dining room serves breakfast ($3.00–$6.00) and dinner ($6.00–$14.00). An adjacent coffee shop serves lunch. A fast-food restaurant is open from 10:30 A.M. to 5:00 P.M. during summer. Limited groceries are available from May through October in the store near the campground.

- **TRANSPORTATION:** The nearest major airports are in Louisville, Kentucky, and Nashville, Tennessee, where rental vehicles are available. Scheduled bus service is available in nearby Cave City, Kentucky.

- **FACILITIES:** Gas station, pet kennels, restaurant, coffee shop, fast-food restaurant (summer only), gift shop, craft store, tennis courts, shuffleboard courts, nature trails, laundry, post office.

- **ACTIVITIES:** Hiking, cave tours, boat tours, tennis, fishing, canoeing, evening campfire programs, ranger talks.

Cave tours are the most popular activity at Mammoth Cave National Park. Approximately a dozen tours are offered, depending on the season and demand. Some tours are easy and last about an hour. Others are strenuous and last from three to six hours. A schedule of each day's cave tours is posted in the visitor center. Cave temperatures are in the fifties, and the paths can be slick, with many steps, so it is important to dress properly. Most tours fill rapidly, so, if possible, make a reservation by mail or phone (800–967–2283) prior to arrival or online at reservations. nps.gov. Reservations may be made up to five months in advance of the tour date you desire. If you arrive at the park without a reservation, be sure to head for the visitor center, where reservations can be made and tickets purchased. You will also be able to obtain information about the various tours that are offered.

# MICHIGAN

STATE TOURIST INFORMATION
(800) 543–2937
www.michigan.org

## ISLE ROYALE NATIONAL PARK

800 East Lakeshore Drive
Houghton, MI 49931
(906) 482–0984
www.nps.gov/isro

Isle Royale National Park comprises 572,000 acres, including the largest island in Lake Superior. Eighty percent of the park is under water. Isle Royale, approximately 45 miles long and 9 miles wide, is a roadless island of forests, lakes, and rugged shores. There are 166 miles of foot trails and numerous inland lakes on the island, where travel is via foot, boat, or floatplane. Isle Royale is located in northwestern Lake Superior, 22 miles southeast of Grand Portage, Minnesota. No roads or bridges provide access to the island.

**PARK ENTRANCE FEE:** A user fee of $4.00 per person per day.

## Lodging in Isle Royale National Park

The only overnight accommodations inside the park are at Rock Harbor, on the south shore of the northeastern tip of the island. Rock Harbor Lodge features motel-type buildings and duplex housekeeping cabins, for a total of eighty rooms. Access to Rock Harbor is via seaplane or scheduled passenger boats from Houghton and Copper Harbor in Michigan's Upper Peninsula and from Grand Portage on Minnesota's north shore.

# ISLE ROYALE NATIONAL PARK

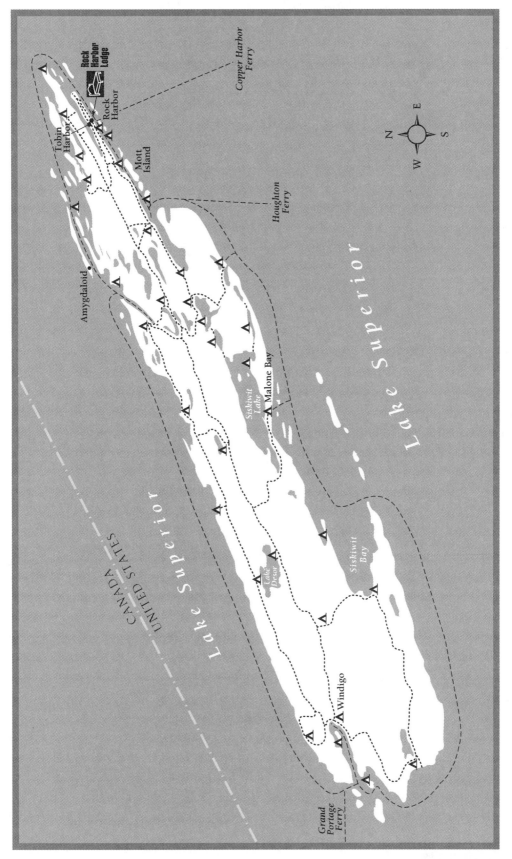

# ROCK HARBOR LODGE

P.O. Box 605 • Houghton, MI 49931-0405 • (906) 337–4993
www.isleroyaleresort.com

*Rock Harbor Lodge*

Rock Harbor Lodge is a complex of four motel-type lodge buildings, twenty housekeeping cabins, a dining room, a meeting hall, a gift shop, a store, and a marina, all located on or near the shore of Lake Superior. The four two-story lodge buildings sit side by side on each side of a meeting hall (actually, an old lodge building) used as a gathering place for guests. All these buildings are directly on the shoreline. The dining room is a short distance behind the lodge buildings. The housekeeping cottages are nearby and convenient to the dining room and store.

The four identical lodge buildings house a total of sixty rooms, each with a private bath and combination shower-tub. The buildings have a stone-and-wood exterior and cement block interior walls. Lodge rooms have steam heat but no television or telephone. Beds vary from one double, to two twins, to two doubles. Rooms on the first floor each have a balcony. Second-floor rooms have a better window view but no balcony. Three meals a day in the dining room are included in the rental of lodge rooms.

Ten stone-and-wood duplexes offer twenty housekeeping cottages, which each have an electric stove, a refrigerator, dishes, and utensils. These units have a double bed and two bunk beds, with linens, blankets, and electric heat but no maid service. The cottages are located near Tobin Harbor, a short distance from the four lodge buildings. An asphalt walkway connects the cottages with the dining room and lodge buildings. Units 1–12 have a view of the harbor, while units 13–20 are deeper in the woods. Meals are not included in cottage rentals, but guests are permitted to eat in the dining room at extra cost.

Isle Royale appeals to visitors who want to try something different. There are no roads, no vehicles, and few people. You won't pass through this park on your way to some other destination, and neither will anyone else. The lodge allows you to experience nature while enjoying nice accommodations and good food. The dining room serves three meals daily; a snack bar is open from 7:00 A.M. to 7:30 P.M. A marina store sells a variety of groceries, fishing equipment, and personal supplies. The nearby marina will accommodate boats of up to 65 feet. Motorboats and canoes are available for rent. Charter fishing boats and sightseeing boats are also at Rock Harbor. The lodge operates a water taxi service daily, dropping off and picking up campers, canoers, and kayakers at numerous points on the island.

> Isle Royale has a rich history to share with present-day visitors. Native tribes had mined copper here thousands of years before the French claimed possession of Isle Royale in 1671. The island became a possession of the United States in 1783 and was identified as Chippewa Territory until the mid-1800s. Copper mining continued during the latter half of the 1800s, when large areas were burned and logged.

- **ROOMS:** Doubles, triples, and quads. Housekeeping cottages can accommodate up to six people. All rooms in the lodge buildings and housekeeping cottages have private baths. Handicap-accessible rooms are available in the lodge and the housekeeping cabins. (Note: No trails are handicap accessible.)

- **RESERVATIONS:** From May through September, Rock Harbor Lodge, Isle Royale National Park, P.O. Box 605, Houghton, MI 49931-0405. Phone (906) 337–4993. From October through April, Rock Harbor Lodge, P.O. Box 27, Houghton, MI 49931. Phone (270) 773–2191 or www.isleroyaleresort.com. A deposit of $75 per room is required. A five-day cancellation notice is required to receive a full refund.

- **RATES:** Lodge rooms with meals ($186); housekeeping cottages without meals ($119). Rates quoted are for two adults. Each additional person is $62 per night ($25 for children under twelve) in lodge rooms (meals included), and $25 in housekeeping cottages.

- **LOCATION:** South shore on the northeastern tip of Isle Royale.

- **SEASON:** The lodge is open from the second week in June through the first week in September. Housekeeping units are available from Memorial Day weekend through mid-September.

- **FOOD:** A dining room serves three meals daily (included in price of lodge room). Snack bar service is available throughout the day. Groceries can be purchased in the store.

- **TRANSPORTATION:** Passenger boats leave for Isle Royale from Copper Harbor and Houghton in Michigan's Upper Peninsula and from Grand Portage on Minnesota's north shore. A seaplane leaves from Houghton. The boat from Grand Portage, Minnesota, circumnavigates the island and will drop off and pick up passengers at various points. The lodge's water taxi will drop off and pick up campers, caonoers, and kayakers at numerous places on the island.

- **FACILITIES:** Dining room, snack bar, store, gift shop, laundry facilities, marina with boat and canoe rentals.

- **ACTIVITIES:** Hiking, fishing, canoeing, charter fishing, and sightseeing via boat.

# MINNESOTA

**STATE TOURIST INFORMATION**
(800) 657–3700
www.exploreminnesota.com

## VOYAGEURS NATIONAL PARK

3131 Highway 53
International Falls, MN 56649-8904
(218) 283–9821
www.nps.gov/voya

Voyageurs National Park preserves 218,000 acres of beautiful forested lake country that was once inhabited by French-Canadian fur traders, who used canoes to transport animal pelts and other trade goods through this area during the late eighteenth and early nineteenth centuries. A 1783 treaty established the U.S.–Canadian boundary along the waterway used by the voyageurs. The south side of the Kabetogama Peninsula is dotted with numerous islands, while the north shore is broken with many coves and small bays. One of the park's visitor centers is in its southwest corner, on Country Road 123. Voyageurs National Park stretches 55 miles along the U.S.–Canadian border, east of International Falls in northern Minnesota. Summer travel within the park is confined to watercraft or floatplane.

**PARK ENTRANCE FEE:** No charge.

## Lodging in Voyageurs National Park

Overnight accommodations within Voyageurs National Park are available only at the Kettle Falls Hotel. Kettle Falls, in the northeast corner of the park, is reached via private boat or by private water taxi. Accommodations are available outside the park in Ash River, Crane Lake, Kabetogama Lake, and International Falls.

# VOYAGEURS NATIONAL PARK

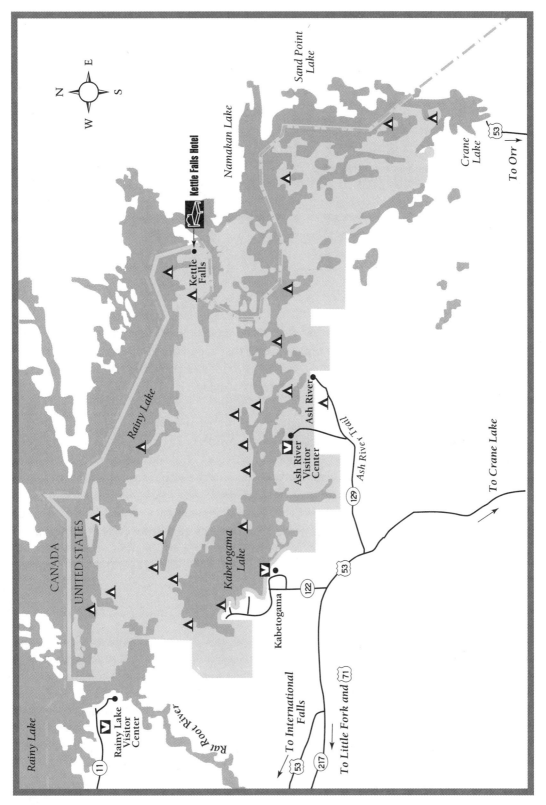

# KETTLE FALLS HOTEL

10502 Gamma Road • Ray, Minnesota 56669 • (888) 534–6835
KFH@uslink.net • www.kettlefallshotel.com

*Kettle Falls Hotel*

Kettle Falls is a relatively small lodging complex consisting of a historic two-story frame hotel plus three newer nearby wooden lodges that each contain from two to four lodging units, for a total of twenty-two rooms. The hotel is part of a National Register of Historic Places District that also includes the historic dam, a dam tenders cabin, and other sites and features. The main building has a lobby, a dining room and a saloon (with a tilted floor) on the first floor and twelve overnight rooms on the second floor. The hotel sits in a small clearing surrounded by woods, and the lodges overlook the rocky shore of Rainy Lake. A quarter-mile gravel road leads from the dock to the hotel. Transportation from dockside to the lodging complex is available. Kettle Falls Hotel is in the northeast corner of Voyageurs National Park and is reached only by boat or seaplane.

Transportation to the Kettle Falls Hotel via a hotel-operated boat is available (fee charged) on a daily basis from the Frontier Resort dock at the end of Ash River Trail. There is no charge for parking at the resort. Call the Kettle Falls Hotel for information.

For day visitors, the park offers three concessioner-operated guided tour boat trips to Kettle Falls each week from the Kabetogama Lake visitor center. Guests of the hotel can arrange to use these trips as transportation to the hotel. Call the visitor center for more information.

Several types of rooms are available. None of the rooms have a telephone or television, although a telephone is in the lobby and televisions are in the lobby and in the saloon. The least expensive rooms, all without private bath, are in the hotel, which was constructed from 1910 through 1913 to house construction workers on the nearby dam. The twelve hotel rooms are furnished with antiques and have either one double bed or two single beds. All these rooms are approximately the same size. The twelve hotel rooms and three centrally located modern community bathrooms with showers are on the second floor of the hotel. Coffee and rolls are served on the second floor each morning.

Kettle Falls also offers ten units in three separate lodge buildings on the Rainy Lake side of the Kettle Falls Dam. These buildings, constructed in the early 1990s, are finished with a pine and oak decor. Each unit has a screened porch and a private ceramic-tiled bathroom that includes a shower. One single-story lodge building with two units is handicap accessible (as is the first floor of the hotel). The other two lodge buildings each have two first-floor units and two second-floor units. Five of the lodge units have a fully equipped kitchen, including utensils. Beds in the lodge units range from bunk beds to full-size beds. The units can sleep up to ten persons when an adjoining door is used to convert two units to a suite. A three-night minimum stay is required when renting any of the lodge rooms. While the lodge rooms are newer and nicer than rooms in the hotel, you will save some money and probably enjoy a more intimate lodging experience by choosing to stay in the hotel. Keep in mind that guests who stay in the hotel must use community bathrooms.

*The Kettle Falls Hotel was built in 1913 by W. E. Rose, reputedly with money from famous madam Nellie Bly. According to legend, "fancy ladies" practiced their trade at the hotel. Other buildings predated the hotel, but little is known about them, and only traces of these structures remain. The hotel that once served as a relatively luxurious refuge for lumberjacks and construction workers for the Kettle Falls Dam now provides food and lodging to modern-day voyageurs.*

Staying at Kettle Falls Hotel is a restful and refreshing experience in a historic location where fur traders and trappers once portaged canoes and goods. If you want to get away from it all, and do so in the great outdoors, this may be just the place. The hotel has a large screened veranda, where guests can sit and drink coffee or have a meal. Most activities center on the water, where fishing and canoeing are the most popular activities. Guide service is available when arrangements have been made ahead of time, and boats and canoes can be rented.

- **ROOMS:** Singles, doubles, triples, and quads. Lodge units with connecting doors can be converted to suites that accommodate up to ten people. All lodge rooms have private baths. Guests at the main hotel have access to community bathrooms. Two lodge rooms are handicap accessible.

- **RESERVATIONS:** Kettle Falls Hotel, 10502 Gamma Road, Ray, MN 56669. Phone (888) 534–6835 or (218) 374–4404; (218) 875–2070 during the off-season.

- **RATES:** Hotel rooms, summer (single, $50; double, $70); lodge rooms per unit (night, $140; week, $650); lodge rooms with kitchenette per unit (night, $170; week, $850); suite per unit (night, $250; week, $1,250). A three-night minimum stay is required in any of the lodge units.

- **LOCATION:** Kettle Falls Hotel is in the northeast corner of Voyageurs National Park.

- **SEASON:** Mid-May through the first week of October.

- **FOOD:** A hotel dining room serves meals from 7:00 A.M. to 9:00 P.M. daily (dinner $12–$16). Morning coffee and rolls are served to guests of the hotel. Limited groceries are available at the trading post.

- **TRANSPORTATION:** The nearest scheduled air service is 50 miles from Kettle Falls, in International Falls, Minnesota, where rental cars are available. With advance notice the hotel will arrange for pickup at the airport. Daily boat service is available to Kettle Falls from Ash River (a fee is charged).

- **FACILITIES:** Dining room, saloon, boat rental, trading post with souvenirs, gifts, and groceries.

- **ACTIVITIES:** Hiking, bird-watching, fishing, canoeing, kayaking.

# MISSOURI

**STATE TOURIST INFORMATION**
(800) 877–1234
www.missouritourism.org

## OZARK NATIONAL SCENIC RIVERWAYS

P.O. Box 490
Van Buren, MO 63965
(573) 323–4236
www.nps.gov/ozar

Ozark National Scenic Riverways comprises nearly 80,000 acres of forested hills and mountains along 134 miles of the beautiful Current and Jacks Fork Rivers. The rivers are especially popular for fishing and for float trips in canoes, rafts, kayaks, and inner tubes, all of which can be rented. The park includes large freshwater springs and caverns. Ozark National Scenic Riverways is located in southeastern Missouri, 150 miles south of St. Louis.

**PARK ENTRANCE FEE:** No charge.

## Lodging in Ozark National Scenic Riverways

The riverways has a single lodging facility at Big Spring, 4 miles south of the town of Van Buren. Other accommodations are available outside park boundaries in Eminence, Mountain View, Salem, and Van Buren.

# OZARK NATIONAL SCENIC RIVERWAYS

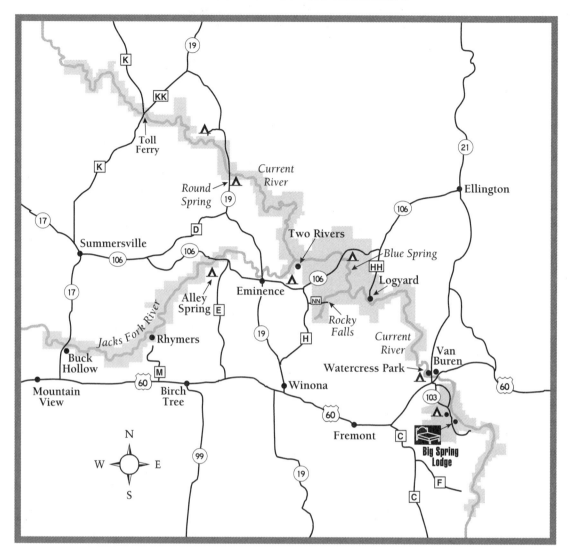

# BIG SPRING LODGE

P.O. Box 697 • Van Buren, MO 63965 • (573) 323–4332

*Cabin at Big Spring Lodge*

Big Spring Lodge consists of a main lodge building plus fourteen freestanding cabins. The timber-and-stone lodge building houses the registration desk and dining room on a bluff overlooking the Current River. The cozy dining room has a small wing with windows that provide a view of the river. The wood-and-stone cabins on a hill above the lodge building provide the only overnight accommodations at Big Spring. A paved road leads up the hill from the lodge to the cabins. Adequate parking is beside each of the cabins. The lodge building and cabins were constructed by the Civilian Conservation Corps in the 1930s; the entire complex sits amid a thick forest of hardwood trees. Big Spring Lodge is in southeastern Missouri, 4 miles south of the small town of Van Buren on Highway 103.

The fourteen cabins at Big Spring are available in four sizes that sleep two, four, six, or eight persons. The rate charged is determined by the cabin that is rented, not by the number of persons. Thus, two people who rent a six-person cabin must pay the same price as a family of four who rent the same cabin.

All the cabins have a private bath with shower but no tub. The cabins are quite roomy, with hardwood floors, stained wood walls, and a private screened porch. They also have fans but no air-conditioning, telephone, or television. All except the two six-person cabins have kitchen facilities and a stone fireplace. Wood is provided for a nominal fee. The kitchens have a cooktop stove, refrigerator, and freezer but no oven or utensils. Outside each cabin is a grill and picnic table. The cabins are widely spaced along both sides of a paved road to provide relative privacy.

Big Spring Lodge, a small lodging complex in a quiet rural area of Missouri, is a good place to get away from the hustle and bustle. Plan to read a few books, play some cards, and do a little hiking. On a rainy day you can sit in front of the stone fireplace in the small lobby area of the lodge building. Another stone fireplace is in the dining room. Van Buren is an especially good place to visit if you enjoy a leisurely float down a beautiful river. The Ozark National Scenic Riverways includes 134 miles of clear, spring-fed streams, including the Current River, which flows past Big Spring Lodge.

- **ROOMS:** From doubles to eight persons per unit. All cabins have a private bath with a shower but no tub. There are no handicap-accessible cabins.

- **RESERVATIONS:** Big Spring Lodge, P.O. Box 130, Van Buren, MO 63965. Phone (573) 323–4332. A two-night-minimum stay may be required on weekends. A three-day cancellation is requested.

- **RATES:** Two-person cabin ($40); four-person cabin ($55); six-person cabin ($70); eight-person cabin ($90). The cost is based on the size of the cabin, not the number of persons. Weekend rates are increased by $15 to $20 per day.

- **LOCATION:** In southeast Missouri, 4 miles south of the town of Van Buren on Highway 103.

- **SEASON:** April through October.

- **FOOD:** A cozy dining room serves breakfast ($3.00–$5.00), lunch ($4.00–$8.00), and dinner ($8.00–$14.00). Groceries are available in Van Buren.

- **TRANSPORTATION:** The nearest scheduled airline service is in St. Louis and Springfield, Missouri.

- **FACILITIES:** Dining room.

- **ACTIVITIES:** Hiking, fishing, canoeing, tubing, swimming.

Many of the visitors to Ozark National Scenic Riverways come here to float on one or both of the Class II rivers. Nineteen National Park Service–authorized concessionaires rent canoes at or near Alley Spring, Big Spring, Pulltite, Round Spring, Two Rivers, and Watercress. Inner tubes are available for rent at several locations. Floaters are permitted to camp overnight on the river gravel bars.

# MONTANA

**STATE TOURIST INFORMATION**
(800) 541–1447
visitmt.com

## GLACIER NATIONAL PARK

West Glacier, MT 59936
(406) 888–7800
www.nps.gov/glac

Glacier National Park, covering more than one million acres, features towering mountains, glacial valleys, sparkling lakes, and more than thirty glaciers. Visitor centers are on the west side at Apgar, on the east side at St. Mary, and in the high country at Logan Pass. The high country is best seen by driving Going-to-the-Sun Road, a 50-mile paved road that bisects the park via the Continental Divide at 6,646-foot Logan Pass. If time permits, drive the Chief Mountain International Highway to Canada's Waterton Lakes National Park and the quaint town of Waterton Park. The 12-mile paved road to Many Glacier also offers beautiful views. The park is in northwestern Montana. The west entrance is 32 miles east of Kalispell, Montana.

**PARK ENTRANCE FEE:** $10.00 per vehicle or $5.00 per person, good for seven days.

### Lodging in Glacier National Park

Six facilities offer guest accommodations within Glacier National Park. Three of the facilities are on the west side of the park near Apgar, one is toward the east side on the Going-to-the-Sun Road, and two are at Many Glacier on the park's east side. We have also included two unique lodges that are near the park. Glacier Park Lodge is just outside the park's east boundary in the town of East Glacier. Glacier's sister national park just across the border in Canada, Waterton Lakes, has one of the most beautiful lodges to be found anywhere.

# GLACIER NATIONAL PARK

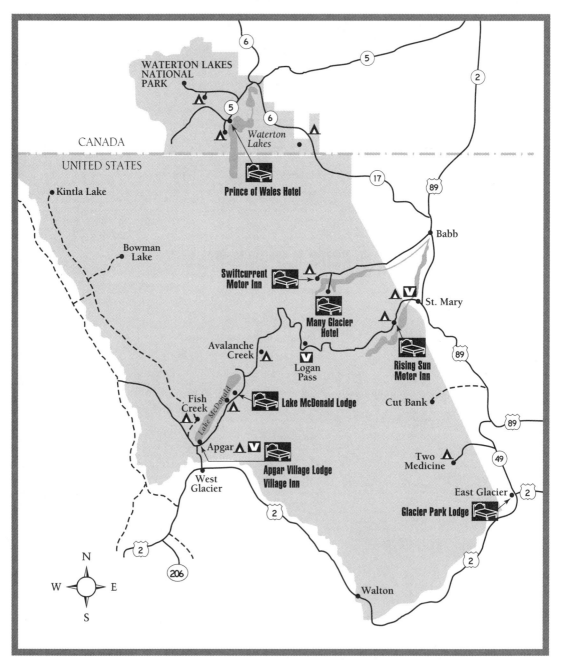

# APGAR VILLAGE LODGE

P.O. Box 410 • Apgar, MT 59936 • (406) 888–5484
www.westglacier.com

*Cabin at Apgar Village Lodge*

Apgar Village Lodge is a cluster of two motel buildings and twenty-eight rustic cabins. The wooden structures were constructed over a period of years, with the oldest cabin dating from 1900. The motel units were built in the early 1940s. The complex covers a fairly large area between the road through Apgar Village and McDonald Creek, which is fed by Lake McDonald. One motel building and seven cabins are located beside the creek. The other motel unit is on the road that leads to the lake. None of the lodging units are on Lake McDonald, although the entire complex is only about a half block away from the lake. No pets are permitted. Apgar Village Lodge is in Apgar Village, 3 miles inside the west entrance to Glacier National Park. The lodge is just up the street from Village Inn, another Glacier Park lodge.

Apgar Village Lodge offers a wide variety of accommodations. All the rooms have electric heat and private baths with showers but no air-conditioning or telephone. Some of the rooms have a television. Picnic tables are scattered about the complex. The least expensive rooms are in the motel building on the creek. These units do not have balconies, but the back window offers a view of the creek. These small rooms have either one double bed, one queen-size bed, or one double bed and a single. The beds pretty much fill the room. The other motel unit on Apgar Road has eleven rooms facing the road. These rooms are somewhat larger than the rooms in the other motel unit. Rooms have one queen-size bed and double bed or two queen-size beds.

All but two of the twenty-eight cabins have a kitchen with refrigerator, stove, oven, and sink. The oldest log cabins were mostly constructed in the early 1900s; other cabins were built in the 1910s and 1930s. All of the cabins have knotty pine interior walls. The smallest of the cabins has one double bed and no kitchen, while the largest has a kitchen and two bedrooms with five queen-size beds. Cabins 6, 7, and 8 have kitchens and are situated directly on McDonald Creek. These three cabins offer the most desirable location in the complex. Four other cabins with kitchens (cabins 10, 11, 12, and 22) are across a small parking area from the creek. Most of the cabins have adjacent parking.

Apgar Village Lodge offers rustic buildings in a relatively quiet setting. The complex tends to be quiet and is suited for people who like this type of environment. Walks, viewing and wading in the lake, fishing and boating are several of the activities that are available here. The National Park Service visitor center is about a half block away. Although the lodge doesn't have its own eating facility, a restaurant flanks the building. Gift shops and a grocery are a short walk away.

- **ROOMS:** Singles, doubles, triples, and quads. A few large cabins can hold six or more persons. All rooms have private baths with showers but no tubs. There are no handicap-accessible cabins.

- **RESERVATIONS:** Apgar Village Lodge, P.O. Box 410, West Glacier, MT 59936. Phone (406) 888–5484; fax (406) 888–5273. A deposit of one night's stay or one-third the total cost, whichever is larger, is required. A seventy-two-hour notice is needed for cancellation.

- **RATES:** Riverview Motel units ($59–$67); Lakeview Motel units ($78); cabins without kitchens ($73–$75); cabins with kitchens ($105–$120); three-room cabin ($115–$190). Rates for motel units and small cabins quoted are for two adults. Rates on medium and large cabins are for four adults.

- **LOCATION:** In the village of Apgar, Montana, 3 miles from the West Glacier entrance station.

- **SEASON:** May 1 through mid-October.

- **FOOD:** No food service is available at Apgar Village Lodge. Next to the lodge, Eddie's Cafe serves breakfast, lunch, and dinner from 7:00 A.M. to 9:30 P.M. Depending on the weather, the restaurant is open from mid-May through most of September. A store sells limited grocery items, beer, and wine.

Milo Apgar, an early homesteader in the area where Apgar Village now stands, arrived soon after the Great Northern Railway reached Belton (now called West Glacier) in the early 1890s. Unable to make it as a farmer, Apgar started offering overnight accommodations for miners and visitors to this beautiful area. Some of Apgar's original cabins are still standing as part of Apgar Village Lodge. Cabin 21 was part of Apgar's first home.

- **TRANSPORTATION:** Scheduled airlines serve Kalispell, Montana, where rental cars are available. An airport shuttle service from Kalispell serves West Glacier. Tours of the park can be arranged from West Glacier. Amtrak service is available to Belton/West Glacier (800–872–7245). A rental car agency is across the street from the Amtrak station.

- **FACILITIES:** The village of Apgar has gift shops, a restaurant, an ice cream shop, boat rentals, and a National Park Service visitor center. An ATM machine is next door in a gift shop.

- **ACTIVITIES:** Nightly ranger/naturalist talks at the Apgar campground, boating, swimming (very cool water), fishing, hiking, horseback riding. Sightseeing tours of the park leave from Apgar.

# GLACIER PARK LODGE

East Glacier, MT 59434 • (406) 226–5600

www.glacierparkinc.com

*Glacier Park Lodge*

Glacier Park Lodge is one of the classic Great Northern Railway park lodges. In fact, freight and passenger trains still operate little more than a stone's throw from the impressive hotel entry. The main lodge building was constructed in 1912, and the adjacent annex building was built in 1913. The two buildings have a similar outside appearance and are connected by a covered walkway. The massive three-story lobby with 40-inch-diameter fir and cedar pillars and surrounded by interior balconies covers most of the first floor of the main building. The annex has more than twice as many guest rooms. A large front lawn has flowers from the entrance to the train station. Adequate parking is near the hotel, but you will want to drop off luggage at the front door. No elevators are in the hotel, but bellhops are available to assist with luggage. The lodge is in the southeast corner of Glacier National Park, in the town of East Glacier, Montana. It is at the intersection of Highways 2 and 49.

Glacier Park Lodge has 162 guest rooms that fall into a number of classifications and a two-bedroom chalet that is located next to the golf course. Rates are set by room size and not by view. Rooms on the west have a view of the Rocky Mountains, while rooms on the east view the front lawn and distant rolling hills. All the rooms have heat, telephone, and private bath with a shower or shower-tub combination. None of the rooms have air-conditioning or television. Beds in nearly all the rooms vary from two twins to two double beds. Some of the rooms have balconies.

All of the fifty rooms in the main building are on the second and third floors. Thirty-four are the hotel's least expensive "value" rooms, which tend to be relatively small. This building also has ten larger lodge rooms that rent for about $20 per night more than the value rooms. Four corner "Big Sky" rooms on the third floor have two queen-size beds and are quite a bit larger. The other two rooms in this building are very large suites, with one king-size bed and a sitting area with a sofa bed. The suites also have a balcony.

Most of the 111 rooms in the annex are classified as "annex rooms" and are a nice size, with hardwood floors and bedding that ranges from two twins to two double beds. The annex rooms are a little bigger and rent for slightly more than the main lodge rooms. Most annex rooms on the first and second floors have balconies. Three family rooms are very large, with three double beds. Six corner mini-suites each have one queen-size bed. The annex also has one handicap-accessible room. Our choice would be a value room facing the west in the main lodge building. Ask for one with a balcony. Situated approximately 50 yards from the main lodge on the ninth hole of the golf course is a one-story chalet with a small living room, a full kitchen (utensils and dishes supplied), two bathrooms with a combination tub/shower, and two bedrooms, each with two queen-size beds. The chalet has an outside deck, flower beds, and a rustic fence. A telephone but no television is included.

Glacier Park Lodge is a handy place to spend a night or more on the east side of Glacier National Park. It's perfect if you travel on the train, because the station is only a short walk from the hotel entrance. It is also a good place to stay if you plan to take a day trip across the park's Going-to-the-Sun Road. The hotel has a nine-hole golf course and a pitch and putt. Horseback riding and hayrides are also available. If food in the hotel restaurant isn't to your liking or you consider it too expensive, a short walk takes you to several restaurants and a grocery in the town of East Glacier. The lodge is one of the few where you will find a swimming pool.

- **ROOMS:** Singles, doubles, triples, and quads. Three family rooms hold up to six persons. All rooms have a private bath. The annex has one handicap-accessible room.

- **RESERVATIONS:** Glacier Park, Inc., 106 Cooperative Way, Suite 104, Kalispell, MT 59901. Phone (406) 756–2444. A deposit of one night's stay is required. Cancellation notice of forty-eight hours is required to receive a full refund less a $10 fee.

- **RATES:** Value room ($135), main lodge ($155), annex ($160), family room ($185), Big Sky room ($195), mini-suite ($195), suite ($299). Rates quoted are for two adults. Children eleven and under stay free. Each additional person is $10 per night. Rates are reduced from mid-May to mid-June and in mid-September.

- **LOCATION:** In East Glacier, Montana, at the intersection of Highways 2 and 49. The lodge is at the southeast corner of the park.

- **SEASON:** Mid-May to mid-September.

- **FOOD:** The dining rooms offer a buffet breakfast ($9.75), lunch ($6.00–$13.00), and dinner ($14–$22) until 10:00 P.M. The lounge serves snacks and sandwiches. A snack shop in the lobby sells cold sandwiches, ice cream, and drinks. Additional restaurants and a grocery are nearby in the town of East Glacier.

- **TRANSPORTATION:** Great Falls and Kalispell, Montana, have scheduled air service and rental vehicles. Amtrak stops directly across the street from the hotel.

Glacier National Park is famous for the red "Jammer" motor coaches that transport people between the park hotels and sites. The coaches, built by the White Motor Company between 1933 and 1939, have black canvas tops that can be rolled back for greater visibility by occupants. The coaches derive their name from the drivers who at one time had to "jam" the gears to get up the mountain roads of Glacier. Because of structural problems, the Jammers were temporarily retired from use in August 1999. Efforts are underway to return the Jammers to Glacier's roads.

- **FACILITIES:** Restaurant, cocktail lounge, gift shop, swimming pool, golf course, ATM. Restaurants, gas stations, and a grocery store are across the road in the town of East Glacier.

- **ACTIVITIES:** Hiking, horseback riding, swimming, golf, evening entertainment by employees.

# LAKE McDONALD LODGE

P.O. Box 210052 • Lake McDonald, MT 59921-0052 • (406) 888–5431
www.glacierparkinc.com

*Lake McDonald Lodge*

Lake McDonald Lodge is a complex consisting of a large main lodge building, fourteen structures with cabin accommodations, two two-story motel units, several support buildings for employee housing, and a store. The main structure is a classic old lodge with a terrific lobby and restaurant on the main floor, and guest rooms on the second and third floors. The main lodge building, which sits on a small hill overlooking Lake McDonald, was constructed in 1913 and partially renovated in 1988. It is an attractive building with comfortable guest rooms. A huge stone fireplace dominates the three-story lobby with log beams and interior balconies. Two second-floor mezzanine areas with tables and chairs look out over the lobby and provide a place to write letters, play cards, or just relax. A covered back patio has chairs and benches for relaxing while viewing Glacier National Park's largest lake.

Lake McDonald Lodge offers rooms of various sizes and beds in the main lodge, cabins, and motel-type buildings. All the rooms have heat, a telephone, and a private bath with a shower (no tub) but no air-conditioning or television. The main lodge has thirty-two rooms, nearly all of which are on the second and third floors. Two handicap-accessible rooms are on the first floor. The building has no elevator. Rooms in the lodge are priced the same regardless of size, beds, and view. Some enjoy a great view of the lake, while others have no view at all. Beds range from one to two double beds. Rooms 202, 212, 302, and 312 are corner rooms with two windows. Rooms 201, 213, 301, and 313 are quite large, with windows toward the lake.

Fourteen separate buildings, some log and some frame, house a total of thirty-eight cabin rooms. Most of these buildings contain two, three, or four cabin rooms, although one building has six units. While all of the cabins are on the lake, trees and plants obscure most views. Beds in the cabins range from one to two double beds. Twenty-one smaller cabin accommodations rent for about half the price of seventeen larger cabin rooms.

Two wooden two-story motel buildings sit parallel to one another and offer a total of thirty rooms. Both the buildings and the rooms are pretty ordinary. One of the buildings has an interior hallway for entry to the rooms. The other building has entry from an outside balcony and walkway. The motel rooms rent for more than the small cabins and are probably the least desirable rooms at Lake McDonald Lodge. Our first choice would be the larger lakeside rooms in the main lodge. The best value is the small cabins. In fact, cabin 12-B, with a nice front porch overlooking the lake, is our favorite accommodation in the entire complex.

Lake McDonald Lodge is a great place to spend a vacation in Glacier National Park. It is a beautiful lodge with attractive rooms in both the main lodge and the cabins. The lake offers boating and fishing, although the water is a little cool for swimming. Boat tours of the lake leave from the back of the lodge. The complex also includes a general store with gifts, supplies, and limited groceries, as well as a gas station (regular unleaded only) and post office. An attractive restaurant with a decor similar to that of the lobby has large windows that overlook the lake. This restaurant serves three meals a day, with a buffet breakfast, while a smaller restaurant across the road has a more limited and less expensive menu.

*The site of Lake McDonald was homesteaded in 1895 by George Snyder, who built a small hotel here. Ownership later passed to John Lewis, who operated a fishing and tourist camp. In 1910 Lewis built the log cabins, and three years later he added the present lodge building at a cost of $48,000. The fireplace was originally used as both a kitchen and a furnace for the lodge. His many hunting trophies remain on display in the lodge lobby. The two motel units, additional cabins, and camp store were added later. The lodge was included in the National Register of Historic Places in 1978.*

- **ROOMS:** Singles, doubles, triples, and quads. All rooms have a private bath with shower but no tub. Cabins 2 and 5 and two rooms on the first floor are handicap accessible.

- **RESERVATIONS:** Glacier Park, Inc., 106 Cooperative Way, Suite 104, Kalispell, MT 59901. Phone (406) 756–2444. A despoit of one night's stay is required. Cancellation notice of forty-eight hours is required to receive a full refund less a $10 fee.

- **RATES:** Main lodge ($135); small cabins ($86); large cabins ($135); motor inn ($88–$92).

- **LOCATION:** Ten miles inside the west entrance to Glacier National Park. The lodge is on Lake McDonald, just off the Going-to-the-Sun Road.

- **SEASON:** Early June to late September.

- **FOOD:** A restaurant in the main lodge serves a buffet breakfast ($9.75), lunch ($6.50–$11.00), and dinner ($12–$20) until 10:00 P.M. No reservations are taken. Across the road Charlie's Pizzeria is open from 7:00 A.M. to 9:30 P.M. with a somewhat limited menu for breakfast ($4.50–$7.00), lunch ($6.00–$9.00), and dinner ($6.00–$14.00). Charlie's also has a take-out counter. The Stockade Lounge in the main lodge serves sandwiches, salads, and snacks. Limited groceries, beer, and wine are sold in the general store.

- **TRANSPORTATION:** The nearest scheduled airline service is to Kalispell, Montana, where rental cars are available. Amtrak and buses serve West Glacier. A park shuttle stops at Lake McDonald Lodge during July and August.

- **FACILITIES:** Restaurants, gift shop, post office, ATM machine, cocktail lounge, boat rental.

- **ACTIVITIES:** Boating, hiking, fishing (no license required), boat tours of Lake McDonald, sightseeing tours, horseback riding, evening ranger programs.

# MANY GLACIER HOTEL

P.O. Box 147 • East Glacier, MT 59434 • (406) 732–4411
www.glacierparkinc.com

*Many Glacier Hotel*

Many Glacier Hotel is a classic old national park lodge. The five-story wooden structure with shake roof and numerous gables and balconies is situated on the edge of Swiftcurrent Lake. Although it appears as a single structure, the hotel is actually two separate buildings connected by an enclosed walkway. The main floor is highlighted by an outstanding three-story lobby with log beams, interior balconies, and a huge conical metal fireplace suspended from the roof. The lobby also has a traditional stone fireplace. Many guest rooms in both the main hotel and the annex have an outstanding view of Swiftcurrent Lake and the surrounding mountains. Parking is on a steep hill above the hotel, so register and drop off luggage before parking your vehicle. No elevators are in the hotel, but bellhops are on duty to assist with luggage. Many Glacier Hotel is in the northeastern section of Glacier National Park, 11 miles west of Babb on Many Glacier Road.

The hotel offers a total of 211 rooms of varying size, beds, and view. All of the rooms have heat, telephone, and a private bath but no television. Most rooms fall into three categories: Lakeside, Standard, and Value. A sloping roof causes rooms on the fourth floor of both buildings to offer less headroom. Surprisingly, lake-level rooms have been assigned 500 room numbers. Lakeside and the slightly less expensive Standard rooms are virtually identical except for the view. Size and beds for these rooms vary considerably, although each of the rooms in a category rents for the same price. Also, some rooms have balconies with chairs, while others do not. Beds vary from two twin beds to two double beds. Large Lakeside rooms in the main lodge include rooms 222, 322, and 332. Bigger Lakeside rooms in the annex with balconies include rooms 102, 104, 112, 114, and corresponding rooms on the second and third floors. Larger Standard rooms in the annex include rooms 105, 205, and 305. Sixty-seven Value rooms, which rent for $12 less per night than a Standard, tend to be very small, have an obscured view, or are located on a main hallway in a heavy-traffic area. The hotel has three handicap-accessible rooms on the first floor. One is a Value room, and two are Lakeside rooms.

Six family rooms consist of two bedrooms and a bath. One bedroom has a double plus a single bed, while the other bedroom has a double bed. Three are Lakeside and three are not, although all six rooms rent for the same price, which is about $72 per night more than a Standard room. Two suites each consist of a bedroom with a king bed and a living room with a sleep sofa. These corner rooms also have a private bath. Lakeside rooms with a great view of the lake are worth the $12 difference in price.

Many Glacier Lodge is a wonderful old hotel. An inviting restaurant at one end of the building has a large stone fireplace and big windows that allow diners to look out over Swiftcurrent Lake. The lounge, with a large nonsmoking area, is located just outside the restaurant. Soup, sandwiches, and snacks are available in the lounge. Nightly entertainment (fee charged) is offered by employees of the lodge. Take a few steps outside the hotel and you can canoe, fish, or enjoy a boat tour accompanied by a park naturalist. Or perhaps you would rather relax in one of the chairs or benches on the large porch that wraps around two sides of the first floor. A stable next to the parking area offers horseback riding. Evening natural history programs are presented in the hotel basement by National Park Service rangers. All in all, this is a great place to spend several days or a week.

Construction on Many Glacier Hotel commenced in 1914, and the first guests were welcomed on July 4 of the following year. The annex next door was completed two years later. The Great Northern Railway, which built the hotel, erected a sawmill and drying kiln near the site to process timber used in the construction. Trees for the lobby columns were harvested from the upper end of nearby Lake Josephine. Even though most of the timber and rocks came from the local area, the high cost of fixtures, glass, and boilers resulted in construction costs of $500,000. A swimming pool that sat beside the dining room and a stone fountain near the current St. Moritz Room have both been removed. The hotel once had its own hydroelectric plant at Swift Current Falls, but the unit was put permanently out of operation by a 1964 flood.

- **ROOMS:** Singles, doubles, triples, and quads. Six family rooms hold five persons. All the hotel rooms have private baths. The hotel has three handicap-accessible rooms.

- **RESERVATIONS:** Glacier Park, Inc., 106 Cooperative Way, Suite 104, Kalispell, MT 59901. Phone (406) 756–2444. A deposit of one night's stay is required. Cancellation notice of forty-eight hours is required to receive a full refund less a $10 fee.

- **RATES:** Value rooms ($106); Lakeside ($135); Standard ($123); family rooms ($180–$185); suites ($205–$209). Room rates quoted are for two adults. Each additional person is $10.00 per night. Children eleven and under stay free.

- **LOCATION:** In the northeast section of the park, at the end of Many Glacier Road, 11 miles east of Babb, Montana.

- **SEASON:** Mid-June to mid-September.

- **FOOD:** A restaurant offers a breakfast buffet ($9.75), lunch ($6.50–$11.00), and dinner ($14–$20). Soup, sandwiches, and snacks are available in the lounge. A small store sells hot dogs, ice cream, yogurt, snacks, drinks, and wine from 6:30 A.M. to 11:00 P.M. Limited groceries are available in a general store 1 mile up the road at Swiftcurrent Motor Inn. The motor inn also has a less expensive restaurant.

- ■ **TRANSPORTATION:** The nearest scheduled air service is in Kalispell, Montana, where rental vehicles are available. Commercial bus service is available in Great Falls and Kalispell, Montana. Amtrak stops in East Glacier, Montana.

- ■ **FACILITIES:** Restaurant, cocktail lounge, snack bar, gift shop, tour desk in lobby, horse stable, boat rentals, ATM.

- ■ **ACTIVITIES:** Hiking, fishing, boating, horseback riding, evening naturalist programs, evening talent shows, boat tours of Swiftcurrent Lake and Lake Josephine.

## PRINCE OF WALES HOTEL

Waterton, Alberta, Canada TOK2MO • (403) 859–2231
gcjensen@telusplanet.net • www.glacierparkinc.com

*Prince of Wales Hotel*

The Prince of Wales Hotel is a single seven-story alpine chalet that may be the most picturesque of all the national park lodging facilities. The only Canadian park lodge constructed by the Great Northern Railway, the hotel sits high on a hill overlooking Waterton Lake and the quaint town of Waterton. Built in 1927, the hotel features two-story windows across one end of a five-story lobby. Interior balconies on each floor and huge timbers near the roof highlight the attractive lobby filled with chairs, tables, and sofas. While standing in the lobby, look up at the ceiling and notice a dark panel. This trap door hides a pulley that is used to lower a rope to an employee who is hoisted to change burned out lightbulbs in the massive chandlier that hangs between the second and third floors. The hotel is about 48 miles northwest of the town of St. Mary, Montana, via Highway 89 and the Chief Mountain

International Highway, which turns off 4 miles north of Babb, Montana. You must pass through a Canadian port of entry and pay a Canadian park fee to enter Waterton Lakes National Park, where the hotel is located.

The hotel has eighty-six rooms, each with heat, telephone, and private bath. None have television or air-conditioning. A small elevator (the oldest in Alberta) in the lobby stops at floors 2, 3, and 4. Most rooms in the hotel fall into two classifications: Lakeside or Standard. Lakeside rooms offer a view of Waterton Lake, while Standard rooms, which rent for about $30 per night less, do not. These rooms are a nice size, with beds ranging from two twins to two doubles. Bathrooms have a shower-tub combination. Lakeside and Standard rooms comprise most of the accommodations on the second, third, and fourth floors. All third-floor rooms have balconies, and smoking is permitted. Second- and fourth-floor rooms are nonsmoking, and only some have balconies. The wind is generally strong enough that you won't want to spend much time on the balconies, so a balcony shouldn't be a major consideration in choosing a room.

The hotel offers twenty fifth-floor Value rooms that are smaller, with variable views. About half face Waterton Lake. These rooms require climbing an additional flight of stairs, and the hotel's sloping roofline reduces headspace in some of these rooms, which rent for about $20 to $40 less than the Standard and Lakeside rooms. Value rooms have one double or two single beds. Bathrooms have a shower but no tub. Keep in mind that the lobby elevator does not provide access to the fifth floor. On the positive side, rooms on the fifth floor tend to be quieter, with the exception of 505, which is located next to the elevator and can be noisy. The hotel's sixth floor (yet another flight of stairs) has four rooms, two of which have two bedrooms and one bath. The other two rooms have a single bedroom. One in each category is on the lakeside but rents for the same price, so request lakeside if possible. These are really nice rooms if you don't mind the additional stairs.

The hotel offers three mini-suites, each with a king-size bed and a sofa or sofa bed. Two upscale suites on the third floor, the Prince and Princess, were completely renovated in 1999. Each suite has a living room, with a wet bar and refrigerator, and a separate bedroom with a king-size bed. The bathroom in each suite has a large bathtub and a separate shower. These suites are expensive and exquisite, with custom-designed furniture.

The Prince of Wales Hotel offers a touch of English tradition. Tea is served each afternoon in the lobby, where you can relax and look out over Waterton Lake. The hotel's main floor has a restaurant and a lounge, both of which provide great views of the lake and surrounding mountains. The building's only fireplace is in the lounge, which serves sandwiches and snacks. A large gift shop is also on the main floor. The town of Waterton, with additional restaurants, clothing stores, and gift shops, is a short distance down the hill. Keep in mind

*The original plans for the Prince of Wales Hotel called for a long, three-story structure similar to the Many Glacier Hotel, another hotel built by the Great Northern Railway. Louis Hill, president of the railroad, changed plans for the Prince of Wales several times during its construction, and what began as a three-story building became a seven-story rectangular hotel that cost three times the original estimate. Strong winds that twice blew the building off center during construction caused the contractor to fear the project would not be completed.*

that lodging rates are quoted in Canadian dollars, which in recent years have traded at a significant discount to U.S. dollars. If you pay with a credit card, you won't have to worry about obtaining Canadian currency or getting a bad exchange rate.

- **ROOMS:** Singles, doubles, triples, and quads. All rooms have private baths. There are no handicap-accessible rooms.

- **RESERVATIONS:** Glacier Park, Inc., 106 Cooperative Way, Suite 104, Kalispell, MT 59901. Phone (406) 756–2444. A deposit of one night's stay is required. A forty-eight-hour cancellation notice is required for a full refund less a $10 fee.

- **RATES:** Value room with mountain view ($259); sixth-floor one bedroom ($259); Value room with lake view ($269); Standard room ($279); Lakeside room ($309–$339); sixth-floor two bedroom ($279–$339); mini-suite ($420); suite ($799). Rates quoted in Canadian dollars are for two adults. Each additional person is $10 per night. Children eleven and under stay free with an adult. Rates are reduced during the month prior to mid-June and the week after mid-September.

According to legend, the Prince of Wales Hotel is haunted by a former female employee who jumped naked off a top floor balcony to her death. Sarah, the hotel employee, committed her desperate act after the hotel manager, with whom she was in love, spurned her advances. Sarah is especially fond of haunting the rooms of newlyweds. Various unexplained events include lights flicking on and off, doors being locked from the inside when no one was in the room, and luggage being found in a running shower. Employees of the hotel sometimes call upon Sarah to rectify a problem they encounter in the hotel.

- **LOCATION:** In Canada's Waterton Lakes National Park, about 48 miles northwest of St. Mary, Montana.

- **SEASON:** Mid-May to late September.

- **FOOD:** A restaurant serves a breakfast buffet ($13.95), lunch ($9.00–$16.00), and dinner ($18–$30). The lounge serves soup, sandwiches, and snacks. An afternoon tea is served in the lobby ($19.95). Several restaurants are in the town of Waterton.

- **TRANSPORTATION:** Scheduled air service is available to Calgary and Lethbridge, Alberta, and Great Falls and Kalispell, Montana, where vehicles can be rented.

- **FACILITIES:** Gift shop, restaurant, cocktail lounge. Additional facilities are in the town of Waterton, a short distance away.

- **ACTIVITIES:** Hiking, golf, tennis, horseback riding, boat rentals, lake cruises, and national park programs are offered in Waterton.

# RISING SUN MOTOR INN

P.O. Box 147 • East Glacier, MT 59434 • (406) 732–5523

www.glacierparkinc.com

*Cabin at Rising Sun Motor Inn*

Rising Sun Motor Inn, initially known as East Glacier Auto Camp, is a complex of wooden buildings, including a main registration/restaurant building without guest rooms, a separate general store with attached lodging rooms, nineteen cabins, and two motel-type structures. There are seventy-two rooms in total, with nineteen cabins dating from 1941. Registration for all guest rooms is in the main building, which houses a restaurant and a small gift shop. The general store is across the parking lot, and the cabins and motel buildings are up a small hill but within easy walking distance of both buildings. Rising Sun is in a scenic area overlooking St. Mary Lake and surrounded by tall mountains. Rising Sun Motor Inn is located on the east side of the park on the Going-to-the-Sun Road, 6 miles from the park entrance at St. Mary.

Rising Sun offers three types of rooms. All the rooms have heat and private baths with showers but no tubs. No air-conditioning, telephone, or television is in any of the rooms. The least expensive rooms are thirty-five duplex cabin units that sit fairly close to one another. The cabins are the same size, with varnished plywood interiors. Beds vary from two twins to two double beds. The toilet and shower are in a small bathroom, and the sink is in the bedroom. The cabins provide fair to good views of the mountains from relatively small windows.

The general store has nine rooms that rent for the same price as the cabins and are accessed from an interior hallway. Beds vary from a double to two double beds. All of the rooms have hardwood floors, but some have relatively dark interiors. Room 33 is one of the larger and brighter rooms, with two double beds. The most expensive rooms at Rising Sun, only a few dollars more than the other rooms, are in two one-story motel-type buildings that hold twenty-eight rooms. These rooms are basically identical except for beds, which vary from two twins to two double beds. Units 8 through 14 in one building and 22 through 28 provide good views of the mountains and a fair view of St. Mary Lake. Two handicap-accessible

*The 52-mile Going-to-the-Sun Road, one of the country's most scenic drives, is the product of more than a decade of work that commenced in 1921. Although several routes were considered, 6,664-foot Logan Pass was chosen, partially because greater exposure to the sun would help clear the road of snow. It takes up to two months each spring to clear the road of snow, which can reach a depth of 80 feet in places. The road provides spectacular views of mountains, lakes, waterfalls, and glacial valleys in the heart of Glacier National Park. The road is winding and quite narrow. Vehicles longer than 21 feet or wider than 8 feet are prohibited from travel between Avalanche Campground and the Sun Point parking area.*

rooms are available. The cabins appear to offer the best value at Rising Sun Motor Inn.

Rising Sun Motor Inn is in a very scenic location, where the blue waters of St. Mary Lake glimmer from down a hill. The lake is mostly out of direct view of the lodging units, and the surrounding mountains are only partially visible from some of the units. Still, this is a quiet place to relax in a natural setting. Walk a short distance from your room and gaze at some of the prettiest landscape in the United States. Rising Sun certainly isn't a busy or congested area, since most people on the Going-to-the-Sun Road drive right by. The restaurant, with a vaulted ceiling and large windows facing the lake and mountains, offers three meals a day. The general store has limited groceries, camping supplies, fishing supplies, and souvenirs. You can hike, fish, or just experience nature without bumping into hundreds of other vacationers. You can also take a boat tour of St. Mary Lake. No pets are permitted at the inn.

- **ROOMS:** Singles, doubles, triples, and quads. All rooms have a private bath with a shower but no tub. There are two handicap-accessible rooms.

- **RESERVATIONS:** Glacier Park, Inc., 106 Cooperative Way, Suite 104, Kalispell, MT 59901. Phone (406) 756–2444. A deposit of one night's stay is required. A forty-eight-hour cancellation notice is required for a full refund less a $10 fee.

- **RATES:** Cottages ($86); store motel rooms ($82); motel-type units ($92). Rates quoted are for two adults. Children eleven years and under stay free. Each additional person is $10 per night.

- **LOCATION:** East side of Glacier National Park, 6 miles west of the park entrance station at St. Mary.

- **SEASON:** Early June to mid-September.

- **FOOD:** A coffee shop/grill in the main building serves breakfast ($5.00–$7.00), lunch ($6.00–$13.00), and dinner ($6.00–$13.00). Limited groceries are sold in the general store.

- **TRANSPORTATION:** The nearest airport is in Kalispell, Montana, on the west side of the park. Amtrak provides service to East Glacier, where rental cars are available. Rising Sun is served by a park shuttle that operates in July and August.

- **FACILITIES:** Restaurant, gift shop, general store with camping and fishing supplies and limited groceries.

- **ACTIVITIES:** Hiking, fishing, boating, boat tour of St. Mary Lake, National Park Service evening naturalist program in campground amphitheater.

# SWIFTCURRENT MOTOR INN

P.O. Box 147 • East Glacier Park, MT 59434 • (406) 732–5531
www.glacierparkinc.com

*One-Bedroom Cabin without Bath at Swiftcurrent Motor Inn*

Swiftcurrent Motor Inn is a complex consisting of a registration building that also houses a store and restaurant, four motel buildings, twenty-six cabins, and a central bathhouse. In all, Swiftcurrent offers eighty-eight lodging rooms. The cabins and motel units sit behind and to the side of the registration building, which has no accommodations. Plenty of parking is available outside the registration building and beside the cabins and motel units. The cabins were constructed in 1937 after a fire destroyed cabins built several years earlier. The motel-type buildings were constructed in 1955. Swiftcurrent Motor Inn is in the northeast section of Glacier National Park, at the end of Many Glacier Road, 12 miles west of the town of Babb.

Two types of accommodations are available at Swiftcurrent. Both types have electric heat but no air-conditioning, television, or telephone. The least expensive lodging is in cabins without bath. A community bathroom has toilets and pay showers. The cabins are rustic and plain but clean. They are nicely spaced, and all are single units (no duplex units, common among other lodges). Eighteen small one-bedroom cabins each have a double bed in one room and a sink (cold water only) and small picnic table in a separate room. Two one-bedroom cabins with a private bath rent for about $30 per night more than the one-bedroom units without a bath. Six two-bedroom cabins have a small bedroom with a double bed on each side of a small room, with a sink and picnic table. These cabins do not have a private bathroom. The two-bedroom units rent for about $10 per night more than the one-bedroom units without bath. Cabins in Loop C are closest to the community bathhouse.

Four one-story motel buildings have a total of sixty-two rooms. The Pinetop unit, near the front of the complex, has twenty rooms, all but two of which have two double beds and a private bath with a shower but no tub. The rooms are entered from a central hallway that runs the length of the building. Three additional one-story motel units, near the back of the

A number of interesting hikes begin from the Many Glacier/Swiftcurrent area. Grinnell Glacier Trail leads 5.5 miles to one of the park's best-known and most visible glaciers. Tour boats on Swiftcurrent and Josephine Lakes can be used to reduce the length of the hike. Another 4.7-mile trail from Swiftcurrent Motor Inn leads to Iceberg Lake, on which icebergs can be seen well into the summer.

complex, each have fourteen rooms that are slightly larger and $10 more expensive than the Pinetop rooms. Each room has two double beds and a private bath with shower but no tub. Two handicap-accessible rooms have two twin beds. Rooms in these buildings back up to one another and are entered from an outside doorway. A small cement porch runs the length of each side of the buildings, but there are no outside chairs.

Swiftcurrent offers lodging at a reasonable price in a very beautiful area of Glacier National Park. In fact, the one-bedroom cabins without bath are about as cheap as you will find in any national park area. The complex is across from a campground and only a mile down the road from the fancier and more expensive Many Glacier Hotel. The registration building has a small lobby area and a large covered porch with chairs. All of the lodging buildings at Swiftcurrent Motor Inn are surrounded by trees, so you won't have any great vistas from your room. On the other hand, Swiftcurrent is a pleasant and relatively inexpensive place to stay. The restaurant serves three meals a day, and a modest walk takes you to more elegant dining at Many Glacier Hotel. Hikers frequently choose Swiftcurrent because of the many trails that originate in the Many Glacier area.

- **ROOMS:** Singles, doubles, triples, and quads. All the motel rooms have private baths. Most cabin guests must use a community bathroom. Two handicap-accessible rooms are located in the Motor Inn.

- **RESERVATIONS:** Glacier Park, Inc., 106 Cooperative Way, Suite 104, Kalispell, MT 59901. Phone (406) 756–2444. A deposit of one night's stay is required. A forty-eight-hour cancellation notice is required for a full refund less a $10 fee.

- **RATES:** One-bedroom cabin without bath ($41); two-bed cabin without bath ($51); one-bedroom cabin with bath ($70); Pinetop Motor Inn ($82); Motor Inn ($92). Room rates quoted are for two adults. Each additional person is $10 per night. Children eleven and under stay free with an adult.

- **LOCATION:** In the northeast section of the Glacier National Park at the end of Many Glacier Road, 12 miles east of Babb, Montana.

- **SEASON:** Mid-June to mid-September.

- **FOOD:** A restaurant in the registration building offers breakfast ($4.50–$7.00), lunch, and dinner ($6.00–$14.00). Lunch and dinner have the same menu. Limited groceries are available in the general store.

- **TRANSPORTATION:** The nearest scheduled air service is in Kalispell, Montana, where rental vehicles are available. Commercial bus service is available in Great Falls and Kalispell, Montana. Amtrak stops in East Glacier, Montana.

- **FACILITIES:** Restaurant, laundry, and camp store with gifts, groceries, and supplies.

- **ACTIVITIES:** Hiking, fishing, horseback riding, evening campfire programs, boat tours of Swiftcurrent Lake and Lake Josephine.

# VILLAGE INN

1038 Apgar Street • Apgar, MT 59936 • (406) 888–5632
www.glacierparkinc.com

*Village Inn*

Village Inn is a long, two-story motel-style wooden building with thirty-six rooms. The inn is at the end of the road, directly on the shore of scenic Lake McDonald. The building, constructed in 1956, was flooded and remodeled in the mid-1960s. Each room enjoys an excellent view of the lake and the mountains beyond. The small registration area at the front of the building offers coffee but no chairs or lobby area. The inn also has no restaurant, although Eddie's Cafe is a short walk up the street. Village Inn is located in Apgar, Montana, 3 miles inside the west entrance to Glacier National Park.

The inn offers four types of rooms. All the rooms are nicely furnished and have heat and a full bath but no air-conditioning, telephone, or television. All are wood paneled, and each room has a large window and an outside balcony or patio that offer excellent views of Lake McDonald. The rooms all have doors that open to the balcony or patio. Larger rooms on the first floor can also be entered from the parking lot behind the building. Unless you specifically desire one of the kitchen units, we recommend a second-floor room for increased privacy and a better view of the lake. The twelve least expensive rooms sit at one end of the building, six on the second floor and six on the ground floor. Half the rooms have one double bed, and the other half have two twin beds, which almost fill these small rooms.

Ten two-bedroom family units, all on the second floor, have a double bed in one bedroom and either a double and twin bed or a double bed and a sofa bed. These rooms cost $35–$55 more per night and are quite a bit larger than the least expensive rooms described above. On the first floor twelve rooms have a bedroom and a kitchen with a refrigerator, sink, oven, and stove. These are the same size as the two-bedroom units on the second floor and have a kitchen in place of the second bedroom. The inn also offers two suites at each end of the second floor that have a living room and two back bedrooms, each with a double bed. A sofa bed is in the living room.

Village Inn is a quiet place to spend a night or two on the west side of Glacier National Park. The inn's location at the end of a short road allows you to avoid the crowds while enjoying a view of Lake McDonald and some of the park's scenic mountains. A gravel beach just outside the rooms leads to the cool waters of the lake. The inn is located less than a block from a restaurant that serves good food at reasonable prices. It is also a short walk from a National Park Service visitor center. Park Service rangers are at the visitor center to answer questions about the park. You will also find three gift shops and an ice cream shop nearby. A store offers limited groceries, beer, and wine.

- **ROOMS:** Singles, doubles, triples, and quads. Some of the family units and the two suites can hold up to six persons. All rooms have private baths. Two kitchen units are handicap accessible.

- **RESERVATIONS:** Glacier Park, Inc., 106 Cooperative Way, Suite 104, Kalispell, MT 59901. Phone (406) 756–2444. A deposit of one night's stay is required. A seventy-two-hour cancellation notice is required for a full refund less a $10 fee.

- **RATES:** One bedroom ($95); kitchen units ($131); two-bedroom family units ($150); three-room suites ($150). Rates quoted are for two adults. Children eleven and under stay free with an adult. Additional adults are $10.

- **LOCATION:** In the village of Apgar, Montana, 3 miles from the West Glacier entrance station.

- **SEASON:** Mid-May through late September.

- **FOOD:** No food service is available at Village Inn. Within one block Eddie's Cafe serves breakfast, lunch, and dinner from 7:00 A.M. to 9:30 P.M. Depending on the weather, the restaurant is open from mid-May through most of September. A store sells limited grocery items, beer, and wine.

- **TRANSPORTATION:** Scheduled airlines serve Kalispell, Montana, where rental cars are available. An airport shuttle service from Kalispell goes to West Glacier. Tours of the park can be arranged from West Glacier. Amtrak service is available to Belton/West Glacier (800–872–7245), where car rental agencies are across the street from the station.

- **FACILITIES:** The village of Apgar has gift shops, a restaurant, an ice cream shop, boat rentals, and a National Park Service visitor center.

- **ACTIVITIES:** Nightly ranger/naturalist talks at the Apgar campground, boating, swimming (very cool water), fishing, hiking, horseback riding. Sightseeing tours of the park leave from Apgar.

# NEVADA

## LAKE MEAD NATIONAL RECREATION AREA

601 Nevada Highway
Boulder City, NV 89005
(702) 293–8907
www.nps.gov/lame

Lake Mead National Recreation Area comprises nearly 1.5 million acres of desert landscape surrounding Lake Mead and Lake Mohave. The 290 square miles of clear water in the two lakes is supplied by the Colorado River. Lake Mead is 110 miles long and results from the famous Hoover Dam near Boulder City, Nevada. Farther south, 67-mile-long Lake Mohave is formed by Davis Dam near Bullhead City, Arizona. The recreation area is particularly popular for water-related activities such as boating, fishing, and waterskiing. Areas near the lake are often five to ten degrees warmer than Las Vegas, which means that summer temperatures frequently rise to 110° Fahrenheit and above. The recreation area is located in southern Nevada and northwestern Arizona. Main access is via U.S. 93, which connects Las Vegas, Nevada, and Kingman, Arizona.

**RECREATION AREA ENTRANCE FEE:** $5.00 per vehicle or $3.00 per person, good for five days.

### Lodging in Lake Mead National Recreation Area

Five lodging facilities are scattered throughout Lake Mead National Recreation Area. Echo Bay Resort, Lake Mead Resort at Boulder Beach, and Temple Bar Resort are each on Lake Mead in the northern half of the recreation area. Cottonwood Cove Resort and Lake Mohave Resort at Katherine Landing are on Lake Mohave in the southern half of the recreation area. The three facilities on Lake Mead and Lake Mohave Resort on Lake Mohave are operated by Seven Crown Resorts of Irvine, California. Cottonwood Cove is operated by Forever Resorts. All five facilities are geared to visitors interested in water-based activities, in particular boating and fishing.

# LAKE MEAD NATIONAL RECREATION AREA

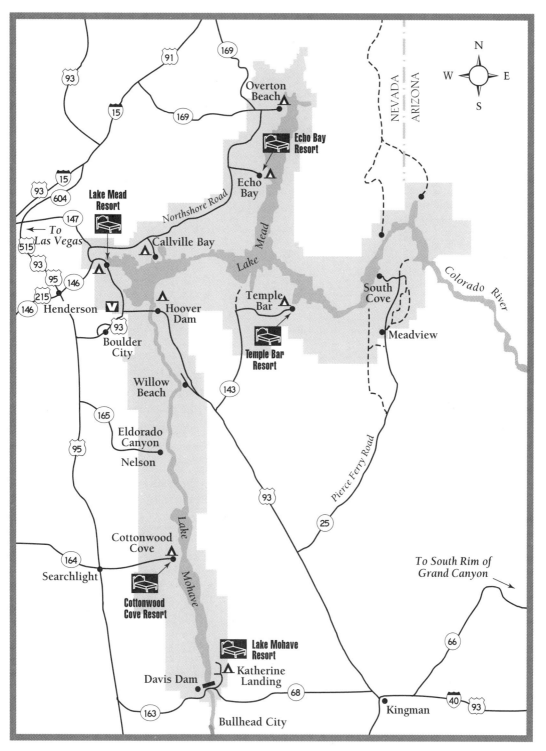

# COTTONWOOD COVE RESORT

Box 1000 • Cottonwood Cove, NV 89046 • (702) 297–1464

*Cottonwood Cove Resort*

Cottonwood Cove is a family resort with overnight accommodations, a restaurant, and a large marina, all on the Nevada shoreline of Lake Mohave. The cement block motel building, with twenty-four guest rooms, was renovated in 1995. The separate restaurant was renovated in 1996. Cottonwood Cove Resort is on the west side of Lake Mohave, 14 miles east of the intersection of Highway 164 and U.S. Highway 95. It is 70 miles southeast of Las Vegas, Nevada, via U.S. 95.

The one-story motel's twenty-four guest rooms each offer lake views. The rooms have either one king-size bed or two double beds and a private bath with a combination shower-tub. All rooms are the same size, and those with a king-size bed cost about $5.00 extra. Each room has a patio that provides access to a swimming beach and harbor.

- ■ **ROOMS:** Doubles, triples, and quads. All rooms have a full bath. Handicap-accessible rooms are available.

- ■ **RESERVATIONS:** Cottonwood Cove Marina, P.O. Box 1000, Cottonwood Cove, NV 89046. Phone (702) 297–1464. A deposit of one night's stay is required. A seventy-two-hour cancellation notice is required for a full refund.

- ■ **RATES:** All rooms ($90–$95) from May through October; ($55–$60) during Value Season, from November to May. Value Season rates not applicable during national holidays. Rates quoted are for two adults. Each additional person is $10 per night. Rollaway beds are $6.00 extra. Children four and under stay free.

- ■ **LOCATION:** Fourteen miles east of Searchlight, Nevada, on Highway 164. The resort is approximately 70 miles southeast of Las Vegas, Nevada.

- ■ **SEASON:** The resort is open year-round. High season is from March 16 to October 31, when rates are highest.

- **FOOD:** A full-service restaurant serves breakfast ($3.00–$6.00), lunch ($4.00–$7.00), and dinner ($7.00–$13.00). A store sells groceries and supplies.

- **TRANSPORTATION:** No public transportation serves Cottonwood Cove. The nearest major airport is in Las Vegas, where rental cars are available. An airport is also in Laughlin, Nevada.

- **FACILITIES:** Restaurant, convenience store, full-service marina.

- **ACTIVITIES:** Fishing, boating, and waterskiing. Numerous casinos are about forty-five minutes away in Laughlin, Nevada.

## ECHO BAY RESORT

Overton, NV 89040 • (702) 394–4000

info@sevencrown.com • www.sevencrown.com

*Echo Bay Resort*

A marina complex, Echo Bay Resort includes a 1970s two-story cement block motel that sits on a hill overlooking the west side of the Overton Arm of Lake Mead. Approximately half of the resort's fifty-two rooms face the water; a marina is in front. The motel, with several nearby palm trees, has an appearance similar to what you might expect near the Florida coast. A large wooden deck on the lake side is accessed from the second floor. Plentiful parking is directly beside the building and close to the main entrance to the registration area. Pets are permitted with a $25 deposit and an additional daily charge of $5.00. The resort is 60 miles northeast of Las Vegas, Nevada, and the farthest north of the five lodging facilities in Lake Mead National Recreation Area. It is located at the end of a paved road, 5 miles east of Northshore Road.

All of the rooms at Echo Bay have air-conditioning, heat, television, and a telephone. Furniture includes a dresser, a table, and three chairs. Nearly all of the rooms have two chairs on a private balcony or patio. Rooms on both sides of the building are accessed through a central corridor that can be entered at either end of the building or near the registration area on the main floor. Three categories of rooms are offered. The least expensive rooms have two double beds and face west, toward the parking lot. A few face a large cement block wall and have no balcony or patio—try to avoid these. Twenty-five rooms face the water and have a single king-size bed; these cost $15 more than rooms on the opposite side of the building. Three extra-large rooms have two double beds and a Hide-A-Bed. Several rooms on the south side of the building appear to have considerably more floor space than the other rooms but rent for the same daily rate.

Echo Bay is a water-based resort that appeals primarily to visitors who boat and fish. A National Park Service ranger station and campground are nearby, but most facilities are some distance away. A marina rents boats of all types, from personal watercraft to large houseboats. The main resort building has a 2,500-square-foot conference room on the second floor. A restaurant, Tail O'The Whale, has a nautical decor, with a wall of large windows that provides a view of the lake. A cocktail lounge located next to the restaurant is accessed through the same outside door. A snack bar/store with supplies and limited groceries is at the marina.

**M**any people who visit Lake Mead National Recreation Area are interested in houseboat rentals, which are available at the marinas. Most houseboats are about 14 feet wide, with lengths that range from 40 to nearly 60 feet. The smaller units sleep six or eight persons, while the larger units can sleep a dozen or more. Be forewarned that houseboats aren't cheap to rent. Smaller houseboats often cost $200 to $300 per night for weeklong rentals and more for shorter rentals. Larger houseboats that hold up to ten or twelve persons rent for $400 to $500 per night for weeklong rentals and even more for two- or three-night rentals. Rental fees are often reduced during the off-season of mid-September to mid-June (excluding Memorial Day weekend). Houseboats are available at 7:00 A.M. on the first day and need to be returned by 4:00 P.M. on the last day. Reservations and deposits are required.

- **ROOMS:** Doubles, triples, and quads. All rooms have a full bath. One room is handicap accessible.

- **RESERVATIONS:** Seven Crown Resorts, P.O. Box 16247, Irvine, CA 92623-0068. Phone (800) 752–9669. A deposit of one night's stay is required. A seventy-two-hour cancellation notice is required for a full refund.

- **RATES:** Nonwaterside ($85); waterside ($100); extra large room ($115). Rates quoted are for two adults per room. Extra persons and rollaway beds are $6.00 additional per night. Children five and under stay free. Pets are $5.00 per night each, with a refundable pet deposit. Snowbird specials are available October through April.

- **LOCATION:** Sixty miles northeast of Las Vegas via Highway 147 and Northshore Road. The resort is at the end of a paved road, 5 miles east of Northshore Road.

- **SEASON:** The resort is open year-round except Christmas Day. High season is during summer months, when the resort often fills on weekends.

- **FOOD:** A full-service restaurant serves breakfast ($3.00–$6.00), lunch ($4.00–$7.00), and dinner ($8.00–$15.00) and is open from 7:00 A.M. to 9:00 P.M. in-season. Hours can change during the off-season. The cocktail lounge is open from 4:00 P.M. to midnight. A snack bar/store at the marina is open from 7:00 A.M. to 8:00 P.M.

- **TRANSPORTATION:** The nearest major airport is in Las Vegas, where rental cars are available. An asphalt landing strip 3 miles from Echo Bay provides access for private planes. The resort has a free pickup service when called ahead.

- **FACILITIES:** A restaurant, cocktail lounge, and conference room are in the main building. An adjacent gas station sells unleaded gasoline, diesel fuel, and propane. A laundry facility is in the nearby RV park. A full-service marina rents a variety of boats, including houseboats, ski boats, patio boats, fishing boats, and personal watercraft.

- **ACTIVITIES:** Fishing, waterskiing, boating.

## LAKE MEAD RESORT

322 Lake Shore Road • Boulder City, NV 89005 • (702) 293–2074
info@sevencrown.com • www.sevencrown.com

*Lake Mead Resort*

Lake Mead Resort is a complex of three one-story cement block buildings overlooking the Boulder Basin section of Lake Mead, with a marina and floating restaurant situated a quarter mile down the road. The lodging buildings are in an area a short distance back from the lakeshore. Lake Mead Resort is located at Boulder Beach, 6 miles north of Boulder

City, Nevada. Of the five lodging facilities in Lake Mead National Recreation Area, this is the nearest to Las Vegas (30 miles).

Most of the resort's forty-three rooms are in U-shaped buildings that are situated parallel to the shoreline of Boulder Basin. Rooms in these buildings are relatively small and have one queen-size bed. The center building houses the registration office, a conference room, and a very nice suite that consists of a living room, bedroom, two bathrooms, kitchenette, and a fireplace. A separate annex has eight larger rooms with two queen-size beds. All the rooms have heat, air-conditioning, and television (with cable). One handicap-accessible room is available. A swimming pool is on the opposite side of the parking lot.

*Lake Mead, with 550 miles of shoreline, is formed by famous Hoover Dam. The dam, completed in 1935, tamed this portion of the often wild Colorado River. The giant concrete structure required more than 5,000 men to work around the clock for five years. Downstream, Davis Dam was completed in 1953. Dam tours once offered have been discontinued indefinitely.*

- **ROOMS:** Mostly doubles, with some triples, and quads. The suite will hold five. All rooms have a private bath. One room is handicap accessible.

- **RESERVATIONS:** Seven Crown Resorts, P.O. Box 16247, Irvine, CA 92623-0068. Phone (800) 752–9669. Reservations require a one-night deposit. A seventy-two-hour cancellation is required for a full refund.

- **RATES:** Regular ($70); Deluxe ($80); suites ($150). Rates quoted are for two adults per room. Extra persons and rollaway beds are $6.00 additional. Children five and under stay free. Rates are reduced in the winter.

- **LOCATION:** Six miles north of Boulder City, Nevada, on Lakeshore Scenic Drive. The resort is 30 miles southeast of Las Vegas.

- **SEASON:** The resort is open year-round except Christmas Day. High season is during summer months, when the resort often fills on weekends.

- **FOOD:** A full-service restaurant, Tail O'The Whale, at the marina serves breakfast ($3.00–$6.00), lunch ($5.00–$7.00), and dinner ($6.00–$16.00). The cocktail lounge, Pelican's Perch, and store are also at the marina.

- **TRANSPORTATION:** The nearest major airport is in Las Vegas, where rental cars are available.

- **FACILITIES:** Swimming pool. A restaurant, cocktail lounge, waterside store, and a tackle and bait shop are at the full-service marina. Ski boats, patio boats, fishing boats, and personal watercraft are available for rent (1–800–752–9669 or www.sevencrown.com).

- **ACTIVITIES:** Fishing, waterskiing, boating, and swimming. No lifeguards.

# LAKE MOHAVE RESORT AT KATHERINE LANDING

Bullhead City, AZ 86430 • (520) 754–3245

info@sevencrown.com • www.sevencrown.com

*Lake Mohave Resort at Katherine Landing*

Lake Mohave Resort is a marina complex situated on a hill above Lake Mohave. The two-story motel, constructed of wood and cement block in the early 1970s, provides a total of fifty rooms in a large grassy area landscaped with palm trees. The resort is located at the south end of Lake Mohave, just off Highway 68, north of Davis Dam. It is the southernmost lodging facility in Lake Mead National Recreation Area. Lake Mohave Resort is 32 miles west of Kingman, Arizona.

The resort offers five types of accommodations. All of the rooms have air-conditioning, heat, a telephone, a television, and a bathroom. Six rooms have a private balcony or patio. Eleven of the resort's least expensive rooms have one king-size bed. Thirty-one rooms have two double beds. Six of these rooms include a kitchen and rent for an additional $10.00 per night. Eight rooms classified as kitchen suites have two queen-size beds. A single deluxe rental house, which sleeps up to ten persons, includes three bedrooms, two baths, and a kitchen. The rental house is across the street from the main building.

Activities at Lake Mohave Resort primarily appeal to visitors who enjoy fishing, waterskiing, and boating. A full marina provides slips, moorage, a gas dock, and repair facilities. The marina has a full-service Tail O' The Whale Restaurant and lounge. Laundry facilities are at the nearby RV park, and a convenience store and tackle shop are adjacent to the restaurant. The booming town of Laughlin, Nevada, and its many casinos is a short drive from the resort.

■ **ROOMS:** Doubles, triples, and quads. All rooms have a bath. The house sleeps up to ten. Handicap-accessible rooms are available.

■ **RESERVATIONS:** Seven Crown Resorts, P.O. Box 16247, Irvine, CA 92623-0068. Phone (800) 752–9669. A deposit of one night's stay is required. A seventy-two-hour cancellation notice is required for a full refund.

- **RATES:** Room with one king-size bed ($80); room with two double beds ($90); kitchen with two double beds ($100); kitchen suite with two queen-size beds ($110); rental house ($200). Rates quoted are for two adults per room, except kitchen units and suites, which are for three adults per room. Extra persons and rollaway beds are $6.00 each. Children five and under stay free.

- **LOCATION:** The resort is located on the shore of Lake Mohave, 32 miles west of Kingman, Arizona. It is 3 miles off Highway 68.

- **SEASON:** The resort is open year-round except for Christmas Day. High season is during summer, and the resort often fills on summer weekends.

- **FOOD:** A full-service restaurant serves breakfast ($3.00–$6.00), lunch ($5.00–$7.00), and dinner ($6.00–$16.00). A store adjacent to the restaurant sells groceries and supplies.

*Lake Mead and Lake Mohave offer excellent fishing and have open season on all species of fish year-round. Largemouth bass, rainbow trout, channel catfish, black crappie, and bluegill are in both lakes. Lake Mead is noted for an abundance of striped bass, some weighing fifty pounds and more. Rainbow trout are the most popular catch in Lake Mohave. Fishing from shore requires an appropriate state fishing license. Fishing from a boat requires a fishing license from either Nevada or Arizona and a special use stamp from the other state. Licenses and stamps are sold at most of the marinas.*

- **TRANSPORTATION:** Kingman, Arizona, and Las Vegas both have airports with rental car service.

- **FACILITIES:** A restaurant, cocktail lounge, store, and tackle shop are at the marina. Laundry facilitiers are at the nearby RV park. A full-service marina located in front of the lodge buildings rents houseboats, ski boats, patio boats, fishing boats, and personal watercraft (1–800–752–9669 or www.sevencrown.com).

- **ACTIVITIES:** Fishing, boating, swimming (no lifeguards), and waterskiing. Numerous casinos are a short distance away in Laughlin, Nevada.

## TEMPLE BAR RESORT

Temple Bar, AZ 86443 • (520) 767–3211

templebaraz@yahoo.com • www.sevencrown.com

Temple Bar Resort comprises an eighteen-unit wood-and-concrete block motel, four free-standing fishing cabins, a restaurant, an adjacent store, and a tackle and bait shop. The complex also includes a full-service marina. The resort is on the south shoreline of Lake Mead within view of a large monolith called The Temple. Temple Bar Resort is located 28 miles northeast of U.S. Highway 93, which connects Las Vegas, Nevada, with Kingman, Arizona. It is 78 miles east of Las Vegas and 85 miles from Kingman.

All of the eighteen motel rooms at Temple Bar have heat, air-conditioning, television, and a private bathroom. There are no telephones in the rooms; pay phones are available.

*Temple Bar Resort*

Twelve of the motel rooms have two double beds and private patios; half of these units are Desert View rooms and the other half are Lake View rooms. Two Traditional rooms offer a double bed and double hideaway. Two Kitchen Units have two double beds and a hideaway bed in one room. The kitchen area includes a stove top, microwave oven, refrigerator, dishes, and basic cooking utensils. Two Kitchen Suites feature two double beds in a separate bedroom with a hideaway bed in the livingroom/kitchen. The four cabins have two double beds, a stove, and a refrigerator but no bath. The bathhouse is adjacent to the cabins. There are no dishes or cooking utensils provided in the cabins.

- **ROOMS:** Doubles, triples, and quads. Suites hold up to six adults. All rooms except cabins have a full bath. One handicap-accessible room is available.

- **RESERVATIONS:** Seven Crown Resorts, P.O. Box 16247, Irvine, CA 92623-0068. Phone (800) 752–9669. A deposit of one night's stay is required. Holiday reservations require full payment in advance. Any reservations made within fourteen days of arrival date must be paid in full. A seventy-two-hour cancellation notice is required for a full refund.

- **RATES:** Traditional rooms ($75); Desert View/Lake View rooms ($85/$95); Kitchen Units ($90); Kitchen Suites ($105); Cabins ($55). Rates quoted are for two adults in regular units and for three adults in kitchen suites. Extra persons and rollaway beds are $6.00 additional. Children six and under stay free. Small pets are permitted (limit two) for a fee of $5.00 each, with a refundable pet deposit.

- **LOCATION:** The resort is 78 miles east of Las Vegas, Nevada. It is at the end of a paved road 28 miles northeast of Highway 93.

- **SEASON:** The resort is open year-round except for Christmas Day. High season is during summer, and the resort often fills on summer weekends.

- **FOOD:** A full-service restaurant serves beakfast ($3.00–$6.00), lunch ($4.00–$7.00), and dinner ($9.00–$17.00). A convenience store sells groceries and supplies.

- **TRANSPORTATION:** Kingman, Arizona, and Las Vegas, both have airports with rental car service.

■ **FACILITIES:** Restaurant, cocktail lounge, store, and tackle and bait shop. The Marina rents ski boats, patio boats, fishing boats, and personal watercraft (1–800–752–9669 or www.sevencrown.com). Laundry facilities are at the nearby RV park.

■ **ACTIVITIES:** Fishing, boating, swimming (no lifeguards), and waterskiing.

# NORTH CAROLINA

## STATE TOURIST INFORMATION

(800) 847–4862

www.visitnc.com

## BLUE RIDGE PARKWAY

200 BBB&T Building

Asheville, NC 28801

(828) 259–0710

www.nps.gov/blri

The Blue Ridge Parkway comprises 81,000 acres in a narrow strip along 470 miles of winding road that follows the crest of the Blue Ridge Mountains. The parkway provides access to craft centers, campgrounds, scenic overlooks, log cabins, rail fences, and beautiful mountain vistas. Lodges, overlooks, restaurants, and other major points of interest along the Blue Ridge Parkway can be located according to milepost markers alongside the road. Mile marker 0 is at Rockfish Gap near Waynesboro, Virginia, the northern entrance to the parkway. Each mile is numbered progressively southward. Be certain to stop at a visitor center and pick up a copy of the parkway folder that provides a map along with the locations of points of interest on the parkway. The parkway is located in western North Carolina and western Virginia. The north end of the parkway connects with Shenandoah National Park, and the south end leads to Great Smoky Mountains National Park.

**PARKWAY ENTRANCE FEE:** No charge.

## Lodging Along the Blue Ridge Parkway

Four lodging facilities are within the boundaries of the Blue Ridge Parkway. Accommodations range from very nice two-story lodges to very rustic cabins without private bath. The facilities are scattered along the parkway from mile marker 86 in the north to very near the south entrance, near Great Smoky Mountains National Park.

# BLUE RIDGE PARKWAY

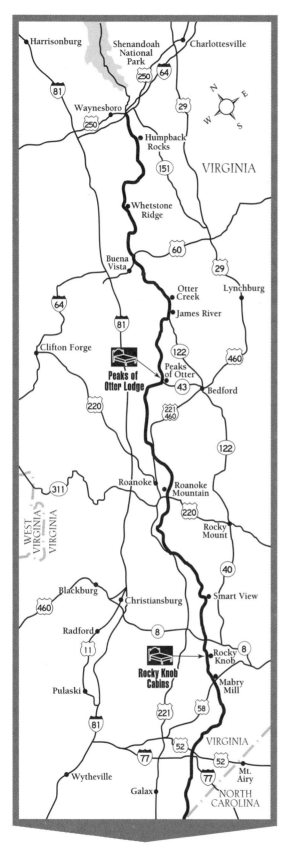

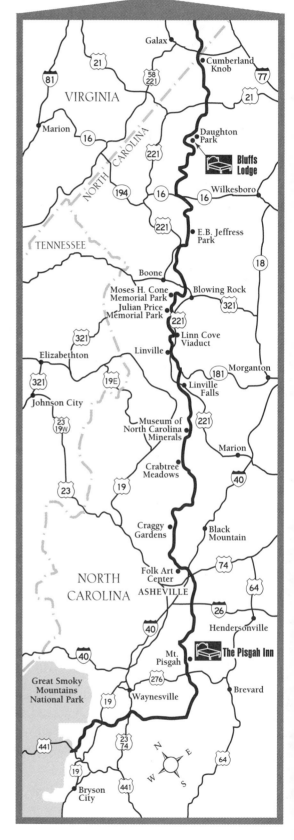

# BLUFFS LODGE

45356 Blue Ridge Parkway • Laurel Springs, NC 28644-9716 • (336) 372–4499

*Bluffs Lodge*

Bluffs Lodge, a Forever Resort, consists of two identical two-story lodge buildings located on a grassy hillside overlooking a meadow and surrounding hills. No other buildings are connected to the lodge, although a coffee shop and gas station are a quarter mile away on the parkway. Each lodge building contains twelve rooms, four on each floor of the back side facing the meadow and four rooms on the front facing the parking lot. A spacious second-floor balcony runs across the back of each building. Chairs are on the balcony and on the rock walkways, as well as the front of the building. A nice rock patio area between the two buildings has a large outdoor stone fireplace and many chairs and tables for viewing the scenery or visiting. The buildings, which opened in 1949, are well maintained. Bluffs Lodge is located in northern North Carolina in the Doughton Park area of the Blue Ridge Parkway. It is at milepost 241, about midway between the north and south entrances to the parkway.

All the rooms at Bluffs Lodge are nearly identical except for the beds and the views. The rooms each have hot-water heat and a full bath with a combination shower-tub but no air-conditioning, telephone, or television. Each room has a desk and several chairs. All but five rooms have two double beds. Three rooms have a queen-size bed, and one has a king. One partially handicap-accessible room has one queen-size bed. The best bet is to try for a second-floor room at the back, which has a superior view. All rooms rent for the same rate.

Bluffs Lodge is a quiet place in a lovely setting. It is a quarter mile off the Blue Ridge Parkway, so you won't be bothered by traffic noise, and since no restaurant or visitor center is at the site, there is no congestion of people or vehicles. You will have to walk (or drive) a quarter mile to the coffee shop in order to eat, but that isn't so bad. Besides, the old-fashioned coffee shop (it still has counter service) with its vaulted ceiling is kind of fun.

- **ROOMS:** Doubles, triples, and quads. All rooms have a private bath with a combination shower-tub. One room is partially handicap accessible.

- **RESERVATIONS:** Bluffs Lodge, 45356 Blue Ridge Parkway, Laurel Springs, NC 28644-9716. Phone (336) 372–4499. During the off-season write Bluffs Lodge, P.O. Box 397, Jefferson, NC 28640. A deposit of one night's stay is required. A forty-eight-hour cancellation notice is required for a full refund.

- **RATES:** All rooms ($74). Rates quoted are for two adults. Each additional person is $8.00 per night. Children twelve and under stay free.

- **LOCATION:** In northern North Carolina, near the midpoint of the Blue Ridge Parkway at milepost 241. The lodge is a quarter mile off the parkway.

- **SEASON:** End of April through the end of October.

- **FOOD:** A coffee shop a quarter mile from the lodge serves breakfast, lunch, and dinner. A special is offered each evening. Snacks are sold at a gas station next to the coffee shop.

- **TRANSPORTATION:** The nearest scheduled airline service is in Charlotte and Greensboro, North Carolina. Both cities are about two hours from the lodge.

- **FACILITIES:** No facilities are at the lodge. A coffee shop, gift shop, and gas station are a quarter mile away on the Blue Ridge Parkway.

- **ACTIVITIES:** Hiking. Park Service rangers present programs on the lodge patio each Sunday evening. Programs are presented on Friday and Saturday nights at the nearby campground.

> Linn Cove Viaduct at mile marker 305 on the Blue Ridge Parkway is considered one of the most complicated concrete bridges ever built. It is one of America's most scenic bridges and has received half a dozen national design awards. The S-shaped viaduct was designed and constructed to minimize environmental damage. Skirting the perimeter of North Carolina's Grandfather Mountain, the viaduct is 1,243 feet long and contains 153 concrete segments, only one of which is straight. Although nearly all of the Blue Ridge Parkway had been completed and open to travelers by 1967, the viaduct was not finished until 1983. A trail leading underneath the viaduct begins at a visitor contact station at the south end of the viaduct.

# PEAKS OF OTTER LODGE

P.O. Box 489 • Bedford, VA 24523 • (540) 586–1081
peaksotter@aol.com • www.peaksotter.com

*Peaks of Otter Lodge*

Peaks of Otter Lodge consists of a main registration and dining building and three adjacent two-story lodging buildings that provide a total of sixty-three overnight rooms. All four of the attractive wood-and-cement block buildings were constructed in the mid-1960s and have a similar appearance. The three buildings with rooms (a few are in the main building) are identical. The buildings are on the grassy bank of Abbott Lake, and all the rooms provide an excellent view of this small but pretty body of water. Peaks of Otter Lodge is located about 25 miles north of Roanoke, Virginia, at mile marker 86 on the Blue Ridge Parkway. It is the farthest north of the four lodging facilities on the parkway.

The twenty rooms in each of the three lodging buildings are almost identical. They are roomy and nicely furnished. Forty-eight of the rooms have two double beds, while the other twelve rooms each have a king-size bed. Each room has a full bath with a combination shower/tub, electric heat, and air-conditioning but no television or telephone. Second-floor rooms have a private balcony with chairs, and first-floor rooms have a patio with a table and chairs, all facing the lake. Two rooms without balconies are offered at a discount.

The lodge has three handicapped-accessible rooms on the ground floor of the main registration building, which has an elevator. The rooms vary in size and the number of beds but, in general, are larger than the rooms in the other buildings. Each room has a television and a telephone but rents for the same amount as a standard room.

Peaks of Otter Lodge is perfect for a weekend getaway. Plan to do a lot of hiking during your visit. A paved walking trail circles Abbott Lake. Three other loop trails are nearby. Daily bus trips to Sharp Top Mountain (nominal fee) leave hourly from the nearby camp store when weather permits. Sitting on one side of small Abbott Lake with a background of tree-covered hills and mountains makes for a tranquil setting. You can fish in the lake using artificial lures. The main lodge has a lobby with a registration desk and a nice gift shop. The sun porch and lounge area have a fireplace and ceiling-height windows that provide a view of the lake and hills. The country-style dining room serves three meals a day, including its famous Friday seafood buffet and a country buffet each Sunday. It is best known for its trout dinners. A coffee shop serves sandwiches and light meals all day (open May–October).

- **ROOMS:** Singles, doubles, triples, and quads. All rooms have a private bath with a combination shower-tub. Three rooms are handicap accessible.

- **RESERVATIONS:** Peaks of Otter Lodge, P.O. Box 489, Bedford, VA 24523. Phone (800) 542–5927. One night's deposit required via check or money order. A twenty-four-hour cancellation notice is required for full refund.

- **RATES:** November 1–April 30 weekdays ($59); November 1–April 30 weekends ($66); May 1–September 30 ($82); holiday weekends and the month of October ($89). Rates are quoted for singles or doubles. Each additional person is $7.00 per night. Children under sixteen stay free. Rollaway beds are $7.00 per night. Call or check the Web site for special packages.

- **LOCATION:** Twenty-five miles north of Roanoke, Virginia, at mileposts 84/87 of the Blue Ridge Parkway.

- **SEASON:** Open year-round.

- **FOOD:** A dining room serves breakfast ($5.50–$8.00), lunch ($5.00–$10.00), and dinner ($8.00–$20.00), including a special seafood buffet on Fridays ($20) and a country buffet on Sundays ($13). A coffee shop in the main building is open for breakfast and sandwiches (May–October). A nearby camp store has limited groceries.

> Several short and intermediate-length hiking trails are near Peaks of Otter Lodge. The nearest is the 1-mile loop trail around Abbott Lake. Directly across the parkway a 2-mile loop trail leads to Johnson Farm, where living history demonstrations are presented on a seasonal basis. The same trail connects with the 3.3-mile Harkening Hill Loop Trail, which leads to a ridge where distant views are possible. The most popular trail leads 1.6 miles from the camp store to the summit of Sharp Top Mountain. The summit offers a 360-degree view of the area. A map and description of these and other trails can be obtained at the lodge or at the National Park Service visitor center across the road.

- **TRANSPORTATION:** Nearby Roanoke and Lynchburg, Virginia, each provide scheduled airline service. Rental cars are available in each town.

- **FACILITIES:** Restaurant, coffee shop, cocktail lounge, gift shop, gas station, camp store, National Park Service visitor center.

- **ACTIVITIES:** Hiking, fishing, interpretive programs, bus trip to Sharp Top Mountain, National Park Service campfire programs on weekend evenings.

# THE PISGAH INN

P.O. Box 749 • Waynesville, NC 28786 • (828) 235–8228
pisgahinn@aol.com • www.pisgahinn.com

*The Pisgah Inn*

The Pisgah Inn consists of three buildings with accommodations, a separate building with a restaurant and gift shop, a gas station, and a store. A National Park Service campground is across the road. All of the buildings are of wood and masonry construction. The registration desk is at the end of the lodging building nearest the restaurant. The three two-story buildings with lodging provide a total of fifty-one rooms, including one suite. All of the rooms are a short walk from the dining room. Each of the rooms offers an excellent view of the distant mountains. The three lodge buildings and the restaurant are situated at 5,000 feet on the side of 5,749-foot Mt. Pisgah. The gas station and camp store are nearby. The inn, constructed in the mid-1960s, is in southwestern North Carolina, approximately 25 miles south of Asheville, North Carolina. It is the farthest south of the four lodging facilities on the Blue Ridge Parkway, at milepost 408.

Two types of rooms and one suite are offered. The difference between the two categories of rooms is that thirty rooms labeled "Deluxe" are slightly larger, have ceiling fans, coffeemakers, refrigerators, and were remodeled in 2001. Twenty rooms rent as "Standard" at a slightly reduced rate. All of the rooms have heat, a full bathroom with a combination shower-tub, and a color television but no air-conditioning or telephone. Each room has a private balcony with rocking chairs. Most of the rooms have two double beds, and some have one queen-size bed. Three handicap-accessible rooms with one queen-size bed are available. Great views from the back windows or balcony are available from each of the rooms, although the second-floor rooms offer the best views. Rooms are entered from an outside door facing the parking lot. More than enough parking is available and close to each of the rooms. The single suite has one large room with a sitting area, one king-size bed, and the only fireplace of any room at the inn.

The Pisgah Inn is a nice place to spend a restful weekend. Temperatures are generally cool, even during summer. The views are great, and the facility is comfortable. The restaurant has ceiling-high windows on three walls that offer views from nearly any table. This is an excellent area for hiking, and good fishing is about 10 miles away. National Park Service rangers conduct evening weekend programs across the road at the campground amphitheater.

■ **ROOMS:** Singles, doubles, triples, and quads. All rooms have a private bath with a combination shower-tub. Three rooms are handicap accessible.

■ **RESERVATIONS:** The Pisgah Inn, P.O. Box 749, Waynesville, NC 28786. Phone (828) 235–8228. One night's deposit is required. Refund requires cancellation notification two weeks ahead of arrival.

■ **RATES:** Standard ($75); Deluxe ($87); suite ($125). Rates quoted are for one adult. Each additional person is $6.00. Rollaways are $6.25 per night. Children eleven and under stay free.

■ **LOCATION:** Southwest North Carolina, 25 miles south of Asheville on the Blue Ridge Parkway.

■ **SEASON:** April 1 through October 31.

■ **FOOD:** An attractive restaurant serves breakfast, lunch, and dinner ($8.50–$12.00). A nearby camp store sells limited groceries.

■ **TRANSPORTATION:** The nearest scheduled airline service is in Asheville, where rental cars are available. No public transportation services the inn.

■ **FACILITIES:** Restaurant, gift shop, laundry, gas station, camp store.

■ **ACTIVITIES:** Hiking, evening weekend programs at the nearby campground amphitheater.

> The Biltmore Estate near Asheville, North Carolina, is one of this region's major visitor attractions. The 250-room mansion was constructed in the late 1800s by George Washington Vanderbilt, grandson of railroad tycoon Cornelius Vanderbilt. Allow at least a half-day for the full self-guided tour (fee charged) of the home, winery, gardens, and greenhouse. The Biltmore Estate is 3 blocks north of I–40 (exit 50) on U.S. Highway 25.

# ROCKY KNOB CABINS

266 Mabry Mill Road • Meadows of Dan, VA 24120-9603 • (540) 593–3503

*Duplex Unit at Rocky Knob Cabins*

Rocky Knob Cabins, managed by Forever Resorts, is a small complex consisting of one registration office/manager's cabin, a central bathhouse, and five older wooden buildings in a semicircle behind the bathhouse. Two of the buildings are constructed as duplex units, for a total of seven rental cabins. The cabins are in a meadow surrounded by heavily wooded hills. The complex has no lobby, dining room, or recreation hall. The buildings are in one of the most remote settings of any national park. The buildings are from the 1930s, erected during construction of the parkway. Rocky Knob Cabins is in southern Virginia, at milepost 174 on the Blue Ridge Parkway. It is 54 miles south of Roanoke, Virginia.

The seven cabins at Rocky Knob Cabins are virtually identical, with two double beds, electricity, and a kitchen with an oven and stove, refrigerator, and sink with cold water only. Linens and utensils, including pots, pans, plates, cups, and silverware, are provided. There is no heat (other than a stone fireplace in two of the cabins), air-conditioning, telephone, or television. Each cabin has a kitchen table and chairs and also an outside porch with table and chairs. None of the cabins have a bathroom, and guests must use the central bathhouse, which has sinks, toilets, and showers. A washing machine is in the women's bathroom, and a clothesline is outside. Two of the buildings are constructed as duplex units, with one unit in each duplex having a stone fireplace (wood not provided). None of the other cabins have a fireplace or heat of any kind. The three other buildings are freestanding cabins. One cabin is handicap accessible.

Rocky Knob Cabins is certainly one of the more unusual lodging units in the national park system. Staying there is like returning to Appalachia in years past—many years past. The cabins are old but clean and comfortable. The deciding factor for many travelers is whether a community bath is a viable alternative. If you don't mind this inconvenience and you want to stay overnight in a very rural setting, Rocky Knob may be your place. Also,

Rocky Knob has no planned activities or other facilities; you are on your own for something to do. You will also enjoy a sense of solitude that many seek in a vacation. If you don't want to cook, a restaurant is a mile down the road. In addition, Mabry Mill, a famous stop on the Blue Ridge Parkway, is 2 miles south.

- ■ **ROOMS:** Doubles, triples, and quads. None of the cabins have a private bath. There is one handicap-accessible cabin.

- ■ **RESERVATIONS:** Rocky Knob Cabins, 266 Mabry Mill Road, Meadows of Dan, VA 24120-9603. Phone (540) 593–3503; during the off-season write Rocky Knob Cabins, P.O. Box 27, Mammoth Cave, KY 42259. Phone (270) 773–2191. One night's deposit is required. Cancellation notice of forty-eight hours is required for a full refund.

- ■ **RATES:** All cabins ($52). Rates quoted are for two adults. Each additional person is $5.00 per night.

- ■ **LOCATION:** Southern Virginia, 1 mile off the Blue Ridge Parkway at milepost 174. The cabins are approximately 55 miles south of Roanoke, Virginia.

- ■ **SEASON:** Last week of May through Labor Day.

- ■ **FOOD:** No dining facilities are available. A restaurant is about a mile up the road near the Blue Ridge Parkway. The Mabry Mill Restaurant is 2 miles south on the Blue Ridge Parkway.

- ■ **TRANSPORTATION:** Scheduled airlines serve Roanoke, Virginia, where rental cars are available.

- ■ **FACILITIES:** Community bathhouse with showers and a washing machine.

- ■ **ACTIVITIES:** Hiking.

- ■ **PETS:** Pets are permitted but must be kept on a leash.

Mabry Mill, at milepost 176, is a favorite stop for travelers on the Blue Ridge Parkway. The mill, operated by E. B. Mabry from 1910 to 1935, today serves country ham, barbecue, homemade biscuits, and corn and buckwheat pancakes. Native handicrafts, including pottery, woodcraft, and metalcraft, are available for purchase. A trail takes you to the original gristmill, sawmill, blacksmith shop, and other outdoor exhibits. Demonstrations are presented in summer and fall.

# OHIO

**STATE TOURIST INFORMATION**
(800) 282–5393
www.ohiotourism.com

## CUYAHOGA VALLEY NATIONAL PARK

15610 Vaughn Road
Brecksville, OH 44141
(216) 524–1497
www.dayinthevalley.com
www.nps.gov/cuva
cuva_canal_visitor_center@nps.gov

Cuyahoga Valley National Park preserves 33,000 acres of a rural river valley that links the two urban centers of Cleveland and Akron. The national park offers a place to enjoy a stroll, hike, or bike along the 19-mile Ohio & Erie Canal Towpath Trail, a primary park attraction. Cuyahoga Valley National Park includes a restored 1800s farm and village, hiking and biking trails, several visitor centers, and the remnants of a company town built in 1906. Throughout the year, the Cuyahoga Valley Scenic Railroad operates the full length of the park and beyond.

**PARK ENTRANCE FEE:** No charge.

### Lodging in Cuyahoga Valley National Recreation Area

A bed-and-breakfast inn with six accommodations, and Hostelling International's Stanford House Hostel are the only lodging facilities within the boundaries of the national park. The Inn at Brandywine Falls is midway between the north and south ends of the park, approximately 4 miles northeast of the crossing of I–80 and I–271. The Stanford House Hostel has men's and women's dormitory rooms, and some family and private rooms are available. The hostel is located on Stanford Road in the village of Boston, approximately 2 miles north of Peninsula, Ohio. A large number and variety of accommodations are available just outside the border of the national recreation area.

# CUYAHOGA VALLEY NATIONAL PARK

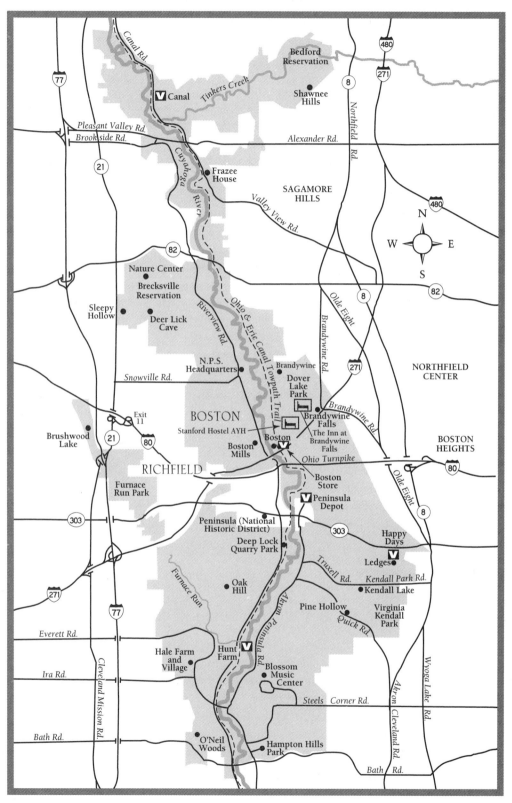

# THE INN AT BRANDYWINE FALLS

8230 Brandywine Road • Sagamore Hills, OH 44607-2810 • (330) 467–1812
brandywinefallsinn@prodigy.net • www.innatbrandywinefalls.com

*The Inn at Brandywine Falls*

The Inn at Brandywine Falls is a renovated farmhouse that an enterprising couple converted into a bed-and-breakfast under a fifty-year lease from the U.S. government. The farmhouse, originally built in 1848, was renovated and opened as a bed-and-breakfast in 1988. The property includes the main house, a separate carriage barn several steps behind the main house, and a nearby stable. Horses, cats, chickens, goats, and an affable dog add to the country atmosphere. Both buildings with overnight rooms have undergone extensive renovations that include heat and air-conditioning. Breakfast is included with the cost of a room. The Inn at Brandywine Falls is located on the east rim of the valley, approximately 3 miles north of I–80. From downtown Cleveland (forty minutes), take I–77 south to Route 82. Drive east about 6 miles to Brandywine Road, then 2.5 miles south.

A total of six overnight rooms are available, including four in the main house and two two-story suites in the adjacent carriage barn. All rooms have heat, air-conditioning, and a private bathroom with a combination shower-tub. Two rooms in the main house have one double bed, while the other two rooms are furnished with two double beds. One of the rooms with two doubles has a small sitting room that can be used as a second bedroom. One of the rooms in the main house is on the bottom floor and is handicap accessible. The two carriage barn suites each have a large Jacuzzi, and a wood-burning stove. The suites have a main floor plus a sleeping loft with a king-size bed.

Located in a quiet, rural area, the Inn at Brandywine Falls offers a great place to relax. Guests are able to walk a short distance to 67-foot Brandywine Falls, hike the 1.5-mile-long Brandywine Gorge Trail, or just stroll around the grounds. They are encouraged to use the inn's living room, library, dining room, and porch. A full breakfast that includes fresh-squeezed juice, homemade bread, an entrée, and much more is served from 7:00 to 10:00 A.M. (8:45 to 10 A.M. on weekends and holidays).

■ **ROOMS:** Doubles, triples, and quads. All rooms have private baths. One room is handicap-accessible.

- **RESERVATIONS:** The Inn at Brandywine Falls, 8230 Brandywine Road, Sagamore Hills, Ohio 44067-2810. Phone (888) 306–3381, (330) 467–1812 or 650–4965. A 65 percent deposit is required with a reservation. A two-week cancellation is required for a full refund unless the accommodation is subsequently booked by another party. The innkeepers recommend that reservations be made at least two months in advance.

- **ARRIVAL/DEPARTURE:** Check-in between 4:01 and 6:45 P.M. and after 8:30 P.M. Checkout at 11:00 A.M.

- **RATES:** Sunday through Thursday non-holiday prices: Main house ($108); carriage barn suites ($184); Fridays are $20 to $30 higher; Saturdays and holidays are about $50 higher. Prices quoted are for two persons and include a full breakfast. Each additional person is $10 to $35 per night, depending on age. There is a 10 percent discount for stays of three or more days.

- **LOCATION:** In north-central Ohio, midway between Cleveland and Akron.

- **SEASON:** Open year-round.

- **FOOD:** Breakfast is included. Refreshments are provided at 4:30 P.M. Alcoholic beverages may be brought by guests. Over a dozen restaurants are within 6 miles of the inn.

- **TRANSPORTATION:** The nearest scheduled airline service is in Cleveland, where rental cars are available.

- **FACILITIES:** Dining room for breakfast.

- **ACTIVITIES:** Hiking. Historic attractions, scenic railroad, museums, golf, and waterpark nearby. Cross-country skiing in the winter.

The James Wallace family, who came to this area in the early 1800s, built the farmhouse that is now The Inn at Brandywine Falls. Although difficult to visualize from today's serene setting, this was once the thriving community of Brandywine Mills. Wallace built a mill powered by the nearby waterfall and used money earned from the business to purchase 600 acres and build a farmhouse. The farmhouse passed through five owners before being purchased by the National Park Service. The property was renovated by innkeepers Katie and George Hoy under an agreement with the NPS.

# OREGON

**STATE TOURIST INFORMATION**
(800) 547–7842
www.traveloregon.com

## CRATER LAKE NATIONAL PARK

P.O. Box 7
Crater Lake, OR 97604
(541) 594–2211
www.nps.gov/crla

Crater Lake National Park encompasses 183,000 acres, including a deep blue lake that resulted from the collapse of Mt. Mazama, an ancient 12,000-foot volcano. A 33-mile paved road circles the lake. The summer days can be cool and the nights quite chilly. Heavy winter snowfall that averages 533 inches can keep portions of the Rim Road closed until July. Crater Lake is located in southern Oregon, 57 miles north of Klamath Falls. The major road into the park is Oregon Highway 62, which enters through the southwest corner.

**PARK ENTRANCE FEE:** $10.00 per vehicle or $5.00 per person, good for seven days.

## Lodging in Crater Lake National Park

The park has two very different facilities that provide overnight accommodations. Crater Lake Lodge offers seventy-one rooms in an old but newly remodeled four-story wooden lodge on the rim of Crater Lake. Mazama Village Motor Inn offers forty basic and less expensive rooms 7 miles south of the rim. While Crater Lake Lodge is one of the classic national park lodges, with a back patio, a large lobby, and two fireplaces, Mazama Village Motor Inn is more of a motel unit. Both locations have eating facilities. At 7,100 feet, Crater Lake Lodge is 1,000 feet higher than Mazama Village, resulting in lower temperatures.

# CRATER LAKE NATIONAL PARK

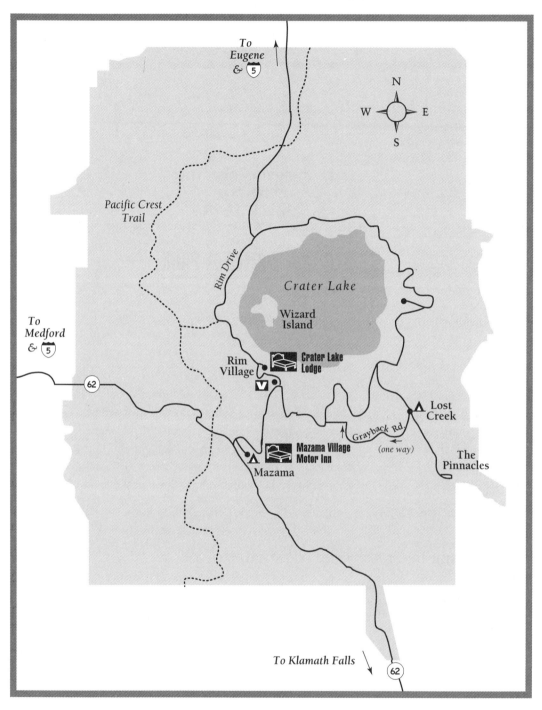

# CRATER LAKE LODGE

Crater Lake National Park, OR 97604 • (541) 594–2255

info@crater-lake.com • www.crater-lake.com

*Crater Lake Lodge*

Crater Lake Lodge offers a total of seventy-one rooms in a restored national park hotel. The four-story stone-and-wood building was originally completed in 1915 and reopened in 1995 after a six-year renovation. The building is on the rim of Crater Lake, allowing guests to view what many consider to be America's most beautiful lake from the window of some rooms. The lodge building has a cozy dining room on the first floor, which also has the registration desk, lobby, and Great Hall with its massive stone fireplace. Another stone fireplace is in the registration lobby. The entire hotel is nonsmoking. Two elevators are near the registration area on the first floor. Parking may involve a short walk, so it is best to unload your luggage from a loading zone in front of the entrance, then locate a parking spot. Bell service is available. Crater Lake Lodge is at the east end of Rim Village. The lodge is 15 miles from the north entrance to the park and 7 miles from the south entrance.

All of the rooms in the lodge vary by size, view, and beds. The remodeled rooms look much newer than the exterior of the lodge would lead you to expect. All are nicely furnished and have heat but no air-conditioning, telephone, or television. A few rooms have bathtubs but no showers. Rooms are entered from a center corridor that is accessed from elevators or a stairway near the registration desk. Beds vary from one to two queen-size beds. Rooms at the back look out on the lake; those at the front look across the parking lot toward the mountains. Prices depend on view and room size. Windows are largest on the second floor. Third-floor windows are high (your chin may rest on the windowsill), and fourth-floor windows are smaller but have window seats. The few first-floor rooms have virtually no view. Room 401, with one queen-size bed, offers a lake view from the claw-footed bathtub. Room 410 is quite large and has two window seats that provide a lake view. Room 220 has one queen-size bed in a large room that faces the lake. Room 221, a corner room with two queen-size beds, has good views of both Crater Lake and Garfield Peak. Four loft suites, each with one bathroom, have bedrooms on two floors and windows that face both the front and the back of the building. These rent for about 50 percent more than view rooms with one bedroom.

Crater Lake Lodge is a comfortable place to stay during a trip to one of America's oldest national parks. The large back porch across most of the length of the original hotel has rocking chairs for relaxing while looking out over the deep blue water of Crater Lake. The Great Hall off the main lobby is covered in pine sheathing and has large windows that provide a terrific lake view. The large stone fireplace has gas logs that are lit each evening. An intimate dining room is just off the Great Hall. All in all, this is one of the nicest lodges of the national park system. Although the rooms have been remodeled enough to lose some of their rustic charm, the lodge building itself radiates its long history.

*C*onstruction on Crater Lake Lodge commenced about a decade after Crater Lake became a national park in 1900. The building, while impressive from the outside, had many structural faults. Over the years major maintenance, including the installation of columns to support the ceiling and walls in the Great Hall, was required to keep the lodge in operation. The National Park Service assumed ownership of the lodge in 1967 and in the early 1980s started considering its demolition. The lodge was closed to visitors in 1989, but public and political pressure resulted in congressional support for a $15 million rehabilitation that included everything from a new foundation to a new roof frame. Essentially, the lodge was torn down and completely rebuilt from the ground up for a reopening in May 1995.

- ■ **ROOMS:** Doubles, triples, and quads. All rooms have a private bath, most with a shower-tub combination. Six rooms on the first floor are handicap accessible.

- ■ **RESERVATIONS:** Crater Lake Lodge, Crater Lake National Park, 1211 Avenue C, White City, OR 97503. Phone (541) 830–8700; fax (541) 830–8514. A deposit of one night's stay is required. A cancellation notice of forty-eight hours is required for a full refund less a $10 fee.

- ■ **RATES:** Most rooms ($115–$160); loft suites ($225). Rates quoted are for two adults except suites, which are for four adults. Children six and under stay free in the same room with an adult. Each additional person is $25. Weekend packages are offered in early spring and late fall.

- ■ **LOCATION:** On the south rim of Crater Lake, 15 miles from the north entrance and 7 miles from the south entrance to Crater Lake National Park.

- ■ **SEASON:** Mid-May to mid-October. The lodge generally sells out from mid-June to the end of September.

- ■ **FOOD:** A small dining room offers breakfast ($5.00–$13.00), lunch ($7.00–$13.00), and dinner ($19–$28). Reservations are only required for the dinner meal. Lodge guests get priority making dinner reservations. Nonguests may make only early or late reservations. A nearby cafeteria at Rim Village offers complete breakfasts, sandwiches, pizza, and salads from 8:00 A.M. to 5:00 P.M. One floor above the cafeteria, a buffet-style restaurant is open for dinner ($10) from 5:00 to 10:00 P.M.

- **TRANSPORTATION:** Scheduled airline service is available to Klamath Falls, Medford, and Eugene, Oregon, where rental cars are available.

- **FACILITIES:** A dining room. Rim Village, a short walk from the lodge, has a cafeteria, a restaurant, and a large gift shop. A National Park Service visitor center is on the rim near the lodge.

- **ACTIVITIES:** Boat tours of Crater Lake, hiking, fishing, and ranger-guided walks.

## MAZAMA VILLAGE MOTOR INN

Crater Lake National Park, OR 97604 • (541) 594–2255
info@crater-lake.com • www.crater-lake.com

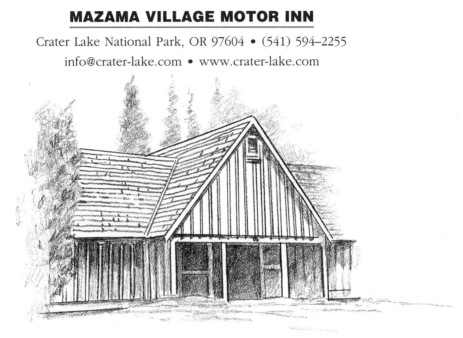

*Mazama Village Motor Inn*

Mazama Village Motor Inn offers a total of forty rooms in ten modern chalet-style wooden buildings. The one-story buildings, constructed in 1983, each contain four guest rooms and are situated around the outside of a paved one-way loop drive. Ample parking is directly in front of each building. The lodging complex is in a heavily wooded area a short distance from facilities in Mazama Village that include a market with a snack area. Mazama Village Motor Inn is in the southern part of the park, at the intersection of Highway 62 and the road to Rim Drive. It is 7 miles from the rim and 22 miles from the north entrance of Crater Lake National Park. At an altitude of 6,000 feet, the complex offers warmer conditions than at the higher rim area.

All of the rooms at Mazama Village Motor Inn are identical in size, beds, and layout except for several that are handicap accessible. The rooms are nice, but this is basic motel-style lodging. Each room is relatively small and has two queen-size beds. The bath has a shower but no tub. There's also a coffeemaker. Each room has an entrance door in the front and a medium-size window in the back. No particularly good views are available from any of the rooms, and so no one room or building is preferable to any other. Each building has a picnic table in front. The handicap-accessible rooms have one queen-size bed and a somewhat larger bathroom.

The motor inn is a convenient place to stay on a one- or two-day visit to Crater Lake National Park. The rooms are basic but relatively close to places in the park you are likely to want to visit—in particular, the rim. The motor inn is within walking distance of Mazama Village, which includes a gas station, a market/snack area, and laundry facilities. Evening programs are presented by National Park Service rangers at the nearby campground amphitheater, which is within easy walking distance. The motor inn is only a 7-mile drive from Rim Village, which has several restaurants and attractive Crater Lake Lodge.

- **ROOMS:** Doubles, triples, and quads. All rooms have private baths with showers only. Several rooms are handicap accessible.

- **RESERVATIONS:** Crater Lake Company, Crater Lake National Park, 1211 Avenue C, White City, OR 97503. Phone (541) 830–8700; fax (541) 830–8514. A deposit of one night's stay is required. A cancellation notice of forty-eight hours is required for a full refund less a $10 fee.

- **RATES:** For all rooms ($95). Rate quoted is for two adults. Each additional person is $7.00 per night. Children six and under stay free with an adult.

- **LOCATION:** On the south side of Crater Lake National Park, 8 miles from the west entrance.

- **SEASON:** Mid-May to mid-October.

- **FOOD:** A snack area in the market is open daily from 7:00 A.M. to 10:00 P.M. The snack area offers prepre-pared sandwiches, ice cream, and beverages. Restaurants are at Rim Village, 7 miles from the inn.

Mazama Village derives its name from the ancient volcano that formed what is now Crater Lake. This dormant volcano is a member of the Cascade Range, a string of volcanoes that extend from Lassen Peak in the south to Mt. Garibaldi near Vancouver, British Columbia. Mt. Mazama may once have towered to 12,000 feet above sea level before a violent eruption occurred about 7,700 years ago. After the chamber inside the mountain was emptied, the walls of the volcano collapsed to form a caldera that filled with water from rain and snow and resulted in the nation's deepest lake, at 1,932 feet.

- **TRANSPORTATION:** Scheduled airline service is available to Medford, Klamath Falls, and Eugene, Oregon, where rental cars are available.

- **FACILITIES:** Grocery store with snack area, laundry, public showers, gas station.

- **ACTIVITIES:** Hiking and evening naturalist programs, depending on snowmelt.

# OREGON CAVES NATIONAL MONUMENT

19000 Caves Highway
Cave Junction, OR 97523 • (541) 592–2100
www.nps.gov/orca/index.html

Oregon Caves National Monument was established in 1909 to protect eleven small caves and a 3-mile-long cave that has rare bats and all of the earth's six main rock types. The area covers 480 acres of old-growth forest, including part of the most diverse conifer forest in the world. The monument is located in southwestern Oregon, 20 miles east of Cave Junction via Oregon Highway 46. Although Highway 46 is paved, the last 8 miles are crooked and hilly. Drivers should be cautious due to icy conditions in late fall or early spring. Parking at the monument is limited, especially for motorhomes and vehicles pulling trailers. Trailers can be dropped off at the Illinois Valley Visitor Center in Cave Junction or at Grayback Campground on Highway 46.

Guided cave tours operate daily from mid-March through late November. Tour times and frequency vary by season, with summer tours beginning at 9:00 A.M. and ending at 7:00 P.M. The cave temperature is 42° Fahrenheit year-round, so be sure to dress properly and wear rubber-soled shoes. Children must be at least 42 inches tall and pass a step test in order to qualify for a tour, but ask about special tours for families with children under 42 inches tall. Canes, staffs, walking aids, and tripods are not permitted in the cave.

**MONUMENT ENTRANCE FEE:** No charge.

## Lodging in Oregon Caves National Monument

A classic six-story lodge with twenty-two guest rooms is the only lodging facility in this relatively small national monument. The lodge is at the end of the road near the entrance to the main cave. Motels and restaurants are in the town of Cave Junction.

### OREGON CAVES LODGE

For most travelers Oregon Caves Lodge remains one of the undiscovered jewels of the national park system. The facility not only calls itself a lodge but really is a lodge. The registration area, lobby, dining room, coffee shop, and all the overnight rooms are in the same alpine-style wooden building that was constructed in 1934 and became a National Historic Landmark in 1987. The lobby is entered on the building's fourth floor (which the lodge calls the first floor), and overnight rooms are on that floor and the two floors above. A restaurant and coffee shop are one floor below. No smoking is permitted anywhere in the lodge. Oregon Caves Lodge is located at the end of Highway 46, 20 miles east of Cave Junction, Oregon.

# OREGON CAVES NATIONAL MONUMENT

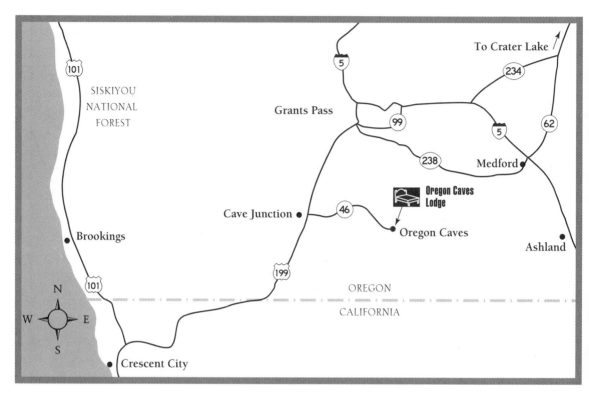

*Oregon Caves Lodge*

Six-story Oregon Caves Lodge retains a coziness and warmth that modern hotels lack. It is completely covered with cedar bark sheathing, and wood shakes top the roof with its many gables. The large lobby area, with huge log supports and giant beams across the ceiling, is dominated by a double-hearth marble fireplace. Some of the original furnishings, including, chairs, card tables, writing desks, and a piano, remain in the lobby. Original furnishings are also in guest rooms on the second and third floors. Parking is directly in front of the lodge. The lodge fills on summer weekends, but rooms are likely to be available on most week-days.

All of the twenty-two guest rooms offer heat but no air-conditioning, telephone, or television. The rooms all differ with respect to beds, size, interior layout, or view. Some rooms are much bigger than others. Some have one queen-size bed, while others have a double and a single bed. A few have two doubles or two queen-size beds. Front rooms face the road or parking lot, while rooms in the back look out over a tree-covered ravine. Several rooms on the top floor are snuggled under gables; these rooms have either a tub or a shower. In general, rooms are classified as either standard or suite. Three suites, composed of two bedrooms and one bath, rent for about $35 daily more than the standard rooms, but the rate is for up to four occupants. Try for one of the rooms at the back of the lodge; these

The first wooden buildings, including the original chalet, were constructed here in 1923 by a group of businessmen who hoped to profit from curious tourists attracted to the caves. The original lodge was expanded in 1941–1942 and currently serves as the visitor center and cave ticket office. The lower story is the original lodge, while the added story now houses employees. The current Oregon Caves Lodge was finished at a total cost of $50,000 in 1934. The lodge remains relatively unchanged since its construction.

offer better views. Several rooms at the front are near a small pond with a waterfall. Keep in mind that there is no elevator, so you will have to climb stairs to your room.

Oregon Caves Lodge is a great place to spend several peaceful days. Spend the first afternoon taking one of the cave tours and the next day walking along the trails. The ticket office for the cave tour is directly across from the lodge. Arrive early enough and you may be able to do the cave tour and some hiking in the same day. On the other hand, maybe you would prefer sitting in the lobby and reading a good mystery. The lodge offers all the facilities you will need for a pleasant stay. The attractive dining room has large windows that look out over the ravine. A 1950s-era coffee shop is on the same floor.

- **ROOMS:** Doubles, triples, and quads. Three suites hold up to seven persons. All rooms have a private bath, although some on the third floor have a tub or a shower. There are no handicap-accessible rooms.

- **RESERVATIONS:** Refer to the information on page 161.

- **RATES:** Standard rooms ($90); suites ($125). Rates for rooms are for two adults, and for suites are for four adults. Children six and under stay free with an adult. Each additional person is $10 each per night. A Lovers Retreat Package, including dinner for two, a cave tour for two, and a standard room for one night, is $135. A bed-and-breakfast rate of $74 is available during early spring and late fall.

- **LOCATION:** Twenty miles south of Cave Junction, Oregon, at the end of Highway 46.

- **SEASON:** The lodge is open from May through mid-October. Cave tours are offered mid-March through late November.

Secluded and tranquil Oregon Caves Lodge served as the meeting place for two men, who together would alter the way people viewed nature . . . and many other things. Harold Graves, a businessman and photographer from Portland, Oregon, was taking photographs in the park one day when he encountered another visitor, William Gruber. Gruber was carrying a tripod on which he had mounted two cameras side by side. The two men met later that evening in Graves's room at the Oregon Caves Lodge, where Gruber described his idea for a viewing device that would place the viewer in the middle of the scene. Gruber's idea, and his meeting with Graves at Oregon Caves Lodge, led to the development of the viewmaster, a viewing device familiar to nearly every child. (From research gathered by Mary Ann and Wolfgang Sell, who are writing a book on the history of the viewmaster.)

- **FOOD:** An attractive dining room is open from 6:00 to 9:00 P.M. for dinner only ($16–$22). Reservations are recommended but not required. A 1950s-era coffee shop on the same floor serves breakfast ($4.00–$7.00), lunch ($4.00–$7.00), real milk shakes, and snacks from 7:00 A.M. to 4:00 P.M. A snack bar in the gift shop serves ice cream and beverages. Beer and wine are available at the registration desk.

- **TRANSPORTATION:** The nearest scheduled air service is in Medford, Oregon, about 50 miles away. A shuttle (fee charged) operates from the lodge to Cave Junction visitor center and the Cave Junction airport.

- **FACILITIES:** Gift shop, restaurant, and coffee shop.

- **ACTIVITIES:** Cave tours, ranger programs and nature walks, and hiking. Three major trails begin at the lodge.

- **NOTE:** No concessioner for Oregon Caves Lodge had been selected at press time. Please contact the Superintendant's office at Oregon Caves National Monument for current information regarding the lodge:

> Superintendant
> Oregon Caves National Monument
> 19000 Caves Highway
> Cave Junction, OR 97523
> (541) 592–2100

# SOUTH DAKOTA

**STATE TOURIST INFORMATION**
(800) 732–5682
www.travelsd.com

## BADLANDS NATIONAL PARK

P.O. Box 6
Interior, SD 57750
(605) 433–5361
www.nps.gov/badl

Badlands National Park comprises 244,000 acres of prairie grassland and scenic eroded landscape created millions of years ago by slow-moving streams. The park is located in southwestern South Dakota, with the Pinnacles entrance 50 miles east of Rapid City off I–90. Highway 240 provides access to the visitor center and much of the park. Three other National Park Service units—Jewel Cave National Monument, Wind Cave National Park, and world-famous Mount Rushmore National Memorial—are south of Rapid City.

**PARK ENTRANCE FEE:** $10.00 per vehicle or $5.00 per person, good for seven days.

## Lodging in Badlands National Park

Cedar Pass Lodge is the only facility providing accommodations in Badlands National Park. The lodge offers twenty-one individual cabins, a dining room, and a gift shop near the park visitor center on the park's east end. The lodge is 8 miles south of I–90 on Badlands Loop Road.

# BADLANDS NATIONAL PARK

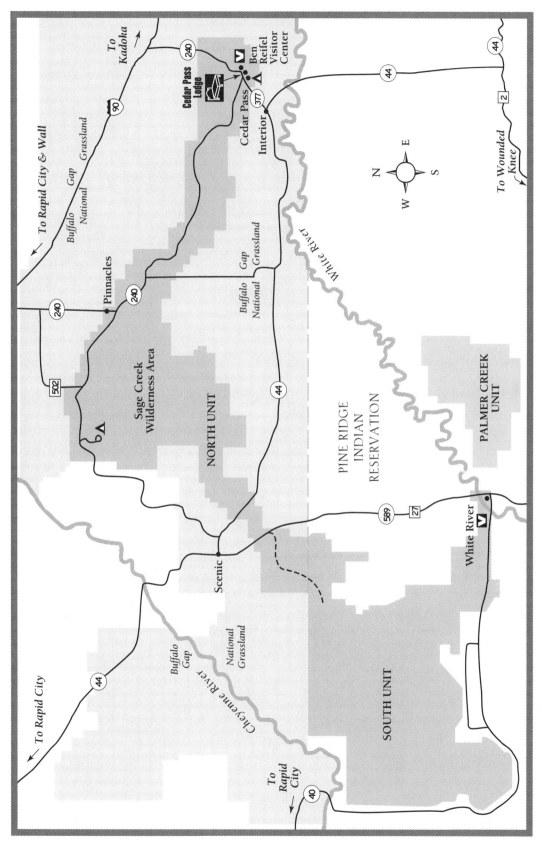

# CEDAR PASS LODGE

1 Cedar Street • P.O. Box 5 • Interior, SD 57750 • (605) 433–5460

*One-bedroom Cabin at Cedar Pass Lodge*

Cedar Pass Lodge is a complex of small, freestanding stucco cabins situated on each side of a U-shaped drive in a grassy area behind a wood-and-stucco registration building. The registration building also houses a restaurant and a large gift shop. No accommodations are in the main building, but all the cabins are a short walk from the registration desk and restaurant. Adequate parking is in front of each cabin and the restaurant. Cedar Pass Lodge is operated by the Oglala Sioux Tribe. The lodge sits in a relatively barren area at the east end of Badlands National Park, within view of the Badlands. It is 8 miles south of I–90, just south of the park's main visitor center.

The lodge offers twenty-one individual cabins with heat and air-conditioning but no telephone or television. They are carpeted and have wood-paneled walls. Each cabin has a small front porch with a bench or chairs but no patio. A one-bedroom cabin has either a double and a single or two double beds. Two-bedroom cabins have two doubles in one bedroom and either a queen-size or a double bed in the second bedroom. All cabins have a private bath, most with a shower but no tub. A few units have a combination shower-tub. Picnic tables are scattered in the grassy area that surrounds the cabins.

Cedar Pass Lodge is a convenient place to stay during your trip to Badlands National Park. The lodge is a short walk from the park's main visitor center, which has exhibits on the Badlands. The lodge is also near the park campground, where summer evening programs are presented by National Park Service rangers. An 80-mile loop drive through the park to the small town of Scenic and back through Buffalo Gap National Grassland on Highway 44 offers an interesting day of sightseeing and hiking. A side trip to the town of Wall (north of the Pinnacles entrance to the park on I–90) takes you to unique Wall Drug.

- **ROOMS:** Singles, doubles, triples, and quads. Three cabins with two bedrooms hold up to six adults. All units have a private bathroom, some with a shower and others with a combination shower-tub. There are no handicap-accessible cabins.

- **RESERVATIONS:** Cedar Pass Lodge, Box 5, Interior, SD 57750. Phone (605) 433–5460; fax (605) 433–5560. A credit card guarantee or deposit of 50 percent of first night's lodging is required. Cancellation requires a twenty-four hours' notice.

- **RATES:** One-bedroom cabins ($46 for one person); two-bedroom cabins ($64 for three persons). Each additional person is $4.00. Prices reduced approximately 20 percent from opening through mid-May and from mid-September through closing. Pets are $5.00 per day. A 10 percent AAA discount is given.

- **LOCATION:** At the eastern end of Badlands National Park, 8 miles south of I–90 at exit 131.

- **SEASON:** April 15 through October.

- **FOOD:** A restaurant serves breakfast ($4.00–$6.00), lunch ($4.00–$6.00), and dinner ($8.00–$15.00). Menu includes buffalo burgers and Indian tacos.

- **TRANSPORTATION:** The nearest airport is in Rapid City, South Dakota, where airline service and rental vehicles are available.

- **FACILITIES:** Restaurant, gift shop, National Park Service visitor center.

- **ACTIVITIES:** Hiking, evening interpretive programs.

> Cedar Pass Camp was opened here in 1928 to provide refreshments to the growing number of sightseers to this area. By the 1930s the facility had become an important stop for Badlands travelers. The owner, Ben Millard, died here in 1956, and Cedar Pass Lodge was purchased by the National Park Service in 1964. Cedar Pass Lodge has been operated by the Oglala Sioux Tribe of the Pine Ridge Indian Reservation since 1971.

# TEXAS

**STATE TOURIST INFORMATION**

(800) 452–9292

www.traveltex.com

## BIG BEND NATIONAL PARK

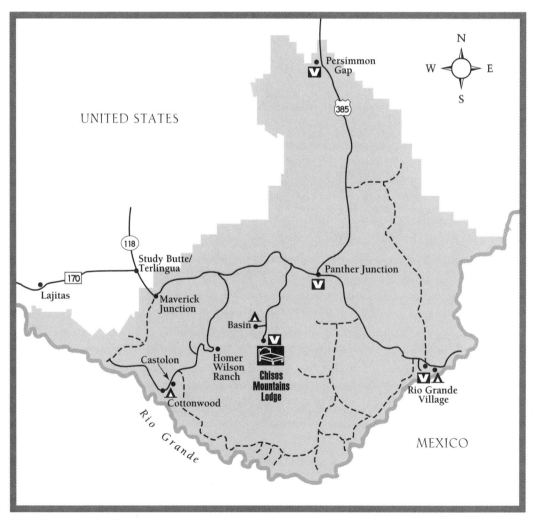

# BIG BEND NATIONAL PARK

Big Bend National Park, TX 79834
(915) 477–2251
www.nps.gov/bibe

**B**ig Bend National Park covers 801,000 acres of wild and scenic desert, mountain ranges, steep-walled canyons, and ribbons of green plant life along the fabled Rio Grande. Because of its remote location, the park is not as crowded as some of the other national parks. Popular activities at Big Bend include bird-watching, hiking, and rafting on the Rio Grande. The park is located on the Mexican border in southwestern Texas.

**PARK ENTRANCE FEE:** $10.00 per vehicle or $5.00 per person, good for seven days.

## Lodging in Big Bend National Park

Chisos Mountains Lodge in the park's Basin area offers the only lodging in Big Bend National Park. The road to the Basin is not recommended for trailers exceeding 20 feet and RVs exceeding 24 feet. A trailer village at Rio Grande Village is available for visitors with trailers and motor homes.

## CHISOS MOUNTAINS LODGE

Basin Rural Branch • Big Bend National Park, TX 79834-9999 • (915) 477–2291
www.bigbendresorts.com

**C**hisos Mountains Lodge, a Forever Resort and concession facility, is a group of modern motel-type units and older stone and adobe cabins and lodge units in the scenic Basin area of Big Bend National Park. All the lodging units rent for about the same price and are open year-round. The Basin area of Big Bend is approximately 40 miles inside the north park entrance, which itself is 40 miles south of Highway 90. In other words, this is a pretty remote lodge in a very remote national park. The good news is the Basin area of the park provides breathtaking scenery along with the outdoor experience you are probably seeking in a national park visit. The lodge is at an altitude of 5,400 feet, which results in moderate summer temperatures when much of the rest of the park swelters in the desert heat. Scenery is provided by the Chisos Mountains, which surround and tower 2,000 to 3,000 feet above the Basin and are fully contained within Big Bend's boundary.

Chisos Mountains Lodge is actually a combination of a main registration and food service building and four types of separate lodging units for a total of seventy-two rooms. About half the rooms are in three two-story motor-lodge-type buildings (called Casa Grande units) that offer private rear balconies with an excellent view of the surrounding mountains. Most of these units, built in 1989, have two double beds, although a limited number of rooms offer a queen-size or a double bed. Each room has a full bath and air-conditioning.

Two one-story motel-type buildings constructed in the late 1970s each have ten rooms. That is, five rooms are located on each side of the building. As a result, these units do not

*Casa Grande Motor Lodge at Chisos Mountains Lodge*

have balconies and views are not as good as those in the Casa Grande section. Rooms have two double beds, a full bath, heat, and air-conditioning. They are somewhat smaller than the rooms in Casa Grande.

The stone lodge units and adobe cottages offer a quieter setting a short distance away from the previously mentioned lodging units. One duplex and four freestanding stone cottages each have three double beds. These buildings, constructed in the late 1930s, have a shower but no tub. They also lack air-conditioning. The thick construction and cross-ventilation generally result in a comfortable inside temperature. Most popular with frequent visitors to Big Bend are cottages 102 and 103, which offer the best mountain views of any of the park's lodging facilities. Cottage 100 is isolated and makes a nice honeymoon cottage. Eight 1950s-era stone lodge units situated near the cottages each have one single and one double bed, a full bath, ceiling fans, and heat. These units are in two buildings, each with four rooms. Access to one of the buildings involves climbing about thirty-two steps.

None of the rooms have a television or telephone, although a number of pay phones are scattered throughout the Basin area. Four Casa Grande motor lodge rooms are handicap accessible. Ice

*Bird-watching is a major activity at Big Bend National Park, where more than 450 species of birds have been identified. Although most are migrants that pass through on their way from wintering in Latin America, occasional rare species end up in Big Bend after wandering off-course. The Chisos Mountains of Big Bend are the only location in the United States where the rare Colima warbler can be observed. Multiday seminars on birding are regularly sponsored by the Big Bend Natural History Association.*

machines are scattered throughout the lodging area. Nonsmoking rooms are available in each of the four types of lodging units. Although you will probably be pleased with any of the lodging facilities, we recommend the Casa Grande units in buildings A, B, and C. Rooms in all three buildings are large, offer great views, and cost about the same as rooms in the other units. Rooms on the second floor have a better view and more privacy.

Other than the cottages and stone lodge units that are located a short distance from the main Basin area, the units are arranged in a circular fashion near the lodge building that houses registration, a small gift shop, and eating facilities. Adequate parking is available near each of the buildings, although a couple of the Casa Grande units require a climb of approximately thirty steps to reach the second floor. If stairs are a problem, you should note this in your reservation request. The stone cottages and lodge units are about a quarter mile away from the other units, but everything in the Basin is within walking distance. Also in the Basin is a small store, with a limited selection of groceries and camping supplies, and a post office substation. A National Park Service visitor center is next to the store. A variety of hikes and nature programs are offered in-season. A self-guided trail and access to several other trails originate near the lodge.

The Chisos Mountains Basin is only a small part of a very large national park that offers much to attract visitors, especially during the spring and fall, when temperatures are mild. The main National Park Service visitor facilities are at Panther Junction. Here you will find the main visitor center and a host of facilities, including a post office and gas station. Other major activity areas of the park center on Rio Grande Village, 20 miles southeast of park headquarters, which offers hiking, camping, a trailer park, a coin laundry, showers, groceries, general merchandise, gasoline, propane, and a visitor center. Castolon, a historic district 35 miles southwest of the visitor center, offers a campground, a ranger station, historic exhibits, and a frontier store that sells picnic supplies, groceries, and general merchandise.

*Although the Rio Grande is one of the major natural features of Big Bend National Park, by the time the river forms the southern boundary of the park, most of the water is supplied by the Rio Conchos, which flows out of Mexico, rather than the headwaters of the Rio Grande. Much of the water of the Rio Grande has evaporated or been diverted for irrigation by the time the river reaches the western border of the park. Abrasive particles carried in the water give the river its impressive power to carve the canyons that have formed along its path.*

- ■ **ROOMS:** Doubles, triples, and quads. A few units sleep up to six. All rooms have private baths. Four Casa Grande units are handicap accessible.

- ■ **RESERVATIONS:** Forever Resorts, Chisos Mountains Lodge, Basin Rural Branch, Big Bend National Park, TX 79834-9999. Phone (915) 477–2291; fax (915) 477–2352. A deposit of one night's stay is required. A cancellation notice of forty-eight hours is required for a full refund; failure to arrive on the designated date means automatic forfeit of the deposit and cancels the reservation. Reservations in any calendar year may be made at the beginning of the previous year.

- ■ **RATES:** Casa Grande ($76); Motel units ($76); Cottage ($84); Lodge units ($75). Rates quoted are for two adults. Each additional person is $10 per night.

- ■ **LOCATION:** About 40 miles south of the north park entrance station and 30 miles east of the west entrance station.

- **SEASON:** All of the lodging units are open year-round. Heaviest season is in the spring up to Memorial Day and in the fall following Labor Day. The lodge is heavily booked during Thanksgiving and Christmas holidays.

- **FOOD:** A full-service restaurant serves three meals a day. Breakfast is served from 7:00 to 10:30 A.M., lunch from 11:30 A.M. to 4:30 P.M., and dinner from 5:30 to 8:00 P.M. Dinner prices range from $6.00 to $17.00. The restaurant is located in the main lodge building and is within walking distance of all the rooms.

- **TRANSPORTATION:** No public transportation is available to or through the park. Train and bus service is provided in the town of Alpine, about 110 miles north of the park. Airlines serve Del Rio, Midland-Odessa, and El Paso, where rental cars are available.

- **FACILITIES:** The Chisos Basin has a store with a post office substation, visitor center, restaurant, and gift shop. All are within walking distance of the lodging units. A gas station, post office, and grocery are at Panther Junction. A variety of supplies and services are at Rio Grande Village, 20 miles southeast of the visitor center.

- **ACTIVITIES:** Hiking, bird-watching, guided walks, and National Park Service programs. Float trips on the Rio Grande are available with your own equipment (permit required) or through one of four local services approved by the Park Service.

# U.S. VIRGIN ISLANDS

## VIRGIN ISLANDS NATIONAL PARK

6010 Estate Nazareth
St. Thomas, VI 00802
(340) 776–6450
www.nps.gov/viis

Virgin Islands National Park, encompassing nearly 14,700 acres, features quiet coves, blue-green waters, and white sandy beaches fringed by lush green hills. The park is located on St. John Island and can be reached via hourly ferry service across Pillsbury Sound from Red Hook, St. Thomas. Ferry service also operates from Charlotte Amalie. Major airlines fly from the U.S. mainland to St. Thomas and St. Croix.

**PARK ENTRANCE FEE:** No charge.

### Lodging in Virgin Islands National Park

Although a variety of lodging is available on the island, Cinnamon Bay Campground, with tents and cottages, offers the only accommodations within the national park. Cinnamon Bay is on St. John Island's north shore, midway across the island via North Shore Road. The campground is a fifteen-minute taxi ride from the town of Cruz Bay, where the ferries dock.

# VIRGIN ISLANDS NATIONAL PARK

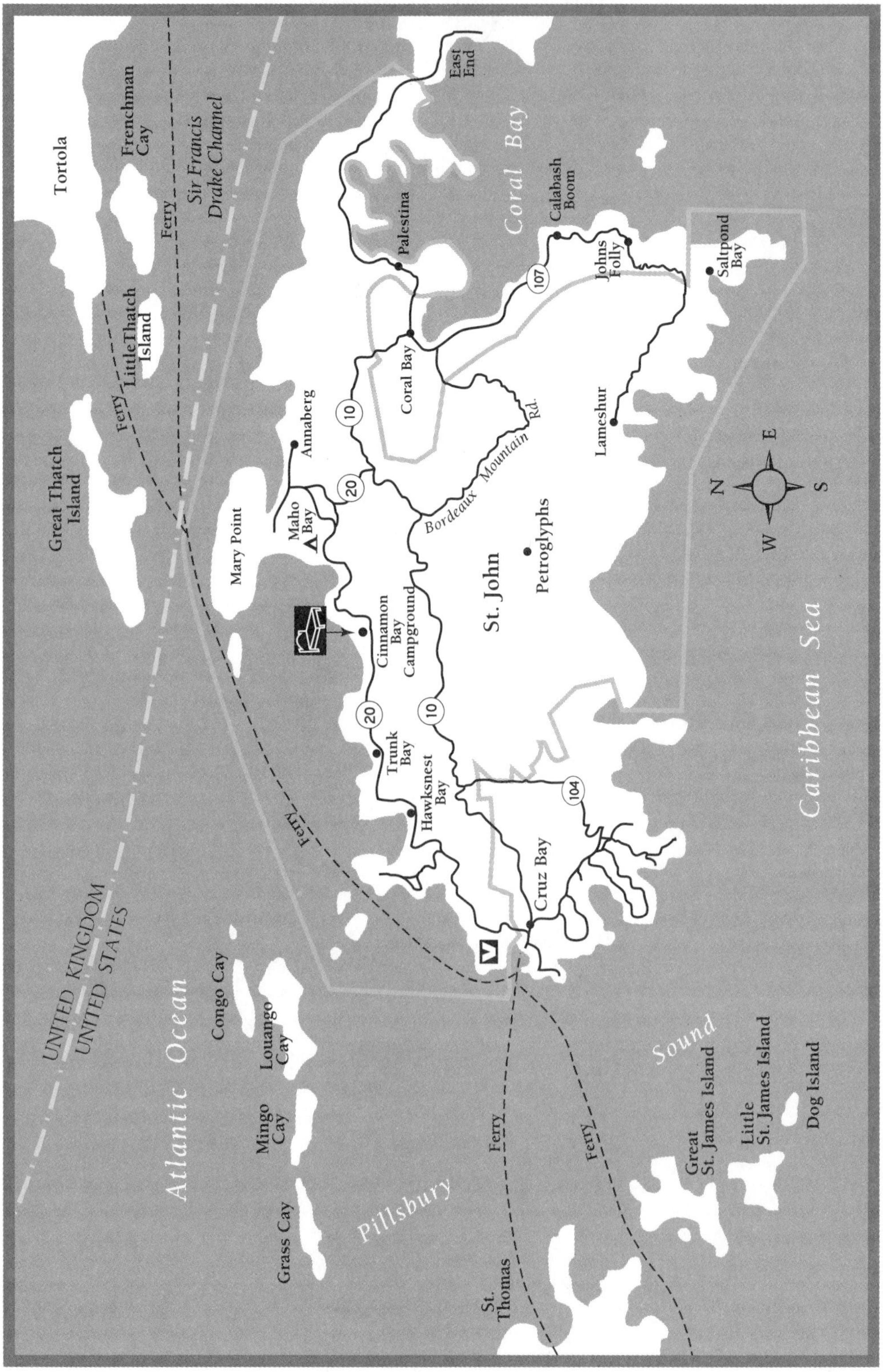

# CINNAMON BAY CAMPGROUND

P.O. Box 720 • Cruz Bay, St. John • U.S. Virgin Islands 00831 • (340) 776–6330
www.cinnamonbay.com

*Cottages at Cinnamon Bay Campground*

Cinnamon Bay Campground is a complex of cottages, tents, separate bathhouses, and a separate main building that houses a registration area, restaurant, and general store. The cottages and tents are grouped separately, with bathhouses available in each grouping. All the buildings are located in a natural area of trees a short walk from half-mile-long Cinnamon Bay Beach. The campground does not have a lodge with accommodations or the wood cabins you might expect to find at a Park Service lodging facility.

The forty cottages are 15 by 15 feet and constructed of cement sides and floor with front and back screening to allow breezes from the trade winds. Each cottage is equipped with electric lights, table and chairs, ceiling fan, picnic table, charcoal grill, propane stove, ice chest, water container, and eating and cooking utensils. Each has four twin beds that are made by the guest on the day of arrival. Additional linens can be obtained twice a week at the front desk. The central bathhouse has cool-water showers. The cost of the cottages varies, because those that are closer to the beach cost more than those farther away.

Forty-four tents, which rent for $12 to $55 less per night (depending on the season) than cottages, have a wood floor and are 10 by 14 feet. Each tent includes four cots with a 3-inch mattress, propane stove, charcoal grill, gas lantern, ice chest, water container, and utensils. A picnic table is under a large canvas flap that extends from the front roof. As with the cottages, beds are made on the day of arrival and fresh linens are available at the front desk twice a week. Three bathhouses scattered throughout the tenting area also have cool-water showers.

Staying at Cinnamon Bay Campground offers a different national park experience, one in which the accommodations permit a full appreciation of the natural surroundings. Both the cottages and the tents are a short walk from Cinnamon Bay Beach. Phones, safe-deposit boxes, and storage lockers are near the lodging facilities. A general store carries grocery items if you are interested in cooking some or all of your own meals. A restaurant is available when you choose to eat out. No laundry facilities are in the campground. Not surprisingly, water-based activities such as snorkeling are popular, and sailboards, sea kayaks, and sailboats are available for rent at a water sports center. Park rangers offer daily activities, which include walks, talks, and snorkeling. Reservations are required for most of the activities with park rangers (340–776–6201).

- **ROOMS:** Doubles, triples, and quads. None of the cottages or tents have a private bathroom. There are no handicap-accessible facilities.

- **RESERVATIONS:** Cinnamon Bay Campground, P.O. Box 720, Cruz Bay, St. John, U.S. Virgin Islands 00831. Phone (800) 539–9998; (340) 776–6330; fax (340) 776–6458. Reservations can be guaranteed with a credit card. A 50 percent deposit is required. Payment must be made in full at the time of check-in (personal checks are not accepted). Cancellations are required at least thirty days prior to arrival for a full refund. Later cancellations will be charged the equivalent of a three-night stay.

- **RATES:** Cottages ($70–$90) from May 1 through December 14, ($105–$135) from December 15 through April 30; tents ($58) from May 1 through December 14, ($80) from December 15 through April 30. Rates quoted are for two adults. Children under three stay free with an adult. Each additional person is $15 per night. Meal packages are available.

- **LOCATION:** On the north shore of St. John Island, approximately 4 miles (fifteen minutes) from the town of Cruz Bay on the island's west end.

- **SEASON:** Open year-round.

> Rosewood Hotels & Resorts, the firm that manages Cinnamon Bay Campground, also operates exclusive Caneel Bay on the same island. Although separated by two bays and only a few miles, in cost and accommodations these two facilities are a world apart. For example, rooms at Caneel Bay run from $400 to $900 daily, depending on season and type of accommodation. The 171 rooms include wall safes, personal bars, and handcrafted furniture. Three restaurants provide a choice of formal, eclectic, and casual dining.

- **FOOD:** A restaurant serves three meals daily. Breakfast ($6.00–$8.00) is served from 7:30 to 9:30 A.M. Lunch ($6.00–$9.00) is served from 11:30 A.M. to 1:30 P.M., and dinner ($9.00–$18.00) is served from 5:30 to 7:30 P.M. Groceries are available at a general store.

- **TRANSPORTATION:** Ferries for Cruz Bay, St. John, leave from Red Hook ($3.00 per person) and Charlotte Amalie ($7.00 per person) on St. Thomas. Taxis (about $3.00 per person) provide transportation from Cruz Bay to the campground.

- **FACILITIES:** Restaurant, general store, beach shop, water sports center with boat rentals.

- **ACTIVITIES:** Swimming, snorkeling, fishing, hiking, National Park Service activities, and commercial guided tours.

# UTAH

(800) 233–8824
www.utah.com

## BRYCE CANYON NATIONAL PARK

Bryce Canyon, UT 84717

(435) 834–5322

www.nps.gov/brca

Bryce Canyon National Park comprises nearly 36,000 acres highlighted by numerous alcoves cut into cliffs along the eastern edge of the Paunsaugunt Plateau. The cliffs are bordered by badlands of vivid colors and strange shapes called hoodoos for which this park is most famous. A paved road with numerous scenic pullouts leads 18 miles south from the entrance to Rainbow Point. Trailers are not permitted beyond Sunrise Point, which lies about 3 miles inside the park entrance. The park is in southwestern Utah and most easily reached via U.S. 89 to Utah Highways 12 and 63.

The National Park Service has implemented a public shuttle service in Bryce Canyon National Park. The shuttle, operated by a private contractor, operates from a boarding area near the park entrance. Visitors can park their cars at the entrance and take the shuttle into the park. The shuttle stops at most of the major destinations served by the park road, and visitors can get off and on the shuttle any number of times. Visitors who choose to drive into the park are required to pay an additional $5.00.

**PARK ENTRANCE FEE:** $20 per vehicle, if vehicle is taken into park; $15 for all occupants of a vehicle, if the vehicle is left at the park entrance and occupants ride the shuttle into the park; good for seven days.

## Lodging in Bryce Canyon

Bryce Canyon Lodge, with several types of accommodations, offers the only lodging in Bryce Canyon National Park. All of the rooms are comfortable and within easy walking distance of both the main lodge and spectacular Bryce Canyon. The lodge is in the northern section of the park, about 1.5 miles south of the park entrance and the visitor center. Privately operated motels are just outside the park entrance.

# BRYCE CANYON NATIONAL PARK

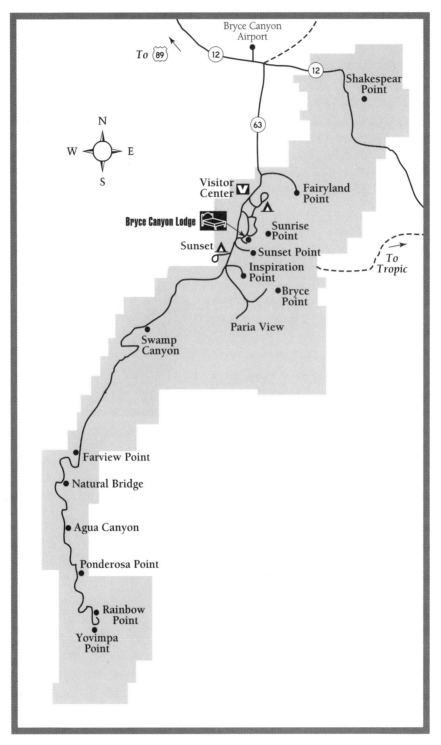

Bryce Canyon Airport

To 89

12

12

Shakespear Point

63

N
W    E
S

Visitor Center

Fairyland Point

Bryce Canyon Lodge

Sunrise Point

Sunset

Sunset Point

To Tropic

Inspiration Point

Bryce Point

Paria View

Swamp Canyon

Farview Point

Natural Bridge

Agua Canyon

Ponderosa Point

Rainbow Point

Yovimpa Point

# BRYCE CANYON LODGE

1 Bryce Canyon Lodge • Bryce Canyon National Park, UT 84717 • (435) 834–5361
www.brycecanyonlodge.com

*Main Lodge at Bryce Canyon*

**B**ryce Canyon Lodge offers a total of 114 rooms in a complex of two motor lodge units, fifteen multiunit cabin buildings with forty rooms, and an impressive wood-and-stone main lodge building that houses the restaurant, registration area, and three suites and a studio. The main lodge was constructed in the 1920s and has been completely renovated. The lodge was designed by Gilbert Stanley Underwood, the same architect who designed the Ahwahnee Hotel in Yosemite, Zion Lodge, and Grand Canyon Lodge on the North Rim. The attractive lobby area has a huge stone fireplace surrounded by chairs. A large brick porch with chairs and benches stretches across the entire front of the building and offers guests a pleasant place to spend idle time. The porch faces a wooded area that separates the lodge from the canyon rim. Bryce Canyon Lodge is located near the rim of the canyon, about 1.5 miles south of the park visitor center and entrance station.

Each of the three types of lodging facilities at Bryce Canyon Lodge is attractive. All of the rooms have heat but no

*C*onstruction on Bryce Canyon Lodge began in 1923, and the foundation and skeletal work were completed the following year. The original building, with upstairs accommodations and an office, lobby, dining room, kitchen, showers, and toilets on the main floor, was completed by May 1925. Wings and a rock facade were added the following year, when the lodge was opened for operation. In September 1927, the recreation hall was added, and sixty-seven standard and economy cabins were grouped around the lodge. The few original cabins that remain are currently used as employee housing. The other economy cabins were sold and moved. By September 1927, five deluxe cabins (the current western cabins) had been constructed. The remaining ten deluxe cabins were completed by 1929.

air-conditioning or television. Forty western cabins are built from two to four to a building. Most of these cabins have two queen-size beds, a gas fireplace, a telephone, a table, a desk, three chairs, and a full bath. The log and limestone cabins, constructed in the 1920s, are roomy and nicely finished. Most of the western cabins have log-beamed vaulted ceilings and shake roofs. Each has a private front porch. Cabins 506, 517, 525, 533, and 537 have porches that face a large wooded area but are a walk from the parking area. Two two-story motor lodge buildings have a total of 70 rooms, each of which has two queen-size beds (a few have one queen), a full bath, a desk, a table, three chairs, and a telephone. These units each have a private balcony with a table and two chairs. Rooms are on either side of the building and are entered through a central corridor that can be accessed at either end or in the middle. Although the lodge classifies these as "motel" units, they are actually larger and the buildings are more attractive than most motels. Rooms on the second floor and in the back of the building provide the most privacy and best view. Two motel rooms are handicap accessible.

The main lodge building houses three second-floor suites and one studio. These are the only sleeping rooms in the main lodge. The suites each have a bedroom with one queen-size bed and a separate sitting area with a desk, a lounge chair, and two rocking chairs; both rooms have ceiling fans. The suites also have a full bath but no balcony. These rooms are nice and roomy, and it is convenient to stay in the main lodge, where the restaurant and lobby are located. The single studio is identical to the suites but without a separate sitting room.

Bryce Canyon Lodge is a pleasant place to spend several relaxing days while you explore this national park. It sits in a heavily treed area with attractive vistas and numerous outdoor activities. The lodge is near Bryce Canyon. A walking trail from the front porch of the lodge leads to spectacular overlooks along the rim. An information desk in the hotel lobby provides information on the area and several tours that originate near the lodge. The main lodge building, with a restaurant and gift shop, is within easy walking distance of all the lodging facilities. The attractive restaurant has two large stone fireplaces and serves three meals daily at reasonable prices. We suggest you choose the western cabins, especially if you plan to stay two or more nights.

- **ROOMS:** Doubles, triples, and quads. All rooms have a full bath. Two rooms are handicap accessible.

- **RESERVATIONS:** Amfac Parks and Resorts, 14001 East Iliff Avenue, Suite 600, Aurora, CO 80014. Phone (303) 297–2757; fax (303) 297–3175; www.brycecanyonlodge.com. Reservations may be made up to twenty-three months in advance. A deposit of one night's stay is required. Cancellation notice of forty-eight hours is required for a refund.

- **RATES:** Western cabins ($102); motel units ($92); suites ($122); studio ($102). Children sixteen and under stay free with an adult. Each additional person is $10 per night.

- **LOCATION:** The lodge is near the north end of Bryce Canyon National Park, about 1.5 miles south of the visitor center that is located near the park entrance station. The lodge is within walking distance of the rim of the canyon.

- **SEASON:** Bryce Canyon Lodge is open from April 1 through November 1. The park is open year-round.

- **FOOD:** A full-service restaurant serves breakfast ($3.00–$7.00), lunch ($5.00–$8.00), and dinner ($10–$22). Reservations are required for dinner. Groceries and snacks are available at a general store at Sunrise Point, about 1 mile from the lodge.

- **TRANSPORTATION:** Airlines serve Cedar City, St. George, and Salt Lake City, Utah, and Las Vegas, Nevada. Rental cars are available at each of these airports. Greyhound/Trailways serves St. George and Cedar City. Amtrak serves Salt Lake City.

- **FACILITIES:** A full-service dining room, gift shop, and post office are in the main lodge building. A general store 1 mile north of the lodge near Sunrise Point has snacks and groceries.

- **ACTIVITIES:** The National Park Service conducts a variety of lectures, nature walks and talks, and slide presentations. A schedule with times is posted at the visitor center. Two-hour and half-day mule and horse trips into the canyon are offered daily. Information on these and other activities is available at the tour desk located in the lobby.

> **B**ryce Canyon is named for Ebenezer Bryce, who assisted in the settlement of this area of Utah and came here to live and harvest timber in 1875. Neighbors called the canyon behind his home Bryce Canyon, a name that carried over to the park when it was incorporated into the national park system in 1928. One of the suites in the main lodge building is named for Ebenezer Bryce.

# ZION NATIONAL PARK

Springdale, UT 84767
(435) 722–3256
www.nps.gov/zion

Zion National Park comprises approximately 147,000 acres of colorful canyons and mesas that create phenomenal shapes and landscapes. Scenic drives and trails provide access to canyons, sculpted rocks, cliffs, and rivers in one of the most beautiful areas operated by the National Park Service. Zion is in southwestern Utah, with the southwest entrance approximately 150 miles northeast of Las Vegas, Nevada.

The National Park Service operates a bus transportation system in Zion National Park. All visitors except those with confirmed reservations at Zion Lodge will be required to use the new system to acces Zion Canyon. The system comprises two loops: The Springdale loop runs from the new Visitor Transit Center (near the current visitor center) to the end of the scenic drive. The admission fee to the park includes access to the shuttle. The Mount Carmel area on the park's east side remains accessible by vehicle.

**PARK ENTRANCE FEE:** $20 per vehicle (all occupants) or $10 per person, good for seven days.

## Lodging in Zion National Park

Zion has only one lodging facility inside the park. Zion Lodge is located on Zion Canyon Scenic Drive, north of Highway 9, which crosses the southeastern section of the park. Additional lodging is available in the town of Springdale, just outside the southwest entrance.

# ZION NATIONAL PARK

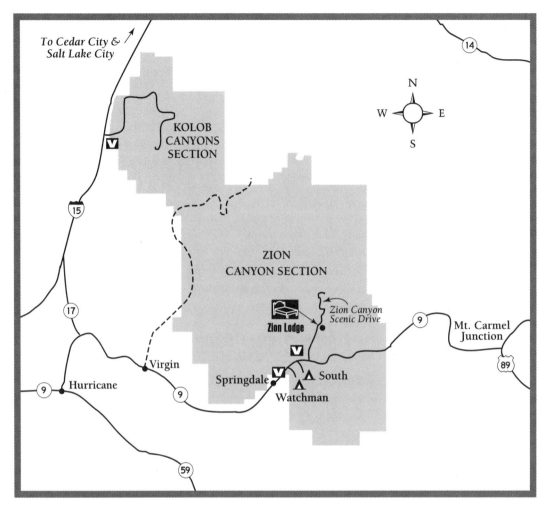

## ZION LODGE

Zion National Park • Springdale, UT 84767 • (435) 772–3213

www.zionlodge.com

Zion Lodge comprises a central lodge building that houses registration and dining facilities, plus seventeen separate but nearby buildings that provide a total of 121 rooms for overnight accommodations. No overnight rooms are in the main lodge building. The lodge is situated in a grassy area of cottonwood trees surrounded by the beautiful red sandstone cliffs that make this such a scenic national park. The North Fork of the Virgin River is across the road from the lodge. The wood and Navajo sandstone main lodge building is a one- and two-story, V-shaped, ranch-style structure that was constructed in 1966 on the site of the original lodge, which burned earlier in the year. The new lodge is attractive but does not have the majestic look of its sister lodges at Bryce Canyon and the North Rim of the Grand Canyon. Zion Lodge is located 3 miles north of the main park road, on Zion Canyon Scenic Drive. The lodge is approximately 3.5 miles north of the National Park Service visitor center.

*Motel Units at Zion Lodge*

Three types of accommodations are available at Zion Lodge. All of the lodging is separate from but near the main lodge building. All rooms have air-conditioning, heat, a telephone, and a hairdryer but no television. Forty western cabins each offer two double beds, a gas fireplace, a table, a desk, chairs, and a full bath. The cabins were constructed either two or four units to a building, in the 1930s, and the interiors were remodeled in 1997–1998. These wood-framed cabins with vaulted ceilings are very similar in design and size to the western log cabins in both Bryce Canyon and the North Rim of the Grand Canyon. The cabins are closely clustered in the front and at the end of one of the motel buildings south of the main lodge. Each cabin has a private porch. Cabins that face west toward the parking lot offer a better location and view. These include cabins 503, 505, 509, 517, 518, 520, and 523.

Seventy-five motel-type rooms are in two large, two-story motor lodge buildings, which were remodeled in 1998–1999. A stone fireplace is in the central lobby area of the larger of the two buildings. Rooms have two queen-size beds (some have only a single queen), a dresser, a nightstand, a table, and two chairs. Each room has a private balcony or patio with two chairs and a table. The rooms are accessed from an interior corridor that runs the length of each building. The best rooms are at the rear of the second floor of each building. These are all odd-numbered. Two rooms are handicap accessible. Six suites located on the second floor each have two rooms, one with a king-size bed and the other with two chairs, a queen-size sofa bed, a refrigerator, a desk, and a chair. The two rooms are separated by a bathroom.

Zion Lodge is a comfortable, quiet place to spend one or more days while you explore magnificent Zion National Park. The setting is both attractive and convenient. Be aware that summer months generally

Navajo sandstone, which forms the canyon walls in Zion National Park, is a porous rock that absorbs rainfall. The moisture percolates through the rock and may require many decades (some say centuries) to reach the base of a large cliff. Perhaps the best example in Zion of this phenomenon is 2,000-foot Weeping Rock, where you can walk under the rock and feel the water dripping. Moisture seeping from the rock results in hanging gardens and spring wildflowers. Weeping Rock is accessed via a quarter-mile trail from Zion Canyon Scenic Drive north of Zion Lodge. This is a stop on the tram tour.

bring hot days to Zion, and daytime temperatures often reach 100° Fahrenheit. The main lodge has most of the facilities you will need for a stay in the park. A large grassy area in front of the lodge provides a nice place to read a book, eat a picnic lunch, or lie on a blanket under a cottonwood tree. A lobby in front of the registration desk has chairs and benches for relaxing. A spacious, wood-paneled restaurant on the second floor serves three full meals a day. The restaurant has large windows that provide a view of the front grounds of the lodge. A balcony is available for outside dining. A cafe at the north end of the main lodge building serves light sandwiches and beverages and has patio seating. The lodge also has a tour desk, auditorium, post office, and gift shop. A 0.6-mile paved trail to Lower Emerald Pools begins opposite Zion Lodge. The longer, 2-mile walk leads to Middle Emerald Pools.

- **ROOMS:** Doubles, triples, and quads. All rooms have a full bath. Two motel rooms are handicap accessible.

- **RESERVATIONS:** Amfac Parks and Resorts, 14001 East Iliff Avenue, Suite 300, Aurora, CO 80014. Phone (303) 297–2757; fax (303) 297–3175. A deposit of one night's stay is required. A cancellation notice of forty-eight hours is required for a full refund.

- **RATES:** Western cabins ($107); motel ($97); suites ($126). All rates quoted are for two adults. Children sixteen and younger stay free. Each additional person is $10. Discount rates are offered December to mid-March.

- **LOCATION:** Three miles north of the main park highway on Zion Canyon Scenic Drive.

- **SEASON:** All of the units of Zion Lodge are open year-round. The lodge is often full from early April through October.

- **FOOD:** An attractive restaurant on the second floor of the main lodge building serves breakfast ($4.00–$7.00), lunch ($5.00–$8.00), and dinner ($10.00–$22.00). Dinner reservations are required. A cafe at the north end of the main lodge building serves light breakfasts, sandwiches, ice cream, and beverages from 10:00 A.M. to 8:00 P.M. in-season.

- **TRANSPORTATION:** Scheduled airlines serve Cedar City, St. George, and Salt Lake City, Utah, and Las Vegas, Nevada, where rental cars are available. Scheduled bus service is available to St. George and Cedar City. Amtrak serves Salt Lake City.

- **FACILITIES:** Post office, gift shop, restaurant, and cafe. Groceries and numerous restaurants are in Springdale, Utah, a short distance outside the park's southwest entrance.

- **ACTIVITIES:** A tour desk in the main lodge building can arrange horseback rides and guided tours. Naturalist programs are offered throughout the park by National Park Service personnel. Schedules are posted at the front desk of the lodge and in the visitor center, which shows a fifteen-minute orientation film. Hiking is a popular activity in Zion National Park.

*A camp of wood-framed tents opened in 1916 on the site of Zion Lodge. The original lodge, designed by Gilbert Stanley Underwood (1890–1961), was constructed in 1925 for the Union Pacific Railroad, which wanted to promote tourism in southern Utah. The current western cabins were constructed in the late 1920s. Fire destroyed the main lodge during renovations in the winter of 1966. The present building, which underwent a major renovation in 1989–1990, was completed only three months after the fire.*

# VIRGINIA

**STATE TOURIST INFORMATION**
(800) 847–4882
www.virginia.org

## SHENANDOAH NATIONAL PARK

3655 U.S. Highway 211E
Luray, VA 22835
(540) 999–3500
www.nps.gov/shen

Shenandoah National Park comprises 196,000 acres of forested mountains through an 80-mile stretch of the Blue Ridge Mountains. Most of the park's features lie alongside 105-mile Skyline Drive, a slow but scenic two-lane road that wanders along much of the crest of the mountain range. The road accesses lodges, campgrounds, and overlooks from the north entrance at Front Royal to the south entrance near Waynesboro, Virginia. The park brochure provided at entry stations identifies places of interest and park facilities according to mile markers alongside the west side of the road. The park has more than 500 miles of hiking trails, including a 101-mile stretch of the Appalachian Trail. Shenandoah National Park is located in northern Virginia, with the northern entrance some 60 miles west of Washington, DC. The south entrance connects with the north end of the Blue Ridge Parkway. The northern section of the park, nearest Washington, DC, tends to be the most crowded. Shenandoah National Park is the northern terminus for the Blue Ridge Parkway, which meanders through Virginia and North Carolina. The parkway is listed in the North Carolina section of this book.

**PARK ENTRANCE FEE:** $10.00 per vehicle or $5.00 per person, good for seven days.

## 🛏 Lodging in Shenandoah National Park

Three locations in Shenandoah National Park provide lodging facilities, all of which are in the central section between mile markers 40 and 60. Big Meadows and Skyland are relatively large complexes with historic lodge and cabins, and modern lodging units. Lewis Mountain is a very small facility with cabins only. All three facilities are operated by the same concessioner, ARAMARK.

# SHENANDOAH NATIONAL PARK

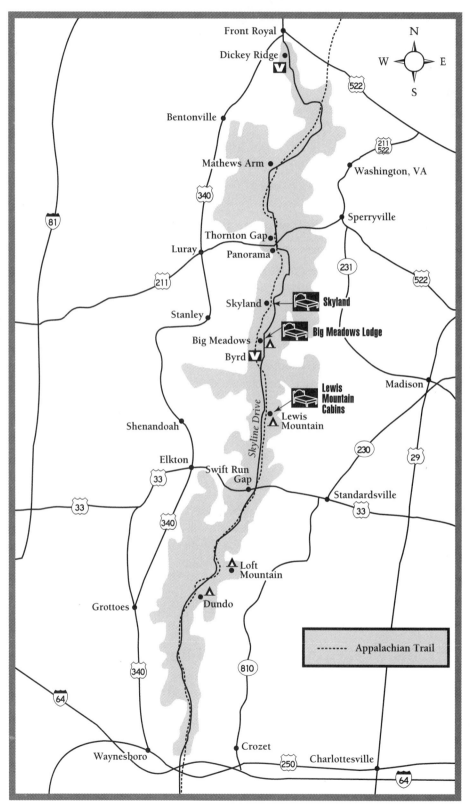

- **RESERVATIONS FOR ALL LODGING FACILITIES:** ARAMARK Convention and Tourism Services, P. O. Box 727, Luray, VA 22835. Phone (800) 999–4714 or (540) 743–5108; fax (540) 743–7883; www.visitshenandoah.com. The first night's deposit by check is required within ten days of booking a reservation. Full refund of deposit requires a seventy-two-hour advance canellation.

- **TRANSPORTATION:** Scheduled airline service is available to several towns surrounding Shenandoah National Park, including Washington, DC (use Dulles), and Charlottesville and Harrisonburg, Virginia. Bus service is available to Waynesboro, just outside the south entrance to the park, and Amtrak (800–872–7245) provides passenger rail service to Charlottesville, Virginia. No public transportation is available in the park.

## BIG MEADOWS LODGE

P.O. Box 727 • Luray, VA 22835 • (540) 999–2221
www.visitshenandoah.com

*One-Story Lodging Unit at Big Meadows*

Big Meadows is a complex consisting of a main lodge building constructed in 1939 and eleven separate but nearby cabins and one- and two-story wooden lodge buildings, for a total of ninety-two rooms. The main lodge and many of the smaller units are on the National Register of Historic Places. Registration is just inside the main lodge building, which also houses the dining room and a large greatroom that each provide spectacular views of the valley below Big Meadows. Registration parking is just outside the building, and adequate parking is near most of the lodging units. No pets are permitted. The main lodge building also has a limited number of overnight rooms. All the lodging facilities at Big Meadows are within close walking distance of the dining room. Big Meadows is in a heavily forested area at an altitude of 3,510 feet and is located at milepost 51, about midway between the north and south entrances to Shenandoah National Park. The northern entry point to Big Meadows is via Highway 211 from Luray, Virginia. The lodge is 15 miles north of Swift Run Gap Entrance and U.S. Route 33.

Big Meadows Lodge offers five categories of accommodations. All of the units have heat and a private bath but no air-conditioning or telephone. Some of the units have a fireplace (wood provided), and mini-suites in Crescent Rock have television. The least expensive option is the main lodge, which has twenty relatively small rooms in a two-story wing of the building. Most of these rooms have one double bed or two twin beds and will accommodate two persons only. Two rooms have two double beds, and one has a queen-size bed. Each room has a private bath with a tub, a shower, or both. Some of the lodge rooms are on the second floor, and some are on the first. Six rooms at the back of the building provide good views of the valley.

Six one- and two-story lodging units provide a total of sixty-two rooms in a combination of six suites, ten mini-suites, and forty-six regular rooms. Four one-story buildings are in a wooded area south of the main lodge, while two newer two-story buildings (Rapidan and Doubletop) are on a bluff overlooking the valley. The regular lodging units each have two double beds and a private bath with a combination shower-tub. These rooms have either a balcony or a patio with a table and chairs. The two-story units have larger rooms and better views, with the top floor offering a great view. Eight mini-suites in the Cresent Rock building, which rent for about $20 a day more than the regular lodge rooms, each have one large room with a king-size bed and a sofa bed. Two other mini-suites in the same building, with one double bed, are handicap accessible. Each of these mini-suites has a private balcony, television, and fireplace. Six regular suites with a separate sitting room have either one king-size bed or two double beds and a sofa bed. These units have a fireplace, small refrigerator, coffeemaker, and a porch.

Ten cabin rooms are constructed two or three to a building in a grassy area between the parking lot and two lodging units. Each of the rooms has one double bed, a fireplace, and a private bath with a shower but no tub. The cabins are relatively close together and do not offer views.

Big Meadows is a relaxing place to spend several days. The views are terrific, and the fall colors can be spectacular. The great room in the main lodge, with a large stone fireplace and many stuffed chairs, sofas, and wooden rockers, is a pleasant place for reading, playing board and card games, and gazing out the large windows at the valley below. A large balcony runs across the back of the building. The country-style restaurant serves three meals a day at reasonable prices. You can enjoy a hike or participate in programs presented by National Park Service rangers. One of the park's main visitor centers near the lodge has exhibits and film programs.

*Big Meadows Lodge, named for a nearby grassy meadow, is constructed of stones cut from the Massanutten Mountains across the Shenandoah Valley. Built by Civilian Conservation Corps and mountain labor, the lodge was completed in 1939 and is listed on the National Register of Historic Places. Paneling in the bedrooms and the dining room came from the native chestnut trees that once grew here on the Blue Ridge but were virtually wiped out by the 1930s blight. Beams in the lounge and dining room are native oak. Heavy cement shingles protect the building from the harsh mountain winters.*

- ■ **ROOMS:** Doubles, triples, and quads. Suites will accommodate up to six adults. Connecting rooms are available in the main lodge and in one of the regular lodging units. All rooms have a private bath, although some have only a shower or a tub. Two mini-suites are handicap accessible.

■ **RATES:** Main lodge ($68–$120); cabins ($75–$87); lodge units ($85–$105); mini-suites ($105–$125); suites ($124–$142). Slightly higher rates for weekends and daily in October. Special packages are offered seasonally.

■ **LOCATION:** At milepost 51.2, about midway on Skyline Drive between the north and south entrances to Shenandoah National Park.

■ **SEASON:** Last week in April to last week of October.

■ **FOOD:** A full-service dining room serves breakfast, lunch, and dinner ($9.00–$19.00). Beer and wine are available. The dining room is fully handicap accessible. A coffee shop and a camp store with groceries are at the Wayside entrance to Big Meadows.

■ **FACILITIES:** Restaurant, gift and craft shop, taproom, conference room, and a nice playground area for children. A gas station, coffee shop, camp store, trails, and National Park Service visitor center are at the nearby Big Meadows Wayside.

■ **ACTIVITIES:** Hiking, National Park Service hikes and programs.

## LEWIS MOUNTAIN CABINS

P.O. Box 727 • Luray, VA 22835 • (540) 999–2255
www.visitshenandoah.com

*A Duplex Cabin at Lewis Mountain Cabins*

Lewis Mountain is one of the smallest lodging units in all the national parks. The entire complex consists of one building with a registration desk and a small store, seven one-story cabins that provide a total of nine overnight rooms, and a hikers' cabin. Lewis Mountain Cabins has no lobby, dining room, swimming pool, or cocktail lounge. A small parking lot is beside the registration building, and all the cabins are a short walk away. A loading area is beside each cabin. The entire complex is in a heavily forested area with no particularly good views but a lot of quiet and privacy. Lewis Mountain Cabins is at mile marker

57.5, in the central section of Shenandoah National Park. It is about 6 miles south of Big Meadows and the farthest south of any of the park's three lodging units.

All of the regular cabins at Lewis Mountain have electric heat and private baths but no air-conditioning, telephone, or television. Each of the units has a small porch with chairs and a covered picnic pavilion with a table, grill, and electrical outlets. Wood is available for purchase. Two of the buildings are constructed as duplexes, with two cabin rooms per unit. These four cabin rooms each have one double bed and a private bath with a shower but no tub. Five of the buildings have two bedrooms, one on each side of a bathroom with a shower but no tub. One of these units is handicap accessible and has a bathroom with a combination shower-tub. The two-bedroom units, which cost about $25 per night more than the one-bedroom duplex cabins, have a double bed in each bedroom. The single hikers' cabin with two bunk beds has a potbellied stove but no bath or running water. Public bathrooms are located in the store and the nearby campground. Bunk beds have mattresses, but guests must supply their own linens for the hikers' cabin.

Lewis Mountain Cabins is one of the least expensive lodging options in Shenandoah National Park. It is also one of the quietest, since you will have few neighbors. The wooden cabins are small and relatively old, with some dating from the late 1930s; however, the interiors are paneled with chestnut or pine and are well maintained. This is a quiet place to stay overnight during a trip down Skyline Drive. It is also a good location for a long weekend of hiking and relaxing. It is not nearly as big as either Big Meadows or Skyland. However, remember to bring food to eat and wood to cook with. A small store in the registration building has limited groceries.

*In the early 1940s, Virginia still had "separate but equal" facilities for African Americans. The Lewis Mountain area was originally designated for blacks and called Lewis Mountain Negro Area. The National Park Service was responsible for caring for the campground, picnic area, and utilities, while the concessioner constructed the original five cabins. An additional two cabins were brought in later.*

- **ROOMS:** Doubles, triples, and quads. Each cabin has a private bathroom. One cabin is handicap accessible.

- **RATES:** Single-bedroom cabins ($65); two-bedroom cabins ($89); hikers' cabin ($20). Slightly higher prices are charged on weekend nights and during October. Special packages are available seasonally.

- **LOCATION:** Between mile marker 57 and 58, near the midpoint of Skyline Drive. Lewis Mountain is about 6 miles south of Big Meadows.

- **SEASON:** First week in May to the last weekend in October. The cabins tend to be full on all weekends and during July, August, and the first part of October.

- **FOOD:** No restaurant or other dining facilities are at Lewis Mountain. A small store with limited groceries is in the registration building.

- **FACILITIES:** Small store, pay showers, and laundry facility, which are all handicap accessible.

- **ACTIVITIES:** Hiking.

# SKYLAND

P.O. Box 727 • Luray, VA 22835 • (540) 999–2211

www.visitshenandoah.com

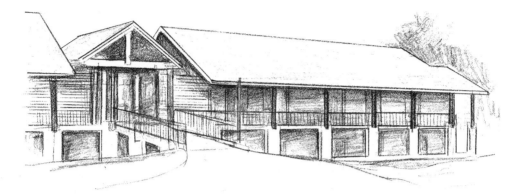

*Laurel Building at Skyland*

Skyland is a group of one- and two-story wooden buildings scattered along a hillside overlooking a large valley. The Skyland area is listed on the National Register of Historic Places. The main registration building has a medium-size lobby with a wall of windows toward the valley. No overnight rooms are in the one-story registration building, although a lodging unit is immediately next door. An adjacent building contains a dining room, a gift shop, a taproom, and a small lounge area. Two lodge buildings (Whiteoak and Stony Man) are nearby, but many of the remaining buildings and cabins are a fairly long walk from the dining room. Nearly all of the 177 rooms at Skyland, which is at an altitude of 3,680 feet, offer good views of the valley. Skyland is at mile marker 42, in the central section of Shenandoah National Park. It is 10 miles north of Big Meadows and the farthest north of any of the three lodging facilities in Shenandoah National Park.

The lodging complex offers four classes of accommodations. Most rooms are in a series of one- and two-story lodge units that overlook the valley. These buildings vary in size and age, but most have two double or two queen-size beds and a private bath with a combination shower-tub. The historic cabins were constructed between 1916 and 1922, when Skyland was a private resort colony. Rooms in the two-story units, including Canyon, Appledore, Craigin, Laurel, Raven's Nest, and Shenandoah, each have a balcony with a view. Rooms in these buildings, except Shenandoah, also have a television. The newest buildings with the largest rooms are Laurel (view rooms) and Franklin (nonview rooms with television). The rooms in Laurel cost only a few dollars more than rooms in the older and nonview buildings, so you should try for one of these.

One of the lodging units has six suites, two with views and four without. These units each have a bedroom with a double and a single bed, and a separate living room with a sofa bed. They rent for $35 to $60 per day more than regular rooms and are the only accommodations at Skyland other than one of the cabins to have a fireplace (wood provided).

The least expensive accommodations are twenty cabins that vary in size and beds. All have private bathrooms. Six cabins have a combination shower-tub, and the remainder have a shower only. Cabins are constructed two or four to a building. Only Byrd's Nest (cabin 68) has a fireplace. These units are scattered about Skyland, and none is particularly close to the registration building or dining room. One cabin (Peak View) has two bedrooms, one with two doubles and one with one double, and a bathroom.

Skyland is the largest lodging complex in Shenandoah National Park. Buildings are widely scattered, which means that you may have to either drive or walk a distance to the dining room. Most of the buildings are sited to take advantage of the views. If location and/or view are an important consideration, be certain this is stated when making a reservation. The large dining room is particularly attractive and offers a pleasant place to eat.

The Skyland area was originally developed in the 1850s to mine copper. Surrounding timber was used to make charcoal for a copper smelter. It was not until 1886 that the son of one of the original mine owners considered the possibility of developing the area as a resort. By the early 1900s Skyland had a dining hall, a recreation hall, bathhouses, and bungalows, all paid for by the sale of cabin sites and loans. The developer ran Skyland as a concessioner for the National Park Service until 1937.

- ROOMS: Doubles, triples, and quads. Suites sleep up to five, and one double cabin accommodates up to six adults. Some rooms, including the suites, can connect with adjacent rooms. All rooms have a private bath with a shower or a combination shower-tub. Handicap-accessible rooms are available in Pinnacles and Laurel.

- RATES: Lodge units ($84–$100); cabins ($53–$103); suites ($150–$170). Slightly higher rates for weekends and daily in October. Rates quoted are for two adults. Each additional person is $5.00 per night. Children under sixteen stay free.

- LOCATION: At milepost 42, about midway on Skyline Drive between the north and south entrances to Shenandoah National Park. Skyland is the northernmost lodging facility in the park.

- SEASON: End of March to the end of November.

- FOOD: A nice dining room serves breakfast, lunch, and dinner ($9.00–$22.00). Beer and wine are available.

- FACILITIES: Restaurant, taproom, gift shop, conference rooms, stables, trails.

- ACTIVITIES: Hiking, horseback riding, National Park Service ranger-led programs, nightly entertainment. Special events are coordinated throughout the season by the concessioner. Call (800) 999–4714 or visit the Web site.

# WASHINGTON

**STATE TOURIST INFORMATION**

(800) 544–1800

www.tourism.wa.gov

## MOUNT RAINIER NATIONAL PARK

Tahoma Woods Star Route

Ashford, WA 98304

(360) 569–2211

www.nps.gov/mora

Mount Rainier National Park is comprised of 235,612 acres, including the greatest single-peak glacial system in the United States. This is one of the most popular mountain-climbing areas in the country. Mount Rainier, the ancient volcano at the center of the park, is surrounded by snow, forests, and subalpine flowered meadows. Visitor centers are at Sunrise, Ohanapecosh, Paradise, and Longmire, the latter being the park's oldest developed area. The Sunrise visitor center, at 6,400 feet, is the highest point in the park reached by road. The road from the Nisqually Entrance in the park's southwest corner to Longmire is considered one of the world's most beautiful forest roads. Mount Rainier National Park is in southwestern Washington, 89 miles south of Seattle. It is 64 miles west of the town of Yakima, Washington.

**PARK ENTRANCE FEE:** $10.00 per vehicle or $5.00 per person, good for seven days.

## Lodging in Mount Rainier National Park

Mount Rainier has two inns, each offering very different lodging experiences. National Park Inn is a relatively small lodge in a heavily forested area with a view of Mount Rainier. The inn is cozy and quiet, with only twenty-five rooms. The much larger and busier Paradise Inn offers more of an alpine experience, at a higher altitude and with better mountain views. Both inns are nonsmoking facilities. Despite the different environments, the two lodges are both in the southern end of the park and only about 13 miles apart.

# MOUNT RAINIER NATIONAL PARK

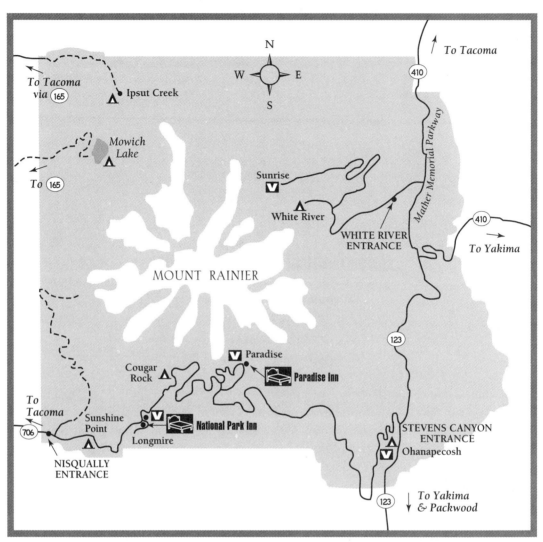

# NATIONAL PARK INN

Mount Rainier National Park • Longmire, WA 98397 • (360) 569–2275
www.guestservices.com/rainier

*National Park Inn*

National Park Inn is a small but nice two-story wooden lodge with twenty-five overnight rooms, all but two of which are on the second floor. The inn is at an altitude of 2,700 feet, surrounded by an old-growth forest of Douglas fir, western red cedar, and western hemlock. National Park Inn retains the character of an early 1900s lodge even though the building has been completely modernized. The inn is entered from the back, where a large parking lot is located. The lodge is on Highway 706, 6 miles from the southwest entrance to Mount Rainier National Park. It is 13 winding miles from the much larger inn at Paradise.

The twenty-five rooms at National Park Inn are all very different in terms of size, beds, and bathrooms. In general, the rooms are comfortable but small. Two suites each have two rooms, one with a double bed and the other with two twin beds. All of the rooms have heat but no air-conditioning, telephone, or television. All but seven rooms have private baths, which have a tub, shower, or both. Rooms without a private bathroom have an in-room sink and access to community showers and baths on the second floor. Beds vary from two twin beds, to a double bed and two twin beds, to two double beds. Although the rooms can be quite dissimilar, with the exception of the two suites, the cost for two adults depends only on whether or not a room has a private bath. Rooms with a bath cost about $30 per night more than rooms without a private bath. Rooms 3 and 7 each have baths and are much larger than average. Rooms along the front of the building, with the exception of room 18, have a view of Mount Rainier when the mountain isn't shrouded in clouds. Room 8 with a private bath offers the best view of the mountain. All rooms are entered from an inside corridor that is accessed via a stairway from the lobby area. No elevator is available. Two handicap-accessible rooms are on the first floor.

National Park Inn is much smaller and cozier than the lodge at Paradise. It is a comfortable place to rest overnight or to stay for several days. There aren't a lot of people here and activities in the immediate vicinity are minimal, but if you desire a comfortable and quiet place to read a book, get to know your spouse and kids, or just recharge your batteries, the National Park Inn can't be beat. A large covered porch with numerous chairs runs the length of the building. A guest lounge just off the lobby has a large stone fireplace, sofas, tables, and chairs. Complimentary tea and cookies are served here each afternoon. Board games are available at the front desk. An informal dining room on the opposite side of the lobby serves three meals a day. A tiny post office is located in a "closet" next to the registration desk. The general store next door sells gifts, limited groceries, beer, and wine. A National Park Service visitor center and a museum with exhibits on geology and wildlife are only a short walk from the inn. No pets are allowed, and no smoking is permitted anywhere in the building.

- **ROOMS:** Doubles, triples, and quads. Eighteen of the twenty-five rooms have private baths. Community baths are on the second floor. Handicap-accessible rooms are available.

- **RESERVATIONS:** Mount Rainier Guest Services, P.O. Box 108, Ashford, WA 98304-0108. Phone (360) 569–2275; fax (360) 569–2770. Credit card guarantee required when the reservation is made. Cancellation requires seven days' notice plus a $10 handling fee. Less than seven days' notice results in a charge for one night's room rate plus tax.

- **RATES:** Rooms with baths ($104); rooms without baths ($74). Rates quoted are for two adults. Two-room unit with bath ($142). Rates are for three adults. Each additonal person is $12. Children under two stay free with an adult, utilizing existing bedding in the room. Special winter bed-and-breakfast packages are available October through April.

- **LOCATION:** Six miles from the southwest entrance to Mount Rainier National Park on Highway 706. The Inn is 13 miles from Paradise, the park's other lodge.

- **SEASON:** Open all year.

- **FOOD:** A pleasant dining room on the main floor is open for breakfast ($6.25–$7.50), lunch ($6.50–$9.00), and dinner ($9.00–$17.00). Snacks and drinks may be purchased at the gift shop/store next door.

The current National Park Inn was the annex of the original lodge, most of which burned in 1926. The inn was subsequently reopened and underwent a major remodeling in 1936. Another extensive renovation occurred in 1989, when the inn was essentially rebuilt from the ground up for reopening in May 1990. The adjacent building currently housing the gift shop was constructed in 1911 and is the only structure at this location that is still on its original site.

- **TRANSPORTATION:** The nearest major airport is SeaTac, located between Seattle and Tacoma, Washington, where rental cars are available. Amtrak also serves these cities. Two ground shuttle services operate between Seattle and Mount Rainier National Park. They are Grayline of Seattle (800–426–7232) and Rainier Shuttle (360–569–2331).

- **FACILITIES:** Dining room, post office, general store that sells gifts and some food items, museum, National Park Service visitor center, hiker information center. Gasoline is not available in the park but may be purchased at Ashford and Elbe.

- **ACTIVITIES:** Hiking, fishing, ranger-guided walks, snowshoeing, skiing.

# PARADISE INN

Mount Rainier National Park • Paradise, WA 98398 • (360) 569–2275
www.guestservices.com/rainier

*Main Lodge at Paradise Inn*

aradise Inn is a large wooden two-story lodge building with an attached four-story annex that offers some of the most striking views of the park's snow-covered peaks, including Mount Rainier. The inn has 117 rooms, most of which are in the annex that is reached via an enclosed walkway from the lobby of the main building. The primary structure was completed in 1917, and the annex was added in the 1920s. The original lodge rooms were renovated in 1990; rooms in the annex were renovated in 1998. Paradise Inn is located at the base of Mount Rainier in the southern end of Mount Rainier National Park, 19 miles from the park's southwest entrance station.

Paradise Inn is built on a hill, so that the outside entry to the lobby is on the third floor. A huge two-story lobby has a vaulted ceiling and runs most of the length of the building. Massive log ceiling beams frame a mezzanine that wraps around the inside of the second floor. The lobby is filled with tables, benches, sofas, and stuffed chairs. Large stone fireplaces are at each end of the room. The registration desk in the corner is beside the stairs to the rooms and the walkway to the annex. The large parking lot is generally crowded, so it may be necessary to temporarily park beside the entrance to unload luggage. Assistance with luggage is available at the registration desk. Access to guest rooms is by stairs. There are no elevators in the hotel.

Paradise Inn has several categories of rooms. All of the rooms are nonsmoking and have heat but no air-conditioning, telephone, or television. The thirty-one least expensive rooms without private bath are all in the main lodge building. These very small rooms (approximately 8 feet by 8 feet, including a small open closet area) have a sink and beds ranging from two twin beds to one double bed, to one double and one single. Common bathrooms and shower rooms are at one end of a long hallway. The next room classification includes seventy-four rooms with bath, nearly all of which are located in the annex. Five handicap-accessible rooms are included in this category. Bathrooms have a tub, shower, or both.

Rooms have two twin beds, two double beds, or one queen-size bed. The rooms with two doubles are larger and cost approximately $20 more per night. Rooms with a private bath rent for about $37 per night more than rooms without a bath.

Ten rooms have two bedrooms and one bath. One bedroom has a double bed, and the other has two twins. The bath is in a small hallway and accessible from either bedroom. These rent for about $30 per night more than the one bedroom with a bath, so you might consider one of these if you are traveling with children. Paradise also offers two suites, each with a bedroom with a queen-size bed, a separate sitting room with a sofa bed, a refrigerator, and a private bath. The suites are about the same size and cost $10 per night more than the two-bedroom units. Rooms in both the main lodge building and the annex offer varying views, so if what you see outside your window is an important consideration, make your interest known when a reservation is booked. Keep in mind that a room with a view isn't guaranteed, and none of the rooms offer a good view of Mount Rainier.

Paradise Inn is a pleasant but sometimes crowded place to stay. At an altitude of 5,400 feet, Paradise can be quite cool and foggy, even during summer. This is a heavily visited area of Mount Rainier National Park, and lots of people, both guests and visitors, seem to constantly browse through the lobby area. Tables and chairs on two sides of the mezzanine offer a more relaxing place to read, play cards, or just people-watch. Complimentary tea and cookies are served for guests here each afternoon from 3:00 to 5:00. An attractive 200-seat dining room with a beamed ceiling is just off the lobby on the main floor. A few entrées served are not found on most menus, such as Buffalo Stew, a luncheon item, and Buffalo Meatloaf with Jack Daniels Sauce, which is on the dinner menu. A lounge, gift shop, snack bar, and post office are on the same floor. A large visitor center within walking distance of the lodge also has an observation floor, exhibits, a grill, and gift shops. The area around Paradise is noted for many varieties of subalpine flowers, which bloom in July and August as the snow is melting.

*Paradise Inn is constructed almost completely from Alaskan cedar taken just a few miles below the Paradise area. The logs were salvaged from an 1885 fire and hauled to the site by horse-drawn wagons. Most of the lobby's woodwork was by a German carpenter who used only an adze in his work. He also built an unusual piano and a huge grandfather clock that remain in the lobby.*

- **ROOMS:** Singles, doubles, triples, and quads. Not all rooms have private baths. Five rooms are handicap accessible.

- **RESERVATIONS:** Mount Rainier Guest Services, P.O. Box 108, Ashford, WA 98304-0108. Phone (360) 569–2275; fax (360) 569–2770. A credit card guarantee is required when the reservations are made. A minimum of seven days' notice must be given for a full refund less a $10 handling fee. Less than seven days' notice results in a charge for one night's room rate plus tax.

- **RATES:** Rooms without a bath ($75); rooms with a bath ($112); double/double with bath ($129); two-room units with a bath ($142); suites with sitting room ($152). Rates for two-room units and suites are for three adults. Rates for a double/double are for four adults.

Each additional person is $12. Children under two stay free with an adult, utilizing existing bedding in the room.

- **LOCATION:** Paradise Inn is on Highway 706, 19 miles from the southwest entrance to Mount Rainier National Park.

- **SEASON:** The lodge is open from mid-May through the first part of October, depending on weather.

- **FOOD:** A large dining room seats 200 and offers breakfast ($5.50–$9.00), lunch ($7.00–$13.00), and dinner ($12–$20) daily, with a special Sunday brunch. No reservations are taken. A snack bar near the gift shop has sandwiches and beverages from 9:00 A.M. to 8:00 P.M. A grill with sandwiches, hamburgers, soups, and beverages is located in the visitor center and open from 10:00 A.M. to 7:00 P.M.

- **TRANSPORTATION:** The nearest major airport is SeaTac, located between Seattle and Tacoma, Washington, where rental cars are available. Amtrak also serves these cities. Two ground shuttle services operate between Seattle and Mount Rainier National Park. They are Grayline of Seattle (800–426–7232) and Rainier Shuttle (360–569–2331).

- **FACILITIES:** Restaurant, gift shop, post office, lounge, snack bar, hiker information center, and nearby National Park Service visitor center. Gasoline is not available in the park but may be purchased at Ashford and Elbe.

- **ACTIVITIES:** Hiking, guided walks, evening programs in the lobby, fishing, mountain climbing, snowshoeing, cross-country skiing, snowboarding, and tubing.

# NORTH CASCADES NATIONAL PARK
# LAKE CHELAN NATIONAL RECREATION AREA
# ROSS LAKE NATIONAL RECREATION AREA

810 State Route 20
Sedro Woolley, WA 98284-1239
(360) 856–5700
www.nps.gov/noca

The North Cascades National Park complex, covering 1,069 square miles, offers magnificent alpine scenery that is unmatched in the continental United States. Heavy precipitation has produced alpine lakes, waterfalls, ice caps, more than 300 glaciers, and glacier-carved canyons such as Stehekin (Native American for "the way through") that sits at the head of 55-mile-long Lake Chelan. Compared to many of the other national parks, this scenic park is relatively wild and uncrowded. The park complex is located in northern Washington (the north boundary borders on Canada). Primary access to the area is via Washington State Route 20, which bisects the park through a portion of the Ross Lake section.

**PARK ENTRANCE FEE:** No charge.

# NORTH CASCADES NATIONAL PARK
# LAKE CHELAN NATIONAL RECREATION AREA
# ROSS LAKE NATIONAL RECREATION AREA

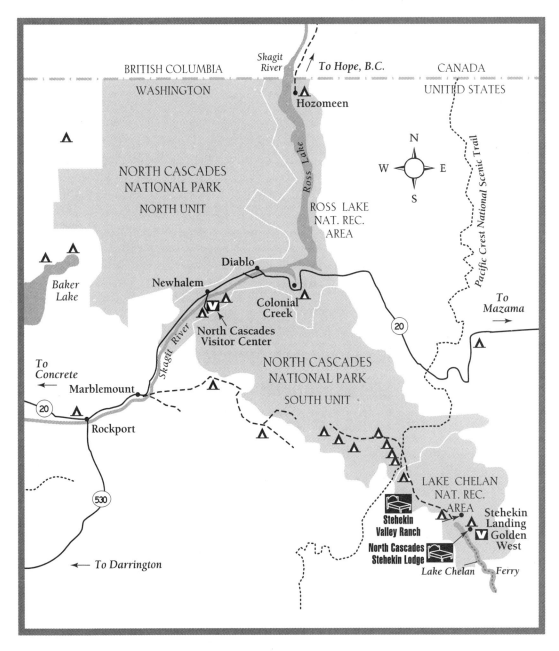

# Lodging in North Cascades National Park Service Complex

Two major lodging facilities within the park are at the north end of Lake Chelan. Only one of the two facilities, North Cascades Stehekin Lodge, is regulated by the National Park Service. The other facility, Stehekin Valley Ranch, is privately owned and on private land. A third and smaller lodging facility (Silver Bay Inn Resort with two cabins, a house, and one room; phone 509–682–2212; or email stehekin@silverbayinn.com) and several privately owned cabins, often with vehicles, are also available for rent near Stehekin. For information on the area, call Lake Chelan Chamber of Commerce at (800) 4–CHELAN.

The lodging facilities at Stehekin are reached only via commercial boats or floatplanes that leave from the town of Chelan. The largest and least expensive boat (approximately $25 round-trip) takes four hours one way and leaves Chelan each morning at 8:30. A faster and more expensive boat ($42 round-trip) takes two and a quarter hours and leaves at the same time. The fastest boat ($89 round-trip) makes two daily round-trips and takes one and a quarter hours each way. All three boats are operated by the same company, Lake Chelan Boat Company. Reservations are required on the two faster boats. For information, call (509) 682–4584, or visit the Web site at www.ladyofthelake.com. Contact Chelan Airways at (509) 682–5065 for information on floatplane service ($100 and up round-trip).

## NORTH CASCADES STEHEKIN LODGE

P.O. Box 457 • Chelan, WA 98816 • (509) 682–4494
www.stehekin.com

North Cascades Stehekin Lodge comprises seven wooden buildings, six of which have a total of twenty-eight overnight rooms. The registration desk is inside the store across a small parking area from the boat dock. The store and restaurant are fronted by a wooden deck with chairs and picnic tables. Both are handicap accessible via an elevator at the corner of the deck. A registration sign is above the entrance. A restaurant in an adjacent building is the only structure in the complex that does not have accommodations. The lodge is on the east bank near the north terminus of Lake Chelan, across the road from the boat dock. There are also a laundry, post office, a few stores, and a large National Park Service visitor center. Shuttle service and tours for the Stehekin Valley begin near the dock.

A total of twenty-eight rooms of various sizes and configurations are available at the lodge. All of the rooms have private baths, heat, and electricity but no telephone, television, or air-conditioning. Ten standard rooms, eight of which are above the store, are the least expensive. These rooms do not have a balcony or a view of the lake, but a sitting area with books, games, and puzzles at the end of the hallway has a good view of the lake. Standard rooms have either one queen-size or two twin beds. Standard rooms 5 and 6 on the lower floor of an A-frame building are preferable to rooms above the store.

Eleven recently renovated Lake View rooms are larger and more expensive, and are located in a two-story building next to the restaurant. These rooms have a twin-size sofa sleeper plus either a king- or queen-size bed and are entered via outside doors at the back of the building. Each Lake View room has a large window and a balcony facing Lake Chelan. Balconies

*North Cascades Stehekin Lodge*

off the five first-floor rooms are significantly larger than balconies for the six second-floor rooms. Three of the Lake View rooms are quite a bit larger and rent for approximately $20 more than the remaining eight rooms. One of these rooms is fully handicap accessible. We think the Lake View rooms are worth the extra $10 per night.

Housekeeping units with kitchen facilities (including utensils) range in size, from two units that accommodate two guests to four units that can accommodate up to six persons. Two units are constructed as A-frames, three units are in a single building, one is by itself on the third floor of the store (this unit can get uncomfortably warm during July and August), and one is a free-standing building. Keep in mind that few grocery items are available for sale at Stehekin, so you must bring food if you wish to use the kitchen of a housekeeping unit.

North Cascades Stehekin Lodge is a convenient and comfortable place to spend a night or two. You might want to take the morning boat from Chelan, stay an evening, then return the

*N*orth Cascades Stehekin Lodge is not the only lodging facility that has served the public at this location. In fact, the current facility is a conglomeration of several hotels that were acquired by the National Park Service in 1968. A small hotel was in operation by 1892 when this area was a major mining center. A larger hotel opened in 1900 and was subsequently enlarged, until by 1910, the three-story building had fifty rooms that accommodate one hundred guests. This hotel was demolished in 1927 before the Lake Chelan Dam raised the water to a level that would have flooded the building. Material from the hotel was used to construct yet another lodge farther up the hill that currently houses the National Park Service visitor center.

morning or afternoon of the following day. The lodge restaurant offers three meals a day, including breakfast and an evening buffet. Shuttle service is available to Stehekin Valley Ranch, which provides an alternative for dining. North Cascades Stehekin Lodge serves as the center for Stehekin activities, including boat and bicycle rentals, snowshoe rental in the winter, bus tours, and hikes. Buses for tours of the valley leave from the lodge.

- **ROOMS:** Doubles, triples, quads, with a few housekeeping units sleeping up to six. Handicap-accessible rooms are available.

- **RESERVATIONS:** North Cascades Stehekin Lodge, P.O. Box 457, Chelan, WA 98816. Call (509) 682–4494. Payment in full is required to book a reservation. Cancellation of sleeping units requires fourteen days' notice. Housekeeping unit cancellation requires thirty days' notice.

- **RATES:** Standard rooms ($90); Lake View rooms ($101.50–$122.50); housekeeping units ($117–$133). Rates quoted are for two persons. Each additional person is $10 per night. Rates for children six through eleven are an additional $5.00 per night. Children under six stay free. Reduced rates of approximately $20 per room per night are offered from October 16 up to the Friday prior to Memorial Day. Special Packages are offered. Check the Web site at www.stehekin.com.

- **LOCATION:** Across from the Stehekin boat dock.

- **SEASON:** The lodge is open all year.

- **FOOD:** An adjacent restaurant offers a breakfast buffet ($7.00), lunch ($5.00–$8.00), and dinner ($13–$17). Dinner reservations are required. A small store sells milk, chips, beer, and wine. The Valley Shuttle offers transportation to Stehekin Valley Ranch, which also serves three meals daily.

- **TRANSPORTATION:** Major airports are in Seattle and Spokane, Washington, where rental cars are available. The lodge is reached from Chelan only via boat or floatplane.

- **FACILITIES:** Dining room, convenience store, post office, laundry, National Park Service visitor center, marina, and boat and bicycle rentals. Snowshoe rentals in winter.

- **ACTIVITIES:** Hiking, fishing, boating, cycling.

## STEHEKIN VALLEY RANCH

P.O. Box 36 • Stehekin, WA 98852 • (800) 536–0745
info@courtneycountry.com • www.courtneycountry.com

Stehekin Valley Ranch is a relatively isolated lodging facility that includes a main two-story wooden building with a dining room, bath and shower rooms, and small upstairs reading room, along with twelve nearby wooden cabins. All of the cabins are a short walk from the dining room and bathrooms. The complex is situated in a grove of maple trees beside a large pasture with a background of snowcapped mountains. The location provides

*Wood cabin with a canvas roof at Stehekin Valley Ranch*

spectacular views, access to great hiking and fishing, and an informal and restful atmosphere. Three meals a day, including an absolutely outstanding dinner, are included in the price of the rooms.

All lodging at the ranch is in two types of cabins. Seven older cabins, constructed in 1983, are hard sided with canvas roofs. Beds are either a double and two twins or a queen-size and one twin. These units have cement floors, only screens over window openings, unfinished interiors, and no electricity, heat, or bathroom facilities. Community bathrooms with showers are in the main building. A kerosene lantern supplies the only lighting. Despite the rustic appearance, these units are clean and comfortable, and the choice of many regular guests. Five of the seven cabins (cabins 1 though 5) are directly beside the pasture and provide an excellent view of the mountains. Two other cabins (cabins 11 and 12) are higher on the hill with views that are obstructed by other cabins.

Five larger and newer cabins constructed in the mid-1990s have metal roofs, electricity, a front porch with chairs, and a private bathroom with a shower but no tub. Beds in three of these cabins include one queen-size and two twin beds. Two of the five cabins (cabins 9 and 10) are newer and larger with a loft bedroom that has two twin beds and a downstairs futon and queen-size bed. These cabins also have cement floors but are considerably larger and brighter than the canvas-covered cabins. However, they are situated behind five of the canvas-roofed cabins, which block their view of the pasture and mountains.

Stehekin Valley Ranch is a fun place to stay, with lots of outdoor activities, including river rafting, horseback riding, mountain biking, fishing, and hiking. The location is spectacular, and both employees and guests are friendly. The dining room, with its three extra-large picnic tables on a floor of wood chips, provides a great atmosphere for enjoying some exceptional meals of fish, chicken, and steak. Best of all are the homemade pies served each evening. After dinner, relax on the porch outside the dining room or walk up the stairs to a small reading room. Guests sometimes linger in the dining room to read or play board games.

- **ROOMS:** Twelve individual cabins, most of which sleep up to four people. Two larger cabins can sleep up to six. Seven canvas-roofed cabins have no private bath. Five newer cabins have a private bath with shower. No handicap-accessible cabins are available.

- **RESERVATIONS:** Write P.O. Box 36, Stehekin, WA 98852. Call (800) 536–0745. A deposit of 50 percent of the total is required at the time the reservation is made. The remainder is due upon arrival by check or can be prepaid by credit card. Cancellation in writing of twenty-one days is required for 75 percent refund. No refunds for later cancellations.

- **RATES:** All prices are per person and include three meals a day. For stays of one or two nights, canvas-covered cabins ($75 per adult; $65 per child seven to twelve; $50 per child four to six; $20 per child three and under); Cabins with bath cost about $10 extra per person per night, with the exception of children three and under, which remains at $20. For stays of three or four nights, all prices are lowered by $10 per night; for stays of five or more nights, all prices are lowered by $15 per night. There's a $5.00 reduction per person per night for guests who provide their own sheets and towels. Packages are available. Check the Web site at www.courtneycountry.com.

*Hugh Courtney, grandfather of the current owners of Stehekin Valley Ranch, homesteaded fifty-two acres in the Stehekin area in 1916. One of his sons, Ray, purchased the twenty-acre dairy farm where the ranch is currently located and started a successful pack trip business. Six of Ray's children are currently involved in a variety of businesses, including the operation of the ranch. The present lodging operation commenced in 1983 with the construction of the main building and canvas-roofed cabins. Stehekin Valley Ranch is on private land that is surrounded by Lake Chelan National Recreation Area.*

- **LOCATION:** Nine miles north of Stehekin Landing. A free shuttle service for guests of the ranch operates four round-trips daily between Stehekin Landing and the ranch.

- **SEASON:** Mid-June to early October.

- **FOOD:** Three excellent meals a day with more food than anyone can possibly eat are served in the dining room and are included in the price of a room. Sack lunches are provided for guests who will be away when lunch is served.

- **TRANSPORTATION:** Major airports are in Seattle and Spokane, Washington, where rental cars are available. Scheduled boat service is available to Stehekin Landing from Chelan. Float planes are available at Chelan. A valley shuttle system operates every three hours beginning at 8:15 A.M. between Stehekin Landing and Stehekin Valley Ranch. The shuttle also stops at the bakery and other points along the road.

- **FACILITIES:** Dining room, small gift shop, library, and reading room.

- **ACTIVITIES:** Fishing, hiking, river rafting, bicycling, volleyball.

# OLYMPIC NATIONAL PARK

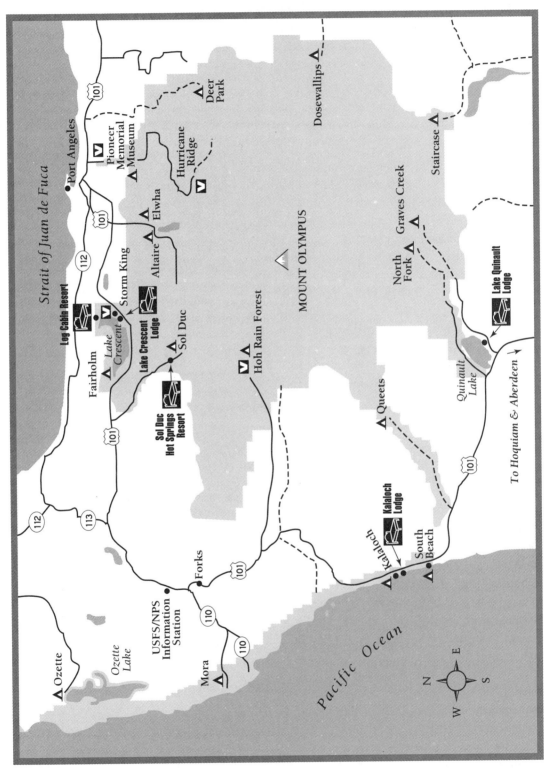

# OLYMPIC NATIONAL PARK

600 East Park Avenue
Port Angeles, WA 98362
(360) 452–0330
www.nps.gov/olym/home.htm

Olympic National Park covers 1,442 square miles of mountain wilderness and includes active glaciers, 57 miles of scenic ocean shore, and the finest remnant of Pacific Northwest rain forest. The strip of the park along the Pacific Ocean has some of the most primitive coastline in the continental United States. Olympic National Park is composed of two sections, located in the northwest corner of Washington. Main access is via U.S. Highway 101, although roads penetrate only the perimeter of the park.

**PARK ENTRANCE FEE:** $10.00 per vehicle or $5.00 per person, good for seven days.

## Lodging in Olympic National Park

The park has four facilities with overnight accommodations. Kalaloch Lodge is located directly on the coast and is perfect for beach walkers. Sol Duc Hot Springs Resort is great for those who want to spend time relaxing in a hot mineral bath. Lake Crescent Lodge and Log Cabin Resort are situated in heavily wooded areas on opposite sides of beautiful Lake Crescent. We have also included charming Lake Quinault Lodge, which is across Lake Quinault from the park's southern boundary.

## KALALOCH LODGE

157151 Highway 101 • Forks, WA 98331-9396 • (360) 962–2271
www.visitkalaloch.com

Kalaloch Lodge is a complex of wooden buildings that include a main lodge, forty-four freestanding cabins, a motel-style unit, and a store, all situated on a bluff overlooking the Pacific Ocean. Only a few overnight rooms are in the main lodge building. The registration desk for all rooms is in the gift shop of the main lodge, which is on Highway 101. This building also has the restaurant and coffee shop/service bar. All of the cabins and other lodging units are adjacent to and within easy walking distance of the main lodge. Kalaloch Lodge is located on U.S. Highway 101, 35 miles south of Forks, Washington. The lodge is 95 miles southwest of Port Angeles, Washington.

The lodge offers a total of sixty-four guest rooms in four categories, all of which have electric heat and a private bath but no air-conditioning, telephone, or television (except the suites in the main lodge). The main lodge building has ten overnight rooms, including two suites. All but one of the rooms are on the second floor and are accessed from a central hallway that is reached from a stairway in the lobby. These rooms each have a bath with a shower but no tub. Room size varies, with five rooms having one queen-size bed and other rooms having up to two queen-size beds and a sofa bed. Each of the suites has a combi-

*Main Lodge Building at Kalaloch*

nation living room–bedroom with one king-size bed and one has a sofa bed. These are the only rooms in the entire complex with a television. Becker's Suite is only rented as a suite during the summer months; during the remainder of the year, it is used as a library. Rooms 1 (on the first floor), 6, 7, and 8 and the suites provide an ocean view. Rooms 5 and 9, with two double beds and a sofa bed, are quite large.

The two-story Sea Crest House has six regular rooms, plus four suites. This building sits behind two bluff cabins. The six regular motel-style rooms are very spacious and have two queen-size beds and a private bath with a shower but no tub. Each room has its own patio or balcony and large windows that provide an ocean view. The suites have a sitting room with a fireplace (wood provided) and two separate bedrooms with one double and one queen-size bed plus a sofa bed. One bedroom and the sitting room have large windows.

Twenty bluff cabins, most of which were refurbished in 1999, offer a great view of the sea. Bluff Cabins 43 and 44 were newly constructed in 1999. About half of these cabins have either a fireplace or a wood stove (wood provided). All but four have one bedroom, with one queen-size to two double beds. The other four have two bedrooms, with one queen-size bed, one double, one single, and one sofa bed. Several of the bluff cabins have carports and kitchens that include a sink, stove, oven, coffeemaker, and refrigerator, although no cooking or eating utensils are provided. Glass cups and glasses, paper plates, and plastic eating utensils are provided. Three of these buildings are modern duplexes with vaulted ceilings. The six cabins in these three buildings do not have kitchens or carports. Twenty-two log cabins each have a front room with a queen-size bed and a bedroom with a queen-size bed. Two larger log cabins have two separate bedrooms with a queen-size bed in each bedroom and a sofa bed. All the log cabins have a wood stove and a kitchen area with the same provisions as the kitchens in the bluff cabins. These cabins have nice roomy interiors with log walls and tile floors. Most of the log cabins sit fairly close together behind the bluff cabins and do not have a direct ocean view but are nonetheless very close to the bluff overlooking the ocean. These rent for slightly less than the bluff cabins.

Kalaloch Lodge is a great place to stay if you want to experience the Pacific Ocean. The roar of the sea can be heard from your room. A wide sandy beach just below the bluff can be reached via an easy trail. The water is relatively cold and there are riptides, so you probably won't want to swim, but walks along the beach are one of the pleasures of staying here. National Park Service rangers lead daily walks along the beach and to various points in the park during the summer months. The main lodge building has a restaurant and service bar/coffee shop. The restaurant has big windows overlooking the ocean. Keep in mind that this coastal area is often breezy and can get quite foggy, so be prepared for the possibility of chilly weather. Of course, the wind, fog, and cool air are all part of the experience of a visit to the Pacific Northwest.

- **ROOMS:** Doubles, triples, and quads. A few cabins can hold more than four persons. All rooms have a private bath, although many have a shower but no tub. One cabin is handicap accessible.

- **RESERVATIONS:** Kalaloch Lodge, 17151 Highway 101, Forks, WA 98331-9396. Phone (360) 962–2271; fax (360) 962–3391. A deposit of one night's stay is required. A cancellation notice of seventy-two hours is required for a refund less a $10 fee.

- **RATES:** Two sets of rates apply to all rooms; peak rates are from early June through mid-October, plus all weekends and holidays. Off-peak rates are 25 to 30 percent less. Lodge ($80–$125, depending on view); lodge suites ($230); Sea Crest House regular ($125); suites ($145); bluff cabins ($160–$230, depending on size); log cabins ($140–$165, depending on size). Rates quoted are for two persons. Each additional person is $10 per night. Children under five stay free. Pets are $10 per night.

A short distance northeast of Kalaloch Lodge is one of the most interesting and popular areas of Olympic National Park. The Hoh Rain Forest annually receives an average of 140 inches of rain. This heavy precipitation produces a mystical environment in which everything is green. Here you will find some of the world's tallest trees, their bark covered by fuzzy green moss. The heavy rainfall on the west side of the park results from ocean air cooling and dumping moisture as it rises to clear the mountains. Ranger-guided hikes and self-guided trails are available at the Hoh.

- **LOCATION:** Directly on the Pacific Ocean, 35 miles south of Forks, Washington, on U.S. Highway 101.

- **SEASON:** Kalaloch Lodge is open year-round.

- **FOOD:** A restaurant serves breakfast ($5.00–$10.00), lunch ($6.00–$10.00), and dinner ($13–$24). The same menu, plus several additional items, is available in the adjacent coffee shop/service bar, which is open from 7:00 A.M. to 10:00 P.M. Limited groceries can be purchased at the store beside the main lodge building.

- **TRANSPORTATION:** The nearest major city with scheduled air and train service is Olympia, Washington, where rental cars are available.

- **FACILITIES:** Restaurant, coffee shop/service bar, gift shop, gas station, and small store.

- **ACTIVITIES:** Walking, beachcombing, whale watching, kite flying, and surf fishing. Ranger-guided walks are offered each day during summer months.

- **PETS:** Pets are allowed in cabins only.

# LAKE CRESCENT LODGE

416 Lake Crescent Road • Port Angeles, WA 98363-8672 • (360) 928–3211
www.lakecrescentlodge.com

*Main Lodge Building at Lake Crescent Lodge*

Lake Crescent Lodge, a Forever Resort, comprises a classic main lodge building surrounded at each end by several types of cabins and one- and two-story motel structures. The main wooden lodge, constructed in 1916 as the Singer Tavern, has only five overnight rooms, all upstairs and without a private bath. All other accommodations are separate but very near the main lodge. The entire complex is situated on the south shore of Lake Crescent among giant hemlock and fir trees in the shadow of Mount Storm King. Registration for all lodging at Lake Crescent Lodge is just inside the door of the main building in the lobby area highlighted by a huge stone fireplace. A gift shop, a restaurant, a lounge, and a beautiful sunroom are also on the main floor of the same building. Virtually all the accommodations, including the cabins, offer a view of beautiful Lake Crescent. Lake Crescent Lodge is located 21 miles west of Port Angeles, Washington, just off U.S. Highway 101.

The lodge offers several types of accommodations. All rooms have heat but no air-conditioning, television, or telephone. All rooms except those in the main lodge have a private bath. Pets are permitted in the Roosevelt Fireplace cottages and the Singer Tavern cottages. Parking is convenient to all the rooms. The least expensive accommodations are the five relatively small rooms on the second floor of the main lodge building. These rooms have paper-thin walls and are entered from an interior hallway via a lobby stairway. All have a double bed but no private bathroom. Two shower rooms and two small bathrooms are in the hallway. All five rooms are on the west side of the building and offer a terrific view of Lake Crescent and mountains on the opposite shore.

Sixteen one- and two-bedroom Singer Tavern cottages are constructed two and three units to a building. Beds in the one-bedroom units vary from one queen- to one king-size bed, to two doubles. The two-bedroom version has three double beds and a twin bed. These cottages sit back from the lake in a grassy area, although all have a lake view. Units 20 and 21 suffer from substantial foot traffic and should, if possible, be avoided. The Roosevelt Fireplace cottages, with either one room or a living room plus a bedroom, were constructed in 1937. These units are quite a bit larger than the Tavern cottages. The two one-room cottages have two double beds, a sofa, and two chairs. The two cottages with two rooms have three double beds, a sofa, and two chairs. Roosevelt Fireplace cottages are directly on the lake; each unit features a wood fireplace (wood is furnished), spacious rooms, and nice hardwood floors, and all four units have coffeemakers.

Three separate buildings have motor lodge rooms. The Marymere Lodge is a one-story cement block and wood frame building that sits back from the lake but still provides a lake view; trees surround the back and side of the building. All of the ten motel-type rooms at Marymere are large and have two double beds, a desk, a chair, and a luggage bench. Each unit has a large window and a covered porch with chairs on the lakeside. The two-story Storm King Motor Lodge is situated in trees back from the lake but still provides a lake view. These ten rooms all have a queen-size bed and are a little smaller and cost about $10 less than the rooms in Marymere. The Storm King units each have a balcony or patio with chairs. The two-story Pyramid Mountain Lodge was constructed in 1991 and is the newest lodging in the complex. This wooden structure sits back from the lake on a hill and has ten rooms. The rooms in Pyramid Mountain each have two double beds and a private patio or balcony. The one handicap-accessible room has one queen-size bed.

If you don't mind using a common bathroom, the five second-floor rooms in the main lodge provide the best value and the best view. Open the front window in any of these rooms and you will enjoy a picture-postcard view. If a common bathroom is unacceptable and you plan to stay for a week or so, the Roosevelt Fireplace cottages are the best choice. These offer privacy and a view. If the Roosevelt cottages are full, your next choice should be the Singer Tavern cottages.

Lake Crescent Lodge is in a picture-perfect setting. Lake Crescent is one of the country's most beautiful lakes, and the lodge takes full advantage of vistas the lake provides. This is a wonderful place to spend an active day or a restful week. Most of the activities are water-related. A wide grassy area with trees and chairs separates the main lodge from the lake. It is a perfect place to read a book, take a snooze, or watch guests use the swimming beach. Rowboats are available for rent at the lodge.

*Lake Crescent is one of the cleanest and most scenic bodies of water in the United States. Surrounded by tree-covered mountains, the glacier-carved lake reaches a depth of 900 feet and varies in width from 0.5 mile to more than 2 miles along its 8.5-mile length. A dozen tributaries feed the 4,700-acre lake, which has only a single outlet. The steep slopes and cold water temperature cause the lake to be relatively free of algae and to take on a deep blue color.*

- **ROOMS:** Doubles, triples, and quads in most units. Some units hold up to seven persons. All rooms outside the main lodge building have private bathrooms. One room is handicap accessible.

- **RESERVATIONS:** Lake Crescent Lodge, 416 Lake Crescent Road, Port Angeles, WA 98363-8672. Phone (360) 928–3211. A deposit of one night's stay is required. Cancellation of forty-eight hours is required for a full refund.

- **RATES:** Historic lodge rooms ($68.50); Singer Tavern cottages: one-room ($110.00); two-room ($116.50); Roosevelt Fireplace cottages: one-room ($132.50); two-room ($148.50); motor lodges: Pyramid Mountain ($123.00); Storm King ($106.00); Marymere ($116.50). Rates quoted are for two persons. Each additional person is $11.50 per night. Pets are $10 each per night. An additional $2.00 per night Resource Education fee is also collected.

- **LOCATION:** Twenty-one miles west of Port Angeles, Washington, on U.S. Highway 101.

- **SEASON:** Late April through October. Four Roosevelt Fireplace cottages are open on winter weekends, but no dining service is available.

- **FOOD:** A dining room on the main floor serves breakfast ($5.00–$10.00), lunch ($6.00–$12.00), and dinner ($12–$22). Wine and beer are available in the lounge and dining room. A few snacks and beverages are available in the gift shop.

- **TRANSPORTATION:** Scheduled airline service is in Port Angeles, Washington, where rental cars are available. A city bus from Port Angeles to the lodge operates daily during the summer.

- **FACILITIES:** Boat rental, restaurant, lounge, swimming beach, and gift shop.

- **ACTIVITIES:** Swimming, hiking, boating, fishing.

- **PETS:** Pets are allowed only in the cottages.

## LAKE QUINAULT LODGE

P.O. Box 7 • Quinault, WA 98575-0007 • (360) 288–2900
www.visitlakequinault.com

Lake Quinault Lodge is a complex of four shake-covered buildings, including a two-story main lodge that has the registration desk/gift shop, dining room, lobby area, indoor heated swimming pool, and men's and women's dry saunas. The main lodge has guest rooms on both floors, but most rooms are in three buildings situated on either side of the main lodge building. The lodge is in the middle of a rain forest, on a hill overlooking the south shore of Lake Quinault. The beautiful setting includes a large lawn that leads to the lake. Lake Quinault Lodge is on South Shore Road, 2 miles east of U.S. Highway 101. The turnoff from Highway 101 is 40 miles north of the town of Hoquiam. The lodge is in Olympic National Forest, across the lake from Olympic National Park. We have included this lodge because of its proximity to the park.

The lodge offers four basic types of rooms, all with heat and private bathrooms, but no air-conditioning, telephone, or television. The main lodge building was constructed in 1926 with thirty-two rooms, including one suite. These rooms differ in size, view, and configuration. In general, rooms in the main lodge are smaller than rooms in the other three buildings. Beds vary from one queen-size to two double beds. About half the rooms have a lake view and cost $25 per night more than rooms that face the road and front drive. For many returning guests, room 223 with a lake view is a favorite. You may want to avoid rooms 206 and 208, which are above the kitchen and can be noisy. Two connecting rooms on the first floor, one with a queen-size bed and the other with a sofa bed, can be rented as a suite.

*Lake Quinault Lodge*

At one end of the main lodge sixteen Fireplace units, constructed in 1972 and refurbished in 1999, have a gas fireplace, coffeemakers, one queen-size bed, a queen-size sofa bed, and a full bath. Each room has chairs and a table on a private balcony or patio that overlooks the lake. Rooms are entered from outside walkways. Rooms 229 and 230 on the second floor offer excellent views of the lake. The Boathouse at the other end of the main lodge is the only original building (it was built in 1923). A large covered porch wraps around the entire building. The nine rooms in the Boathouse vary by size; beds range from a double plus a twin to two doubles plus two twins. These rooms each have a private bath with a shower but no tub. A second-floor suite has a queen-size bed, a dining table, a sitting area, and a combination shower-tub.

Next to the annex are the thirty-six Lakeside units, constructed in 1990 and refurbished in 1999. The rooms are nicely furnished and fairly spacious, with either two double beds or one king-size bed, a sofa bed, a table and chairs, coffeemaker, and a small balcony that over-looks the lake. Two large fixed windows provide a wonderful view of trees and the lake. The suites have two adjoining rooms. Lakeside rooms are entered from an outside walkway on each floor that is reached from either a stairway or a series of ramps. No elevator is in either building, and handicap-accessible rooms are on the first floor.

Lake Quinault Lodge offers plenty to do in a scenic outdoor setting. It is a wonderful place to spend several days or a week. The spacious lobby with a large brick fireplace and windows that overlook the lake is one of the most comfortable common areas you will find in any national park lodge. It is perfect for reading, playing board games or completing jig-saw puzzles, conversing with friends, or just enjoying the fire on a rainy day. When the weather clears, move out to a picnic table on the spacious back porch or down to one of the lawn chairs near the lake. Activities range from games such as badminton and volleyball, to swimming in the lake or indoor pool, to canoeing. The main lodge dining room has a wall of large windows that offer a great view of the lake. Across the road from the lodge, a coun-try store sells general merchandise, sandwiches, and groceries. A service bar in the lobby sells coffee, espresso, beer, wine, cocktails, and other beverages.

- **ROOMS:** Doubles, triples, and quads. A few rooms sleep more than four. Each room has a private bath, although some rooms have either a bathtub or a shower, but not both. Two handicap-accessible rooms are in the Lakeside units.

- **RESERVATIONS:** Lake Quinault Lodge, P.O. Box 7, Quinault, WA 98575-0007. Phone (800) 562–6672 in Washington or (360) 288–2900 outside Washington; fax (360) 288–2901. First night's payment is required. Three days' cancellation notice required for full refund less a $10 cancellation fee.

- **RATES:** Rates are seasonal. Peak rates apply from June through September, plus all holidays. Value season rates apply the remainder of the year. Lakeside rooms ($150/$110); Lakeside suites ($295/$215); Main Lodge lake view ($140/$110); Main Lodge woodside ($115/$88); Main Lodge suite ($210/$160); Fireplace units ($170/$135); Boathouse lake view ($125/$85); Boathouse woodside ($110/$75); Boathouse suite ($250/$200). Rates quoted are for two adults; each additional person is $10. Children under 5 stay free. Pets are allowed only in the boathouse at $10 per night per pet.

- **LOCATION:** On the south shore of Lake Quinault, 2 miles east of U.S. Highway 101 on South Shore Road.

- **SEASON:** The lodge is open year-round.

- **FOOD:** The dining room serves breakfast ($4.00–$8.00), lunch ($7.00–$12.00), and dinner ($15–$24). Reservations are required for dinner. A general store across the road serves hamburgers, pizza, sandwiches, and beverages and sells groceries, beer, and wine.

- **TRANSPORTATION:** The nearest scheduled air and rail service is in Seattle, where rental cars are available.

- **FACILITIES:** Heated indoor pool, men's and women's dry saunas, game room, boat rentals, swimming beach, auditorium, restaurant, service bar, gift shop, gas station, and general store.

- **ACTIVITIES:** Guided walks, canoeing, boating, badminton, volleyball, horseshoes, and evening programs are popular during summer. Fishing, hiking, swimming, Ping-Pong, and board games are available year-round.

The first log structure to accommodate travelers to Quinault was built in the 1890s. Another facility, Lakeside Inn, was constructed here in 1923. The inn eventually changed its name to The Annex (now The Boathouse) following the construction of Lake Quinault Lodge in 1926. Even though lumber, glass, fixtures, and furniture had to be hauled over 50 miles of dirt road, the lodge was completed in only ten weeks at a cost of $90,000. Guests can still view original stenciled designs on the beamed ceiling of the lobby. Lake Quinault Lodge's most famous guest was President Franklin D. Roosevelt, who visited here in 1937, one year before the creation of Olympic National Park.

# LOG CABIN RESORT

3183 East Beach Road • Port Angeles, WA 98363 • (360) 928–3325
www.logcabinresort.net

*Chalets at Log Cabin Resort*

Log Cabin Resort is a complex of freestanding cabins and linked A-frame chalets scattered in front of and beside a main lodge building that houses several motel-type rooms. The one-story wooden main lodge, constructed in the 1950s, houses the registration desk, a restaurant, a cafe, a lobby, and a small store, and has lots of antiques. There's a parking lot immediately in front of the lodge; other parking is near the chalets and cabins. Virtually all of the cabins and rooms offer good views of beautiful Lake Crescent and the mountains on the southern shore. Log Cabin Resort is located in the far northern section of Olympic National Park, on the north shore of Lake Crescent. It is 21 miles west of Port Angeles, Washington, 3.5 miles off U.S. Highway 101 on East Beach Road.

The resort offers four types of accommodations. All of the rooms have electric heat but no air-conditioning, television, or telephone. The main lodge building has four attached motel-type rooms that each have one queen-size bed, one queen-size futon, and a private bath with a shower but no tub. These rooms are paneled and have a large back window that provides a view of Lake Crescent. A table and two chairs are beside the window and a back door that opens to a private patio with table and chairs. The rooms are entered through an outside door directly beside the parking lot. All four rooms are nonsmoking.

Beside the lodge along the shoreline are two buildings that each have six attached A-frame rooms with small lofts. These rooms have a double bed, a futon, a kitchen sink, and a refrigerator, but no cooking or eating utensils are provided. A second double bed is in the loft reached via a stairway. A private bathroom has a shower but no tub. Windows across the back allow good lake views from both the downstairs and the loft. A cement patio across the back of both buildings has a picnic table and grill for each room. These are all nonsmoking rooms.

Eight rustic cabins constructed in 1928, three with kitchens, are available in a variety of sizes, with several types of beds that range upward from a double and a single bed. The cabins each have a private bath with either a shower or a tub. Each cabin has a covered front porch with chairs that allow guests a good view of the lake and mountains. The three cabins with kitchens that cost about $15 extra per night have a stove, oven, sink, and refrigerator, but no cooking or eating utensils are provided. Six of the cabins are arranged in a semi-circle on a grassy hillside overlooking the lake. A picnic table is in front of each cabin. The least expensive accommodation is four relatively new camping log cabins with electricity but no plumbing. Each cabin has two double beds, but guests are required to provide their own bedding or it can be rented. Outside each cabin is a picnic table and a fire barrel. A common bathroom with showers is located just behind the cabins. These buildings are virtually identical to the camper cabins you will find in KOA campgrounds.

Log Cabin Resort is a fun place to spend several days in a magnificent mountain and lake setting inside Olympic National Park. Guests have plenty to do, with a roped lake swimming area just beside the lodge, boat rentals (canoes, paddleboats, and rowboats), and fishing. A 4-mile-long trail along an old railroad bed beside the lake passes by the resort. A nicely decorated restaurant, which serves breakfast, lunch, and dinner, has a wall of windows that looks out over the lake. A patio area directly in back of the main lodge is available for outside dining. A cafe, The Soda Jerk, serves hot dogs, milk shakes, espresso, other beverages, and ice cream from 8:00 A.M. to 8:00 P.M. The store also sells snack foods and beverages.

- **ROOMS:** Singles, doubles, triples, and quads. The A-frame chalets and some of the cabins can hold up to six persons. No handicap-accessible rooms are available.

- **RESERVATIONS:** 3183 East Beach Road, Port Angeles, WA 98363. Phone (360) 928–3325; fax (360) 928–2088. A deposit of one night's stay is required. A cancellation notice of forty-eight hours is required for a full refund less a $12 fee.

- **RATES:** Lodge rooms ($96); A-frame chalet ($115); cabins ($72–$85); camping log cabins ($49). Rates quoted are for two adults. Each additional person is $10 per night in all lodgings, with the exception of the camping cabins where each additional person is $5.00. Children six and under stay free. There is a $6.00 per night charge for pets.

- **LOCATION:** The resort is 18 miles west of Port Angeles, Washington, on U.S. Highway 101, 3.5 miles on East Beach Road on the north shore of Lake Crescent.

- **SEASON:** April 1 to September 30.

- **FOOD:** An attractive dining room in the main lodge serves breakfast, lunch, and dinner ($9–$22). A cafe serves hot dogs, milk shakes, espresso, other beverages, and ice cream from 8:00 A.M to 8:00 P.M.; microwaveable foods are sold in the store, and a microwave is available for use.

- **TRANSPORTATION:** The nearest scheduled air service is in Port Angeles, where rental cars are available. A Port Angeles city bus stops at the resort twice a day, at 1:00 and 6:00 P.M.

- **FACILITIES:** Swimming beach, boat rental, boat launch, gift shop, limited groceries, laundry, and fishing supplies.

- **ACTIVITIES:** Fishing, hiking, boating, swimming.

- **PETS:** Pets are allowed in the cabins only.

# SOL DUC HOT SPRINGS RESORT

P.O. 2169 • Port Angeles, WA 98362 • (360) 327–3583
pamsdr@aol.com • www.northolympic.com/solduc

*Cabin at Sol Duc Hot Springs Resort*

Sol Duc (a Native American term meaning "sparkling water") Hot Springs Resort includes a single two-story wooden lodge building constructed in the 1980s and twenty-nine modern wooden buildings, for a total of thirty-two rooms. The cabins are clustered in a grassy area in front of the main lodge. The resort is known primarily for more than twenty hot mineral springs that feed pools located behind the lodge. A swimming pool is in the same complex. The resort is situated in the Sol Duc River Valley, surrounded by the heavily treed mountains of Olympic National Park. Sol Duc Hot Springs Resort is 42 miles west of Port Angeles, Washington, in the northwest corner of Olympic National Park. It is on a paved road 12 miles southeast of U.S. Highway 101.

The only accommodations at Sol Duc Hot Springs Resort are twenty-nine cabins constructed in the early 1980s. Three cabins are duplex units. No overnight accommodations are in the main lodge building. The lodge houses a lobby, gift shop, convenience grocery store, restaurant, and registration desk. The twenty-nine freestanding cabins are virtually identical in size and come with two double beds or  two queen-size beds. Each cabin has a front porch with bench and heat but no air-conditioning, telephone, or television. All the cabins have a private bath with a combination shower-tub. Three duplex units have cabins with two double beds and a kitchen furnished with a sink, refrigerator and freezer, stove, and oven. These units, which are near the main lodge, rent for about $20 more per night than cabins without a kitchen.

Most visitors take advantage of the natural hot springs. The resort has three circular pools of hot mineral water and a regular swimming pool, all located behind the main lodge building. The largest hot-water pool and a small shallow pool for children each have mineral water at a temperature of 99° to 101° Fahrenheit. Another small pool has mineral water at a temperature of 105° Fahrenheit. These pools are relatively shallow and designed for sitting and walking, not swimming. A larger swimming pool in the same complex has regular water that is heated. Both the larger mineral water pool and the swimming pool have ramps for handicap access. The mineral water pools and the swimming pool are available without charge to resort cabin guests; other visitors can use the facilities for a fee.

Sol Duc Hot Springs Resort is a good place to unwind. You can hike in the morning, soak in the mineral water pool after lunch, get a professional massage in the late afternoon, take a nap in your cabin, then walk to the lodge for supper. After that, it's time for a good night's sleep so you can start all over again the next morning. A restaurant in the main lodge serves breakfast and dinner, while lunch is available at a deli beside the pool. Plenty of hiking trails near the resort lead into the rain forest and to the beautiful Sol Duc Falls. Evening programs on natural history are occasionally offered at the nearby campground by National Park Service rangers.

*The first hotel at Sol Duc Springs was opened in 1912. The elaborate hotel, constructed by a man who claimed the mineral springs had cured him of a fatal illness, included tennis courts, bowling alleys, golf links, a theater, and a three-story sanatorium with beds for one hundred patients. Unfortunately, sparks from the fireplace ignited the shingle roof and burned down the hotel only four years after its completion. According to legend, the fire short-circuited the hotel's wiring, causing the organ to begin playing Beethoven's "Funeral March" while the building was burning.*

- **ROOMS:** Doubles, triples, and quads. All rooms have a full bath. Handicap-accessible cabins are available.

- **RESERVATIONS:** Sol Duc Hot Springs Resort, P.O. Box 2169, Port Angeles, WA 98362. Phone (360) 327–3583; fax (360) 327–3593. A deposit of one-night's stay is required. A cancellation notice of forty-eight hours is required for a full refund less a $5.00 fee. A two-night minimum is required for holidays.

- **RATES:** Cabin without kitchen ($104). Cabins with kitchen ($125). Rates quoted are for two persons. Each additional person is $15 per night. Children under four stay free.

- **LOCATION:** Twelve miles southeast of U.S. Highway 101. The resort is in the northern part of Olympic National Park, 42 miles from Port Angeles, Washington.

- **SEASON:** The lodge is open to overnight guests from April 1 to October 31. Some facilities are limited in April to mid-May and the last week of September to October 31.

- **FOOD:** A restaurant in the main lodge building serves breakfast ($6.00-$9.00) and dinner ($11–$18). Sandwiches and beverages are available at the poolside deli from 11:00 A.M. to 4:00 P.M. A few groceries, beer, and wine are sold near the registration desk.

- **TRANSPORTATION:** No public transportation is available to the lodge. Port Angeles, Washington, is the nearest city with scheduled air service and rental vehicles.

- **FACILITIES:** Swimming pool, heated mineral pools, restaurant, deli, gift shop, convenience store, and licensed massage practitioners.

- **ACTIVITIES:** Swimming, hiking, fishing, and soaking in mineral baths. Occasional evening National Park Service campfire programs.

# WYOMING

**STATE TOURIST INFORMATION**
(800) 225–5996
www.wyomingtourism.org

## GRAND TETON NATIONAL PARK/ JOHN D. ROCKEFELLER, JR., MEMORIAL PARKWAY

P.O. Drawer 170

Moose, WY 83012

(307) 739–3300

www.nps/gov/grte/

www.nps.gov/jodr/

Grand Teton National Park, which covers nearly 310,000 acres, includes the famous Teton Range, considered by many as the most beautiful mountain range in the United States. The park's three visitor centers are at Moose, Jenny Lake, and Colter Bay. A visitor center jointly operated by the U.S. Forest Service and the City of Jackson is at the north end of Jackson. The 24,000-acre John D. Rockefeller, Jr., Memorial Parkway is a 7½-mile corridor that links the south entrance of Yellowstone National Park with the north entrance to Grand Teton National Park. The Snake River, which flows through both parks, offers excellent float trips. The two parks are in northwestern Wyoming, directly south of the West Thumb area of Yellowstone National Park.

**PARK ENTRANCE FEE:** $20 per vehicle, $15 per motorcycle, or $10 per person, good for seven days. This entrance fee also covers Yellowstone National Park.

### Lodging in Grand Teton National Park

Grand Teton National Park and the John D. Rockefeller, Jr., Memorial Parkway together provide a total of seven lodging facilities. Flagg Ranch Village is the only one of the seven that is located in the parkway, which lies between Grand Teton and Yellowstone. Triangle X Ranch, the only working dude ranch in a national park, is the most unusual lodging facility in the park, and maybe in any park. The least expensive facilities are at Colter Bay. The view

# GRAND TETON NATIONAL PARK/
# JOHN D. ROCKEFELLER, JR., MEMORIAL PARKWAY

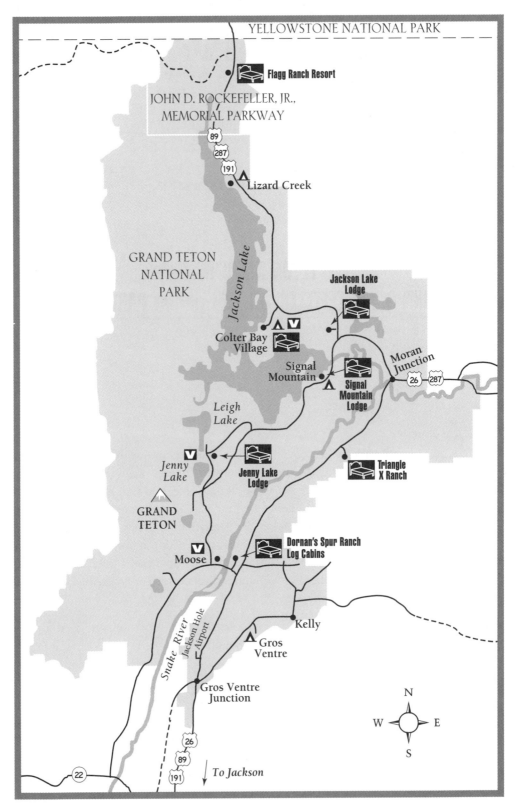

rooms at Jackson Lake Lodge are some of the most upscale accommodations. Jenny Lake Lodge, with a four-star rating, is a quaint facility but is relatively expensive, even considering that horseback riding, bicycles, and breakfast along with a five-course dinner are included in the price.

## COLTER BAY VILLAGE

P.O. Box 240 • Moran, WY 83013 • (307) 543–3100
www.gtlc.com

*Cabins at Colter Bay Village*

Colter Bay Village, a major recreation center for Grand Teton National Park, includes a grocery store, gift and tackle shop, laundromat, the steak & pasta house, deli, and gas station. The lodging facility at Colter Bay consists of 166 rooms in log cabins and sixty-six tent cabins. RV sites and a campground are also available. Colter Bay has no hotel, motel, or main lodge building. A small cabin rental office handles registration for the log cabins, while a separate office farther down the road takes care of registration for the tent cabins. The two types of accommodations are in separate areas, but both are near the restaurants and other facilities of Colter Bay Village. The lodging facilities here are the least expensive in Grand Teton National Park. Colter Bay Village is located on the shore of Jackson Lake, about 15 miles south of the north entrance to Grand Teton National Park.

Colter Bay has two very different types of accommodations. The least expensive lodging is in sixty-six tent cabins. This lodging is about as basic as you will find outside your own tent. The tent cabins are constructed of two canvas walls and a canvas roof connected to two log walls. The cabins each contain a wood stove (wood is not provided but can be purchased), electric light, and two sets of bunk beds with thin vinyl-covered mattresses. A picnic table is on a canvas-covered porch just outside the front door. Guests are responsible for everything else, including sheets, blankets, pillows, and utensils. Sleeping bags, cots, blankets, and pillows can be rented at the registration office. Two rest room facilities without showers are in the immediate area. Showers (fee) are available at a nearby laundry facility. The tent cabins are on a hill and offer views of pine trees, and a few sites have limited views of the Tetons.

Colter Bay also has 166 log cabins clustered in an area of pine trees. Most of the cabins are constructed two, three, or four to a building, but none have a front porch. All except the semiprivate dorm units have a private bath with a shower. All units have heat but no telephone or television. These are nice, roomy units, both inside and out. Parking is immediately in front of each unit. Beds range from one double to two doubles and a single in the one-bedroom units. Forty-two cabins have two bedrooms, one on each side of a common bathroom. These units come with up to two double beds in each of the two bedrooms. One-bedroom cabins 476, 478, 488, and 490 back up to a wooded area and offer more privacy than other cabins. Two-bedroom cabins 480, 484, and 492 are in the same area. One-bedroom cabin 839 and two-bedroom cabin 1055 are freestanding units that probably offer the two best locations for privacy, but both are some distance from the restaurants.

Two log buildings in the cabin area offer a total of nine rooms without private bath. These semiprivate dorm rooms are nice, but occupants must use a community bathroom. Four units in one building each have two twin beds and a hallway bathroom. Five units in a nearby building behind the restaurant are smaller, with a single double bed. Bathrooms here must be entered from outside the building. The building with twin-bed units is far more desirable because the rooms are bigger (especially rooms 466 and 464), the bathroom is inside, and the location is quieter. A guest lounge with couches, chairs, and game tables is nearby.

Colter Bay Village is a pleasant place to spend several days in Grand Teton National Park. Although the main village area, with restaurants, gift shops, grocery store, laundry facility with showers (fee), and the National Park Service visitor center, is generally bustling with people and vehicles, the lodging is far enough away to escape most of the noise and congestion. At the same time, it is close enough that guests can avail themselves of the facilities. If you don't mind a room without a private bath, the semiprivate dorm rooms are the best value, at half the price you will pay for the smallest cabin and the same price as a tent cabin, where you have to supply your own bedding and pay for a shower that is some distance away. Colter Bay Village offers a variety of activities, including horseback riding, raft trips, fishing, lake cruises, and boating. A pool at Jackson Lake Lodge is available to Colter Bay guests.

*Most of the buildings at Colter Bay Village were moved here from other locations around the Jackson Hole area. At one time Jackson Hole had many small dude ranches and tourist resorts, typically consisting of a central lodge building and five to thirty log cabins. After Grand Teton National Park was expanded in 1950 with a gift of 34,000 acres from John D. Rockefeller, Jr., most of the old lodges were closed and many of the cabins were moved via flatbed truck to Colter Bay, where the cabins were modernized with new roofs, electricity, and plumbing. In fact, the existing Colter Bay cabin office was once the old store at Square G Ranch that was located just north of Jenny Lake. The ranch also supplied many of Colter Bay's cabins. Other cabins came from the old Teton Lodge at Moran, the old Jackson Lake Lodge, and the Circle H Guest Ranch. Cabins from several other old resorts were moved to Colter Bay during the 1960s.*

- **ROOMS:** Doubles, triples, and quads. A few two-bedroom units can accommodate up to eight persons. Most of the cabins have a private bath. None of the tent cabins have a private bath. A few cabins are handicap accessible.

- **RESERVATIONS:** Grand Teton Lodge Company, P.O. Box 240, Moran, WY 83013. Phone (307) 543–3100. A one-night deposit is required. A cancellation notice of forty-eight hours is required for a refund less a $10 fee.

- **RATES:** Tent cabins ($33); semiprivate dorm cabins ($33); one-bedroom cabins ($68–$98); two-bedroom cabins ($102–$125). Rates quoted are for two persons. Each additional person is $4.00 per night in tent cabins, $8.50 per night in log cabins. Children eleven and under stay free with an adult.

- **LOCATION:** North section of Grand Teton National Park, 40 miles north of Jackson, Wyoming.

- **SEASON:** Late May to late September for log cabins. Early June to early September for tent cabins.

- **FOOD:** Colter Bay has two relatively inexpensive restaurants. The Chuckwagon Steak & Pasta House serves a hot and cold buffet or a la carte breakfast ($5.50–$8.25) and dinner ($6.75–$17.00). John Colter Deli Court, a cafeteria-style restaurant, serves lunch ($5.00–$7.00), and dinner ($5.00–$7.00). A grocery store is in the village.

- **TRANSPORTATION:** The nearest scheduled air service is in Jackson, Wyoming, where rental cars are available. With advance notice, a shuttle from Jackson Lake Lodge will meet flights. A shuttle (fee charged) operates between Colter Bay and Jackson Lake Lodge.

- **FACILITIES:** Restaurant, food court, snack bar, grocery store, gift shop, tackle shop, stables, marina, boat rental, service station, laundry, National Park Service visitor center with museum and gift shop.

- **ACTIVITIES:** Hiking, fishing, boating, boat cruises, horseback riding, float trips, bus tours to Yellowstone National Park and through Grand Teton National Park, ranger/naturalist talks and walks during the day, evening campfire programs. The swimming pool at Jackson Lake Lodge is available to registered guests from Colter Bay Village.

- **PETS:** Pets are allowed in some cabins.

## DORNAN'S SPUR RANCH LOG CABINS

P.O. Box 39 • Moose, WY 83012 • (307) 733–2522
spur@dornans.com • www.dornans.com

Dornan's Spur Ranch is a lodging complex of twelve modern log cabins clustered in a courtyard behind a log registration building. The cabins are down a small hill from Dornan's, a small commercial center, which includes a grocery and outdoor restaurant. The entire complex sits in a basin next to the Snake River. The cabins are on privately owned land within the boundaries of Grand Teton National Park. Dornan's is located near the south end of the park, at Moose Junction.

*Dornan's Spur Ranch Log Cabins*

The twelve modern duplex log cabins at Dornan's were constructed in 1992. All the cabins have a combination living room/kitchen area, a full bathroom with a shower-tub, and either one or two bedrooms. The kitchen area has a table and chairs. The bedrooms have one queen-size bed with a down comforter, and the living room has a sofa bed. An extra comforter is in the closet. Each cabin has a door off the living room that leads to a small covered wooden deck with table and chairs. A charcoal grill (but not charcoal) is on the porch. The cabins have been sited so that most of the decks offer a view of the magnificent Tetons. Even though the cabins are duplex units, we found that they were designed so that you won't realize you have a neighbor in the same building. The cabins are roomy and have hardwood floors in the living room/kitchen, nice tile in the bathroom, and fully carpeted bedrooms. Voice mail service and Internet access is available in all units. The kitchen is fully equipped, with a full-size refrigerator, stove, oven, coffeemaker, toaster, dishes, and all utensils. All you need to bring is the food. Of course you can walk up the hill and purchase some nice sirloins at the gourmet grocery store. Folks, it doesn't get much better than this.

Dornan's log cabins are among the nicest accommodations in Grand Teton National Park. The cabins are a short walk from Dornan's small commercial area, which has a gas station, a gift shop, a sporting goods store, a chuck wagon restaurant, and a grocery with many specialty gourmet items. A bar/restaurant adjacent to a liquor store, with a sizable variety of wines, has large picture windows that offer spectacular views of the Teton Mountain Range. Dornan's sells and rents various sports equipment and offers both scenic and whitewater float trips. The cabins are open during the winter.

- **ROOMS:** One-bedroom cabins can accommodate up to four persons. Two-bedroom units hold up to six. All cabins have a full bath and full kitchen. One one-bedroom cabin is handicap accessible.

- **RESERVATIONS:** Dornan's Spur Ranch Log Cabins, P.O. Box 39, Moose, WY 83012. Phone (307) 733–2522; fax (307) 739–9098. A deposit of three nights' stay is required during high season, and a deposit for one night is required for the low season. All cancellations result in a $25 charge plus forfeit of deposit if received less than 30 days prior to arrival in high season and less than 14 days prior to arrival in low season.

- **RATES:** Rates are seasonal. High-season rates apply May 20 to September 30 with a three-night minimum; one-bedroom cabin with one to two persons ($140), with three to four persons ($170); two-bedroom cabin with up to six persons ($210). Low-season rates for October 1 to May 19 with a one-night minimum: one-bedroom cabin with one to two persons ($100); with three to four persons ($125); two-bedroom cabin with up to six persons ($150).

- **LOCATION:** South end of Grand Teton National Park, at Moose Junction. The cabins are 12 miles north of Jackson, Wyoming.

- **SEASON:** Open year-round.

- **FOOD:** A chuck wagon outdoor restaurant serves breakfast ($6.00), lunch ($6.00), and all-you-can-eat dinner ($12) during summer months. A bar/restaurant serves salads, pizza, and pasta for lunch and dinner (hours vary). Groceries are available at the store.

- **TRANSPORTATION:** Air service is available to Jackson, Wyoming, where rental vehicles are available.

- **FACILITIES:** Grocery, bar/restaurant, liquor store, outdoor restaurant, gift shop, sports shop, fly-fishing store, gas station.

- **ACTIVITIES:** Hiking, fishing, scenic and whitewater float trips on the Snake River, canoeing, kayaking, mountain biking. Winter activities include cross-country skiing, downhill skiing, and snowmobiling.

> *Dornan's is probably most famous for the gourmet grocery and large wine selection. The grocery has a deli, a bakery, and a selection of gourmet specialty foods. Next door, the liquor store offers 1,500 choices of wine. The chuck wagon dinner offers all you can eat of ribs, roast beef, and stew, beginning at 5:00 P.M.*

## FLAGG RANCH RESORT

P.O. Box 187 • Moran, WY 83013 • (307) 543–2861

info@flaggranch.com • www.flaggranch.com

Flagg Ranch Resort encompasses a modern log-style main lodge building, ninety-two nearby modern log cabin rooms, a service station, and a campground with hookups. Registration for the cabins is just inside the front door of the main lodge, which itself has no accommodations. A large parking lot is in front of the lodge. The main lodge is quite attractive, with a lobby separated from the dining room by a large double-sided stone fireplace. In addition to the dining room and lobby, the main lodge houses a gift shop, grocery with deli, espresso bar/lounge, conference room, and front desk. Flagg Ranch Resort is located at the north end of John D. Rockefeller, Jr., Memorial Parkway, 2 miles south of the south entrance to Yellowstone National Park and 5 miles north of the north entrance to Grand Teton National Park. It is just west of the parkway.

Thirty relatively new buildings house the spacious ninety-two cabin rooms. The buildings are clustered in a natural area of rocks and dirt behind a large parking area (separate from the main lodge parking) and in front of a bluff overlooking the Snake River Valley. Only the rooms in the back with king-size beds have a view of the river valley. They are also in an area with more trees. These back units have a private patio with larger windows and are generally more desirable even though they don't cost more. Sixteen of the buildings are constructed with four cabin rooms each; the remaining fourteen buildings are duplex units with two cabin rooms each. Each cabin unit has heat, telephone, coffeemaker, a full bath with a combination shower-tub, nice furnishings, and a cement porch with two rocking chairs. The units are fully carpeted. None of the rooms have a kitchenette, television, or air-conditioning.

All the cabin rooms at Flagg Ranch are the same size. Your only choice is whether to choose a room with two queen-size beds or a king-size bed plus a lounge chair. Most of the cabin rooms with a king-size bed are in the duplexes. These are farther from the parking area but are probably the best choice. Cabin rooms with two queen-size beds are in the quad buildings located between the parking lot and the duplex units. Three handicap-accessible cabin rooms, each with two queen-size beds, are available. Some cabins are a distance from the parking lot, although sidewalks lead to each building and luggage carts are provided.

*F*lagg Ranch was established between 1910 and 1916 at its present location by an early guide and pioneer in this area, which is believed to have been a favorite camping spot for both native tribes and fur trappers. The ranch is the oldest continually operating resort in the upper Jackson Hole area. It has served as both a dude ranch and a lodging facility, offering overnight accommodations to early trappers and present-day travelers. The ranch name is derived from the flag that flew from the Snake River Military Station, once located here.

*Cabin at Flagg Ranch Resort*

Flagg Ranch offers modern, comfortable lodging at a convenient location between Yellowstone and Grand Teton National Parks. The cabins are relatively large, and the main lodge building has an attractive western decor. Several activities are available for guests, including interpretive tours to Yellowstone and Grand Teton National Parks, one-hour guided trail rides, a 10-mile scenic float trip, and a 30-mile whitewater rafting trip. Flagg Ranch is also a good location to enjoy winter activities in Yellowstone, including heated snowcoach interpretive tours, snowshoeing, cross-country skiing, and snowmobiling. Rentals are available, and an activities information desk is just inside the lodge.

- **ROOMS:** Doubles, triples, and quads. All rooms have a private bath with a combination shower-tub. Three cabins are handicap accessible.

- **RESERVATIONS:** Flagg Ranch Resort, P.O. Box 187, Moran, WY 83013. Phone (800) 443–2311 or (307) 543–2861; fax (307) 543–2356. A deposit of one-night's stay is required. A cancellation notice of six days is required for a full refund, less a $10 cancellation fee.

- **RATES:** Summer ($135); winter ($110). Rates quoted are for two adults. Children seventeen and under stay free. Pets are charged an additional nightly fee. Several packages are available during fall and winter.

- **LOCATION:** North end of John D. Rockefeller, Jr., Memorial Parkway, 2 miles south of the south entrance to Yellowstone National Park. The ranch is just off the highway.

- **SEASON:** Mid-May through mid-October and mid-December through mid-March.

- **FOOD:** A full-service restaurant offers breakfast ($4.00–$6.00), lunch ($5.00–$7.00), and dinner ($10–$20). Groceries are available at a small store in the main lodge. A deli is open from 11:00 A.M. to 5:30 P.M.

- **TRANSPORTATION:** The nearest scheduled air service is in Jackson, Wyoming.

- **FACILITIES:** Restaurant, cocktail lounge, gift shop, grocery store, gas station, coin laundry.

- **ACTIVITIES:** Hiking, river rafting, interpretive tours to Yellowstone National Park and Grand Teton National Park, horseback riding. Winter activities include snowcoach tours, cross-country skiing, snowshoeing, and snowmobiling.

## JACKSON LAKE LODGE

Grand Teton Lodge Company • P.O. Box 250 • Moran, WY 83013 • (307) 543-3100
www.gtlc.com

Jackson Lake Lodge includes a very large central lodge building flanked by numerous multiple-unit wooden buildings that house cottage units. These cottages are hidden from view by surrounding trees. Overnight rooms are also on the third floor of the lodge. The three-story cement lodge sits on a bluff overlooking a large willow meadow and Jackson Lake, both of which are highlighted by the spectacular Teton mountain range. Registration is just inside the main entrance. The lodge building has a large second-floor lobby with two corner fireplaces, many comfortable chairs and sofas, Native American artifacts scattered throughout, and a two-story wall of windows with a picture-perfect view of the Tetons. The lodge also has a dining room, grill, cocktail lounge, gift shop, apparel shop featuring fine western and adventure wear, and a T-shirt shop—all on the second floor; an art gallery on the third-floor balcony has tables and chairs and a great view. A large parking lot is just behind the lodge, and plentiful parking is near each of the cottage units. Arriving guests can use the entrance drive to register and, for guests who will be staying in the lodge, drop off luggage. An elevator is in the lodge. Jackson Lake Lodge is located on the eastern shore of Jackson Lake, 5 miles northwest of Moran Junction, about 35 miles north of the town of Jackson.

The lodge offers four basic types of rooms: view rooms, lodge rooms, cottages, and suites. All rooms have heat, a telephone with data port, and a private bath but no air-conditioning

*Main Lodge Building at Jackson Lake*

or television. Cottages comprise the vast majority of the 385 rooms at the Jackson Lake complex. The thirty-seven rooms in the main lodge, all on the third floor, are mostly alike except for the view. Rooms on the west side of the building, with large windows that provide great views of the Tetons, cost about $90 more per night than similar rooms on the east side. All the rooms have two double beds with a full bathroom. The more costly view rooms also have a refrigerator, a wet bar, and down comforters on the beds. All the rooms in the lodge are quite large and attractively decorated, but none have a balcony. The lodge has one suite, two rooms with a sitting area with a sofa and chairs, one king-size bed, a formal cherrywood dining table, a wet bar, and a refrigerator. The suite offers a view of the mountains.

The 347 cottage rooms each have two double beds, comfortable furniture, a vaulted beamed ceiling, and a full bath. These cottages are quite roomy (bigger than rooms in the main lodge), attractively landscaped, and considerably nicer than a typical motel room. The cottages are mostly one-story with six or eight units to a building. Those with a back patio rent for about $10 per night more than a standard cottage. Twenty rooms in a two-story building with patios and balconies do not offer a mountain view and are categorized as patio rooms. Three two-story buildings house units with a patio/balcony and offer a mountain view. These units offer the same amenities and rent at the same rate as lodge view rooms (about $65 per night more than regular cottage units). Three suites in one of the two-story view buildings have a double-size room, Jacuzzi, one and a half baths, a king- or queen-size bed plus a Murphy bed. One of these suites (room 911) has a full kitchen and

The Amoretti Inn, the original lodge constructed in 1922 at this site, included a main lodge building and thirty cabins. The lodge, which stood near where the 900 building of the current lodge is located, boasted of indoor plumbing in its log cabins. The name was changed to Jackson Lake Lodge in the late 1920s. The old lodge continued to provide overnight rooms until the new Jackson Lake Lodge was completed in June 1955. The old cabins were then moved to Colter Bay, where they were renovated and are still in use today.

wraparound deck. We believe the best value is a nonview room in the lodge. Although limited in number, these are the cheapest rooms available and it is nice being in the same building where all of the facilities are located. If you want a view, walk (or take the elevator) down one flight of stairs to the second-floor lobby.

Jackson Lake Lodge is a pleasant place to stay, especially if you enjoy spectacular scenery. The location offers unsurpassed views, and all of the rooms in the complex are relatively large and comfortable. Several choices are available for dining, and the main dining room on the second floor has western-theme murals and large windows with views that rival those of the lobby. The chef will even cook fish that you catch and clean. The lodge also offers more stores than are usually found in a national park lodge. A variety of activities are available, including swimming in a heated pool, horseback riding, float trips, and park bus tours.

- **ROOMS:** Doubles, triples, and quads. All rooms have a private bath. Several cottages are handicap accessible.

- **RESERVATIONS:** Grand Teton Lodge Company, P.O. Box 240, Moran, WY 83013. Phone (307) 543–3100. If staying two or more nights, a two-night deposit by check or money order is required. Seventy-two-hour cancellation is required for deposit refund less a $25 fee.

- **RATES:** Main lodge: nonview ($120); view ($210); cottages/patios ($146–$156); view rooms ($210); suites ($355–$550). Rates quoted are for two persons. Each additional person is $9.00 per night. Children eleven and under stay free.

- **LOCATION:** Jackson Lake Lodge is located on the eastern shore of Jackson Lake, 6 miles northwest of Moran Junction, about 24 miles north of the town of Moose.

- **SEASON:** Mid-May through mid-October.

- **FOOD:** The main dining room serves buffet or a la carte breakfast ($6.75–$9.95), lunch ($5.50–$10.00), and dinner ($16–$24). Next door, the Pioneer Grill, with U-shaped counters, serves breakfast ($4.50–$8.00), lunch ($6.50–$10.50), and dinner ($8.50–$11). A pool grill with sandwiches, pizza, and ice cream is open for lunch during July and August. An all-you-can-eat barbecue ($15) is offered Monday through Saturday evenings, weather permitting.

- **TRANSPORTATION:** The nearest airport is 26 miles south, in Jackson, Wyoming, where rental cars are available. A shuttle service (fee charged) operates several times a day between Jackson and the Jackson Lake Lodge.

- **FACILITIES:** Restaurant, grill, cocktail lounge, gift shops, apparel shop, newsstand, outdoor heated swimming pool, service station, stable, medical clinic, conference facilities.

- **ACTIVITIES:** Horseback riding, swimming, Snake River float trips, hiking, evening ranger/naturalist programs, boat curises on Jackson Lake, bus tours to Yellowstone National Park and through Grand Teton National Park.

- **PETS:** Pets are allowed in some cottages.

# JENNY LAKE LODGE

P.O. Box 240 • Moran, WY 83013 • (307) 733–4647

www.gtlc.com

*Cabin at Jenny Lake Lodge*

Jenny Lake Lodge features a main log lodge building on a grassy area and thirty-seven log cabins. The complex is located at the base of the Tetons, across the road from beautiful Jenny Lake. The main lodge building, with hardwood floors and vaulted ceilings, houses the registration desk, the dining room, and a cozy lobby with stuffed furniture and a large stone fireplace. Lobby and some dining room windows provide good mountain views. A wooden front deck has chairs and benches that face the mountains. A few of the cabins are freestanding, but most are duplex units. The cabins are nicely spaced in an area of pine trees. The facility is quaint, quiet, well maintained, and expensive. Unlike cabin rates at most other national park facilities, the rates here include breakfast, a five-course dinner, the use of bicycles, and for those so inclined, horseback riding. Lunch is also served for an extra charge. Jenny Lake Lodge is located in the middle of Grand Teton National Park, about 20 miles north of Jackson, Wyoming.

Jenny Lake Lodge has been awarded four stars by Mobil and four diamonds by the American Automobile Association, indicating that it is one of the more upscale lodging units in the United States, let alone in a national park. For example, each cabin is named for a wildflower and has an original watercolor painting of the respective flower. The flower is also painted on a few bathroom tiles. The beds are covered with handmade quilts and down comforters, and robes, an iron and ironing board, and a hairdryer are provided in each cabin.

Two types of cabin accommodations are available at the lodge. Each cabin has a log-beamed vaulted ceiling, hardwood floors, heat, a small refrigerator, a telephone, and a private bath with a shower-tub combination but no air-conditioning or television. Thirty-one one-room cabins vary somewhat in decor, view, and bed configuration, which ranges from one queen-size bed, to a queen-size and a twin, to one king-size bed. Each cabin has a covered front porch with two rocking chairs. Some of the cabins face the mountain range and offer good views from the front porch. Six suites each have a wood stove (wood provided) and sofa bed in the sitting area or living room, an in-wall safe, and a coffeemaker. Configurations vary from two doubles to two queen-size beds to a king-size bed. Five of the suites have two rooms, a living room, and a bedroom. One suite consists of one very large room with a whirlpool tub and a large private patio.

Jenny Lake is a wonderful place where you can relax, hike, and sightsee without worrying about much of anything. The rustic nature of the lodge and cabins provides a taste of the West but with style. Two meals a day and horseback riding are included, the chef will cook any fish you catch, and a valet will take care of your laundry for a nominal charge. Guests of Jenny Lake Lodge have free use of the swimming pools at Jackson Lake Lodge and the Jackson Hole Golf and Tennis Club. If you choose to enjoy an extended stay and want to eat somewhere else, you can obtain vouchers for dinner at Jackson Lake Lodge or the Strutting Grouse Restaurant and Lounge at the Jackson Hole Golf and Tennis Club. Fly into Jackson and the staff will, with prior notice, pick you up. The only downside to Jenny Lake Lodge is the expense. On the other hand, if cost isn't a factor, this is your place to enjoy the Tetons and nature in luxury.

*Jenny Lake Lodge is the descendant of a small 1920s dude ranch called Danny Ranch on the same site. Five cabins and a portion of the original main lodge building remain as part of the existing complex, which gained its current name in 1952. The original log building now houses the lodge dining room. Cabins have been modernized and added to over the years. A major restoration was undertaken in the late 1980s, and four new cabins were added in 1993.*

- **ROOMS:** Singles, doubles, triples, and quads. All cabins have a full bathroom. Handicap-accessible cabins are available.

- **RESERVATIONS:** Grand Teton Lodge Company, P.O. Box 240, Moran, WY 83013. Phone (307) 733–4647. Up to a three-day deposit is required for stays of three days or more. Four-week cancellation is required for a refund less a $35 fee.

- **RATES:** Cabin: one person ($338); two persons ($418); suites: one or two persons ($565–$590). Each additional person is $120 a day. Children two years and under stay free with an adult. Breakfast and dinner are included in the price.

- **LOCATION:** Midsection of Grand Teton National Park, approximately 20 miles north of Jackson, Wyoming.

- **SEASON:** First part of June to early October.

- **FOOD:** A cozy dining room serves breakfast, lunch, and a five-course dinner. Breakfast and dinner are included in the price of a room.

- **TRANSPORTATION:** Daily air service is available from Denver, Colorado, and Salt Lake City, Utah, to Jackson, Wyoming, where rental vehicles are available.

- **FACILITIES:** Restaurant, stables, bicycles, gift shop, concierge service. Guests have free use of the swimming pools at Jackson Lake Lodge and the Jackson Hole Golf and Tennis Club. A National Park Service visitor center is 3 miles away.

■ **ACTIVITIES:** Hiking, fishing, horseback riding, Snake River float trips, and bicycling. Guided walks and evening campfire programs originate at the National Park Service visitor center.

## SIGNAL MOUNTAIN LODGE

P.O. Box 50 • Moran, WY 83103 • (307) 543–2831
signalmtn@rmisp.com • www.signalmtnlodge.com

*Rustic Log Cabins at Signal Mountain Lodge*

Signal Mountain Lodge is a small commercial and lodging complex consisting of seventy-eight cabins and three support buildings, including a registration building, a separate restaurant building, and a convenience store with limited supplies and groceries. The cabins are a short distance from the registration building, but the complex is small enough that guests can walk to the restaurant, store, and registration building. The lodge is in an attractive setting on the east shore of Jackson Lake, with views of the Tetons in the distance. Signal Mountain is in the middle of Grand Teton National Park, 7 miles west of the Moran entrance station and about 4 miles south of Jackson Lake Lodge.

The registration building at Signal Mountain has a small but comfortable lobby area with television, tables, couches, and stuffed chairs. The restaurant building houses The Peaks Restaurant, the Trapper Grill, a lounge, a very nice gift shop, and a clothing store. Both the restaurant and grill have windows that provide an excellent view of Jackson Lake and the Tetons. Food is also available in the lounge and on an outside deck. This building was renovated in 2000 and is handicap accessible.

Five classifications of cabins are offered at Signal Mountain Lodge. The cabins are constructed two, three, or four to a building. All of the cabins have electric heat, a telephone, and a full bath with a combination shower-tub, but no air-conditioning or television. The least expensive accommodation is the Rustic Log cabin, available in both one- and two-bedroom versions. One-bedroom units come with bedding that ranges from one double bed to two double beds and a sofa bed. The two-bedroom units have a bedroom on each side of a bathroom and come with two double beds; two doubles, a twin, and a sofa bed; or three double beds. Five of the one-bedroom units have fireplaces and rent for about $15 per night extra; firewood is provided. Most of the Rustic Log cabins have a porch with chairs, but the views are obscured by other lodging units. Cabins 137, 139, 143, 146, and 147 do provide lake views.

Twelve larger Country Rooms scattered about the complex have a queen-size bed and a sofa bed, two queen-size beds, or one king-size bed. These units are more modern motel-style rooms, and each has a small refrigerator. They rent for about $15 more per night than the one-bedroom Rustic Log cabins. Three Deluxe Country Rooms, all in the same building, each has a living room and a bedroom with a king-size bed. They also have a small refrigerator and stone fireplace and rent for about $50 per night more than the regular Country Rooms.

Twenty-eight Lakefront Retreats are constructed four units to a building, with two units up and two units down. These large one-room units overlook Lake Jackson and offer great views of the mountains. The units have a living room/kitchen with a sofa bed, microwave, stove top, and refrigerator. The bedroom area, with either two queen-size or a king-size bed, can be closed off. A coffeepot and limited cookware are included, but utensils and dishes are not. These rent for about $15 more than the Deluxe Country Rooms.

Hole *is a term that was used by fur trappers to describe a high valley surrounded by mountains. The valley of Jackson Hole is named for trapper David Jackson, who reportedly spent the winter months in 1829 along the shore of Jackson Lake. Jackson Hole is 40 miles in length and varies from 8 to 15 miles in width.*

One Family Bungalow has two units that can be rented as a whole or separately. One unit comprises a bedroom with two queen-size beds and a sofa bed, as well as a separate kitchen with a microwave, stove top, oven, and full-size refrigerator. Limited cookware is provided, but utensils and dishes are not. The attached unit has one room with a queen-size bed, sofa bed, and small refrigerator. The building has a large deck with picnic tables and an outdoor barbecue.

One three-room cabin called the Home Away from Home has two queen-size beds in the bedroom, a sofa bed and a fireplace in the living room, and a kitchen with limited cookware and a laundry area.

Signal Mountain Lodge is a relatively quiet facility in a beautiful setting. Everything is on a small scale, from the registration building, to the dining room, to the individual cabin units. It lacks the large lobby area that makes Jackson Lake Lodge so attractive, but the same views are available with smaller crowds.

■ **ROOMS:** Doubles, triples, and quads. Several rooms with a sofa bed can handle up to six persons. All rooms have a private bath. No handicap-accessible rooms are available.

■ **RESERVATIONS:** Signal Mountain Lodge, P.O. Box 50, Moran, WY 83013. Phone (307) 543–2831, Monday through Friday, from 8:00 A.M. to 5:00 P.M. Mountain Standard Time; open twenty-four hours May through early October. A deposit of one night's stay is required. A cancellation notice of seventy-two hours is required for a refund.

■ **RATES:** Rustic Log Cabins: one room ($92–$105); with a fireplace ($109); two rooms ($119–$125); Country Rooms ($109); Deluxe Country Rooms ($157); Lakefront Retreats ($172); Family Bungalow–one room ($137), two rooms ($184); Home Away from Home ($216). Rates are by the room and not the number of occupants.

- **LOCATION:** On Jackson Lake, 7 miles west of Moran Junction.

- **SEASON:** Mid-May to mid-October.

- **FOOD:** A restaurant and grill offer breakfast ($5.00–$7.00), lunch ($5.00–$7.00), and dinner ($11–$20). Food is also served in the lounge and on the outside deck. Limited groceries are in a convenience store. A short distance down the road is Leeks Marina & Pizzeria.

- **TRANSPORTATION:** The nearest scheduled air service is in Jackson, Wyoming, where rental vehicles are available.

- **FACILITIES:** Marina with boat rentals, restaurant, grill, gift shop, clothing store, convenience store, gas station.

- **ACTIVITIES:** Boating, canoeing, fishing, hiking, guided fishing trips, evening naturalist programs, float trips.

## TRIANGLE X RANCH

2 Triangle X Ranch Road • Moose, WY 83012 • (307) 733–2183
trianglexranch@wyoming.com • www.trianglex.com

*One-Bedroom and Two-Bedroom Cabins at Triangle X Ranch*

Triangle X Ranch is the only operating dude ranch in a national park. It has also been used as the location for several movies, including John Wayne's first picture and the classic western *Shane*. The ranch has all of the buildings you would expect in a working ranch, as well as twenty-one freestanding log cabins that provide overnight accommodations. The ranch is on a hill overlooking Jackson Hole and the Teton Mountain Range. One of the many buildings in the ranch complex has the dining room and a living room with a fireplace. All of the cabins are within a short walking distance of the dining room. Triangle X requires a minimum stay of one week (June through August) beginning and ending on Sunday. The ranch is particularly appealing to people who enjoy horseback riding, since this is the main activity for guests. Triangle X Ranch is on the eastern side of Grand Teton National Park, 25 miles north of Jackson, Wyoming, just off U.S. Highways 26, 89, and 191. It is 6 miles south of Moran Junction.

A total of twenty-one log cabins are available for guests. All of the cabins have electricity, heat, and a private bathroom with a combination shower-tub but no telephone or television. Cabins are available with one, two, and three bedrooms. The two- and three-bedroom units each have two full bathrooms. Each comes with one or two queen-size beds. While all cabins have a very rustic outside appearance, the interiors are quite nice, with paneled walls and heavy pine furniture. Most of the ceilings are slightly vaulted. Each cabin has a covered front porch with chairs and views of the Tetons.

Triangle X Ranch is a wonderful place to stay if you enjoy mountain scenery, horseback riding, and an overall western experience. With each guest spending an entire week at the ranch, it is a certainty you will make some friends during your stay here. Three meals a day, served family-style, and horseback riding (except Sunday) are included as part of the package. Meals are announced by the ring of the dinner bell. Each guest is assigned his or her own horse at the beginning of the week's stay. The evenings each have a different scheduled activity, including square dancing, ranger talks, cookouts, and campfire gatherings. Triangle X offers float trips and pack trips at extra cost.

*Triangle X Ranch has served as home to four generations of the same family. The ranch was purchased by John S. Turner in the summer of 1926. Turner started construction of his home and welcomed guests the same summer. The ranch was self-sufficient, with refrigeration provided by ice cut from nearby ponds and stored in piles of sawdust. In the late 1920s Turner sold the property to a land company owned by John D. Rockefeller, who eventually donated the land to the federal government. Today the grandsons of John Turner operate the ranch as a concessionaire of the National Park Service.*

Children five to twelve receive special attention at Triangle X. They eat in a separate dining room from teenagers and adults, and their activities, including horseback riding, are especially designed for their age group.

Winter brings a different environment with different activities. The ranch reduces the required stay to two nights (except for New Year's), and a shuttle service is available without charge to the Jackson Hole airport and to the Jackson Hole Ski Resort. Triangle X provides complimentary cross-country skis and snowshoes. In addition, guided snowmobile trips can be arranged (fee charged). A hot tub is available for guests. Meals are more formal, with selections served to order.

- **ROOMS:** One to three persons in a one-bedroom unit; three to five persons in a two-bedroom unit; five to six persons in a three-bedroom cabin. All cabins have a private bath with a combination shower-tub. One cabin is handicap accessible.

- **RESERVATIONS:** Triangle X Ranch, 2 Triangle X Ranch Road, Moose, WY 83012. Phone (307) 733–2183; fax (307) 733–8685. Minimum stay of one week during June, July, and August. Four days at other times during the summer season. A two-day minimum is required during the winter season. Required deposit of 30 percent of total cost. Credit cards are not accepted during the summer season. When a cancellation occurs, a refund is given if the cabin can be filled.

- **RATES:** All rates are per person. One-bedroom cabin (one person $1,350, two persons $1,090, three persons $965); two-bedroom cabin (three persons $1,175, four persons

$1,050, five persons $965); three-bedroom cabin (five persons $1,070, six persons $965). Prices reduced before June 1 and after September 1. Winter rates are $90 per night per person. A 15 percent charge for gratuities is added to all bills. Rates include three meals a day and horseback riding (summer).

- ■ **LOCATION:** East side of Grand Teton National Park, 25 miles north of Jackson, Wyoming. The ranch is 6 miles south of Moran Junction, on U.S. Highways 26, 89, and 191.

- ■ **SEASON:** Summer season: late May to the first week in November. Winter season: end of December through the end of March.

- ■ **FOOD:** Three meals a day are served in the ranch dining room. Meals are included in the quoted rates.

- ■ **TRANSPORTATION:** Scheduled airlines serve Jackson Hole, Wyoming, where rental vehicles are available. Salt Lake City, Utah is the nearest large airport.

- ■ **FACILITIES:** Corrals, dining room, laundry, gift shop.

- ■ **ACTIVITIES:** Summer: Horseback riding, breakfast and dinner cookouts, square dancing, fishing, hiking, float trips. Pack trips and hunting trips can also be arranged. Winter: Cross-country skiing, snowmobiling, snowshoeing, wildlife viewing, or just relaxing in the hot tub.

# YELLOWSTONE NATIONAL PARK

National Park Service
P.O. Box 168
Yellowstone National Park, WY 82190
(307) 344–7381
www.nps.gov/yell

Yellowstone National Park, the world's first and probably best-known national park, comprises nearly 3,400 square miles of lakes, waterfalls, mountains, and some 10,000 geysers and hot springs. The park has almost 300 miles of roads. Most of the major attractions are near Grand Loop Road, which makes a figure eight in the park's central area. The road's east side provides access to canyons, mountains, and waterfalls, while the west side leads to areas of thermal activity. Most of the park is in the northwestern corner of Wyoming, with overlapping strips in Montana and Idaho.

**PARK ENTRANCE FEE:** $20.00 per vehicle, $15.00 per motorcycle, or $5.00 per person, good for seven days. This entrance fee also covers Grand Teton National Park and the connecting parkway.

## 🛏 Lodging in Yellowstone National Park

Yellowstone has nine lodging facilities, the best known of which is Old Faithful Inn. Two other lodges are in the Old Faithful area. Other lodges are at Grant Village, Mammoth Hot

# YELLOWSTONE NATIONAL PARK

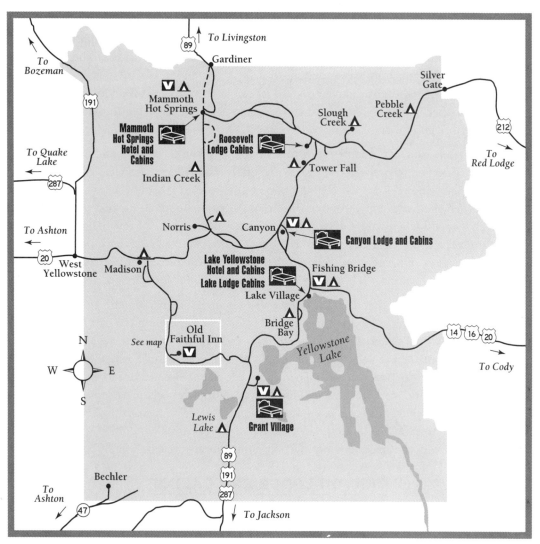

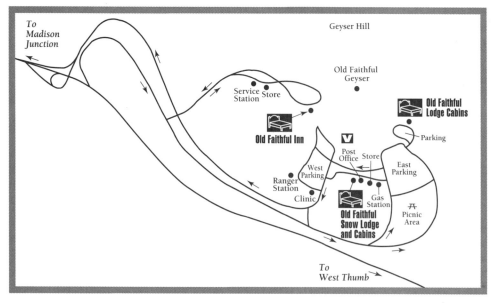

Springs, Roosevelt, Canyon Village, and Lake Village. Accommodations range from very rustic cabins, to a wonderful hundred-year-old hotel, to relatively new motel-type accommodations. All nine of the lodging facilities are operated by the same firm, so the registration desk at any of the lodges can determine whether vacancies exist at any of the other locations. Yellowstone is very busy, so it is important to make reservations as early as possible. If you are unable to obtain a reservation when you first call, it may pay to call periodically, because openings may become available due to cancellations. You may be able to obtain a room as a walk-in, although you aren't likely to have much choice regarding the facility or cost.

- **RESERVATIONS FOR ALL ACCOMMODATIONS INSIDE THE PARK:** Yellowstone National Park Lodges (operated by Amfac Parks & Resorts), Reservations Office, P.O. Box 165, Yellowstone National Park, WY 82190. Phone (307) 344–7311; fax (307) 344–7456; or book on the Web site, www.TravelYellowstone.com. Deposit is required for first night's lodging at each location where you will be staying. Cancellation notice of forty-eight hours during the summer season required for refund of deposit. Fourteen days' advance notice required for cancellation of winter reservations. If traveling in an off-season, be sure to inquire about seasonal specials, such as Early Bird, Fall, and Winter Kickoff specials.

- **TRANSPORTATION:** Scheduled airlines serve Bozeman, Montana, on the northwest side; West Yellowstone, Montana, on the west side; Cody, Wyoming, on the east side; Jackson, Wyoming, south of Grand Teton National Park, and Billings, Montana, which is 129 miles to the northeast. Rental vehicles are available at all five locations. Scheduled shuttle service is available to Bozeman and Livingston, Montana. Bus service operates between Cody and the park. No public transportation system operates within Yellowstone National Park, although scenic bus tours along the upper and lower loop roads are scheduled from various lodging locations in the park. Heavy traffic, poor road conditions, and seemingly continual repairs can make driving in Yellowstone an aggravating affair.

## CANYON LODGE AND CABINS

Yellowstone National Park, WY 82190 • (307) 344–7331

www.TravelYellowstone.com

Canyon Lodge is a large commercial complex that includes hundreds of cabins and two newer lodge buildings. Most of the 613 rooms at Canyon Lodge are one-story cabins constructed four or eight to a building. The village also has a large general store/coffee shop, restaurant, snack bar, lounge, and gift shop. This is a busy commercial center of the park, but most of the overnight rooms are far enough away that you will be able to enjoy a relatively quiet stay. It is also large enough that you may have a hike to the restaurant, depending on the location of your cabin. The registration desk is in a separate building near the cafeteria and restaurant. After registering, you will need to drive to your room. The village takes its name from the Grand Canyon of the Yellowstone River, a half mile away. Canyon Village is near the center of the park, 42 miles from the east entrance and 40 miles from the west entrance at West Yellowstone.

Canyon Lodge and Cabins has four types of accommodations. All of the rooms have heat and private baths but no telephone, television, or air-conditioning. None of the rooms have balconies, including those in the lodge buildings. Adequate parking is available near all the

*Dunraven Lodge at Canyon Lodge and Cabins*

rooms. The least expensive and most plentiful lodging are the 336 Pioneer cabins and ninety-six Frontier cabins built in the 1950s; these are concentrated in two large sections behind the main lodge building. These cabins are all constructed eight to a building. The bathroom has a shower but no tub. Cabin size varies according to beds, which range from two twin beds to two doubles and a single. All of the cabins in each category rent for the same rate even though room size varies, so it is best to ask for a room with two double beds.

One hundred Western cabins are constructed four or six units to a building. These units are larger, are newer (1969), and rent for about $30 more than the Frontier units. Each Western cabin has two double beds, a table with two chairs, and a bathroom with a shower-tub combination. Like most of the Pioneer and Frontier cabins, the Western units are fairly widely spaced among pine trees, which allows for some privacy. Some of the units are constructed with windows on two sides of each room.

Two attractive lodge buildings offer nearly identical accommodations with large rooms, two double beds (in all but a few rooms), exceptional lodgepole pine furniture, and a bath with a shower-tub combination. The two are connected by a cement walkway, and adequate parking is available. Cascade Lodge, constructed in 1993, has thirty-seven rooms on three floors. Dunraven Lodge, completed in spring 1999, with forty-four rooms on four floors, is the newest facility in Yellowstone National Park. A modest lobby on the second floor of Dunraven serves both lodges. The two buildings offer a total of seven handicap-accessible rooms.

The Pioneer cabins are Canyon's best value for budget-conscious travelers. These are the same size as the more expensive Frontier cabins, and the differences aren't worth the extra cost. For those seeking more upscale accommodations, we would choose either of the lodge units over a Western cabin. Of the two, you might want to select the newer Dunraven Lodge, which has an elevator and offers in-room coffeemakers. Try for second- or

*Canyon Lodge is within walking distance of the North Rim of the Grand Canyon of the Yellowstone. A half-mile trail leads from cabin P26 to the North Rim's Grandview Point. From here North Rim Trail leads either 1 mile northeast to Inspiration Point or about 1 mile southwest to the Lower Falls. The entire North Rim Trail, which begins at South Rim Drive Bridge and ends at Inspiration Point, is slightly less than 3 miles, and a portion of it is paved. A variety of trails are also on the south side of the canyon.*

third-floor rooms on the south side (odd-numbered rooms) that face the woods rather than the parking lot. Dunraven rooms on the fourth floor are somewhat smaller than rooms on the other floors. Rooms on the third floor of Cascade, especially 305 and 307, are larger and offer views of the woods.

Canyon Lodge and Cabins is the most centrally located of all the lodging facilities at Yellowstone National Park, so it is a perfect place to settle in and explore this large park. Canyon Village offers just about anything you desire when you return from a long day of touring. The location, number of lodging places, and variety of facilities make this a very busy place. A restaurant, cafeteria, coffee shop, and deli offer an array of meals and prices. You will also find gift shops, a nature store, and a large general store with books, supplies, gifts, and groceries. A cocktail lounge with a large fireplace and post office are also in the village. A National Park Service visitor center has a geology display. Stables are available for horseback riding.

- **ROOMS:** Doubles, triples, and quads. All rooms have a private bath. Seven handicap-accessible rooms are available in the lodge buildings.

- **RATES:** Pioneer cabins ($54); Frontier cabins ($78); Western cabins ($111); Lodge rooms ($121). Each additional person is $10 per night. Children eleven and under stay free.

- **LOCATION:** Near the middle of Yellowstone National Park, 40 miles from the west entrance at West Yellowstone.

- **SEASON:** June through the first part of September.

- **FOOD:** Several eating options are available in the Canyon commercial center, which is a long walk from the two lodge buildings and many of the cabins. A dining room offers breakfast ($4.00–$7.00), lunch ($5.00–$8.00), and dinner ($8.00–$13.00). A less expensive cafeteria serves three meals a day with dinner costing from $5.00 to $10.00. The deli serves rotisserie chicken, sandwiches, salads, drinks, and ice cream. A coffee shop in the Hamilton Stores building serves sandwiches, hamburgers, ice cream, and beverages. A lounge serves appetizers.

- **FACILITIES:** Restaurant, cafeteria, deli, coffee shop, lounge, gift shop, laundry, general store with groceries, nature store, post office, gas station, stables, National Park Service visitor center.

- **ACTIVITIES:** Horseback riding, hiking, motor coach excursions, evening ranger program.

## GRANT VILLAGE

Yellowstone National Park, WY 82190 • (307) 344–7311
www.TravelYellowstone.com

Grant Village includes a registration building plus six modern two-story lodge buildings, each with about fifty rooms. The wooden lodge buildings, constructed from 1982 to 1984, sit staggered across a hillside above the south shore of the West Thumb of Yellowstone Lake. Rooms on each side of the building are entered from a central corridor on each floor. Half the rooms in each of the six lodge buildings face the lake; the other half face parking areas and a pine forest. Each building has a small first-floor lobby with chairs, while

*Grant Village*

the newer buildings also have a small second-floor lobby with tables and chairs. Adequate parking is directly beside each building. There are no elevators in the buildings, but bell service is available at the registration building. Grant Village is located in the south end of Yellowstone, in the West Thumb area. It is the southernmost lodging facility in the park, 20 miles north of the south entrance to Yellowstone.

Two types of rooms are offered at Grant Village. All rooms have heat, a telephone, and a private bath. Most bathrooms have a shower, but some offer a combination shower-tub. None of the rooms have air-conditioning, television, or a balcony. All of the rooms are of good size, but approximately 200 rooms in four newer buildings are a little larger and cost about $20 extra per night. The two classes of rooms are so similar that the small price difference probably isn't worth paying. Rooms facing the lake and rooms facing the parking area rent for the same price, so it is best to request a lakeside room. Second-floor lakeside rooms in Lodge A and Lodge F, which are closest to the lake, have the best window views. The eight corner rooms in the four newer buildings have an extra side window. A total of twelve handicap-accessible rooms are available.

Grant Village is a good place to spend a restful night at Yellowstone, especially if you are arriving late or will be leaving from the park's south entrance. The village is away from the park's heavily visited tourist areas and free from the congestion they attract. Another advantage is that the village is only 19 miles from the park's main attraction, Old Faithful. In addition to lodging, Grant Village also has two restaurants, a grill, a post office, a gift shop, a service station, laundry facilities, a boat launch, and a National Park Service visitor center. Three eating establishments with varying menus and prices are separate but only a short walk from the lodges. The Grant Village Dining Room near Lodge A is an unusual building, with a high vaulted wooden ceiling and windows that offer a view of Yellowstone Lake. A cozy cocktail lounge is just off the entrance area. A less expensive restaurant, Lake House, is directly on the lake and serves breakfast and dinner. Windows on three sides of the building provide good views of the lake. A general store near the registration building houses a grill that serves breakfast, sandwiches, ice cream, and beverages. A salad bar is also available.

- **ROOMS:** Doubles, triples, and quads. All rooms have a private bath with shower or combination shower-tub. Handicap-accessible rooms are available.

- **RATES:** Newer rooms ($111); older rooms ($89). Each additional person is $10 per night. Children eleven and under stay free.

- **LOCATION:** At the south end of the park, 20 miles north of the south entrance.

- **SEASON:** The end of May through the first of October.

- **FOOD:** Grant Village Dining Room serves breakfast ($4.00-$7.00), lunch ($5.00–$7.00), and dinner ($13–$18) in an attractive building. Lake House serves breakfast ($3.50–$6.50) and dinner ($8.00–$11.00) only. A grill in the general store serves breakfast, sandwiches, and beverages. The store also has a good offering of groceries.

- **FACILITIES:** Two restaurants, cocktail lounge, grill, general store, gift shop, service station, boat ramp, picnic area, post office, laundry, National Park Service visitor center.

- **ACTIVITIES:** Hiking, fishing, evening ranger programs at the amphitheater.

## LAKE LODGE CABINS

Yellowstone National Park, WY 82190 • (307) 344–7311

www.TravelYellowstone.com

*Pioneer Cabins at Lake Lodge Cabins*

Lake Lodge Cabins is a complex consisting of a large log lodge building with a registration desk and support services, plus 186 wood cabins situated on a hill overlooking the lodge. No guest rooms are in the main registration building, which has a cafeteria, a gift shop, a cocktail lounge, and a large lobby area with two fireplaces. The lodge building has a large covered front porch with chairs and overlooks Yellowstone Lake. The entire complex sits back from the lake, and the cabins offer no lake views. Parking is adjacent to each cabin unit. The lodge is located at Lake Village, in the eastern section of Yellowstone National Park. It is 30 miles from the east entrance station to the park.

Lake Lodge Cabins offers two types of cabin accommodations. All of the cabins have heat and private bath with shower but no tub. There is no air-conditioning, telephone, or television in any of the cabins. Most of the cabins are constructed four to a building, although a few buildings have two units and others have six. The least expensive alternative is the eighty-six Pioneer cabins. The smallest Pioneer units have one double bed; larger units have two double beds and a single bed. These cabins look very rustic on the outside, but the interior is fairly nice. The cabins are near the lodge in an area devoid of trees.

One hundred Western cabins are identical to those at Canyon Lodge and Cabins. All are the same size and come with two double beds or two double beds and a single bed. These cabins are bigger than the Pioneer units and cost twice as much. All cabins have private bathrooms, most with a combination shower-tub. The layouts differ from building to building so that a few Western cabins have sliding glass doors with a small porch in the back, while others do not. Other units are laid out so that each cabin has windows in two walls. Western cabins toward the rear of the complex (units F, G, H, and J) are spaced farther apart and are surrounded by trees.

Lake Lodge Cabins provides modestly priced accommodations. The Lake Village area is very scenic and relatively quiet, at least compared with the Old Faithful area. These are also the closest accommodations to Fishing Bridge and Bridge Bay Marina. The less expensive Pioneer cabins are a good value but offer little more than basic lodging.

> Lake Lodge was constructed during the 1920s to provide mid-level accommodations to travelers who didn't want to tent camp but who couldn't afford the more expensive hotels. The East Wing was added as a dining area (currently the cafeteria) in 1926, and the West Wing was built as a dance hall (now an employee recreation hall) in the same year. The front porch of Lake Lodge was added in 1929.

- **ROOMS:** Doubles, triples, and quads. A few rooms have a single bed for a fifth person. All cabins have private baths. No handicap-accessible rooms are available.

- **RATES:** Pioneer cabins ($50); Western cabins ($111). Rates quoted are for two adults. Each additional person is $10 per night. Children eleven and under stay free with an adult.

- **LOCATION:** On the north shore of Yellowstone Lake, in the east-central section of Yellowstone National Park. The lodge is approximately 30 miles from the east park entrance and 43 miles from the south entrance.

- **SEASON:** Mid-June to mid-September.

- **FOOD:** A cafeteria is open for breakfast ($2.00–$4.00), lunch ($4.00–$6.00), and dinner ($6.00–$12.00). A nearby general store has a coffee shop and limited groceries. Nearby Lake Yellowstone Hotel has a lovely dining room and a small deli.

- **FACILITIES:** Gift shop, laundry, cafeteria, cocktail lounge. A general store is a short walk from the lodge. Nearby Lake Yellowstone Hotel offers additional facilities.

- **ACTIVITIES:** Hiking, fishing. Nearby Bridge Bay Marina offers boat tours on Lake Yellowstone, boat rentals, and fishing guides.

# LAKE YELLOWSTONE HOTEL AND CABINS

Yellowstone National Park, WY 82190 • (307) 344–7311

www.TravelYellowstone.com

*Lake Yellowstone Hotel*

Lake Yellowstone Hotel and Cabins, also called Lake Hotel, consists of a three- and four-story hotel building, an adjacent two-story Annex, and 110 closely clustered cabin units that are located behind the hotel. The hotel, Annex, and cabins offer a total of 296 rooms. The large hotel is the oldest hotel in the park today. An extensive renovation to return the hotel to its 1920s appearance was completed in 1991. The first floor houses the registration desk, lobby, and dining room. The wonderful lobby and sunroom, with some of the hotel's original wicker furniture, has large windows that overlook Yellowstone Lake. The 1920s-era dining room has windows with a similar view. A drive to the front of the hotel provides access for registration and dropping off luggage. The parking area is on the back side of the hotel. Lake Yellowstone Hotel and Cabins is located in the east-central portion of Yellowstone National Park, on the north shore of Yellowstone Lake. It is 30 miles from the east entrance to the park.

Lake Yellowstone Hotel and Cabins offers three basic types of lodging: hotel rooms, Annex rooms, and cabins. The hotel has 158 rooms on four floors, all attractively decorated. An elevator is located in the East Wing, and bell service is available. Hotel rooms all have full baths, heat, and telephone but no air-conditioning or television. Room size varies, with the largest rooms located in the West Wing. Beds range from one to three queen-size beds. A few rooms have two double beds. Rooms with a lake view are priced about $10 per night higher than rooms facing the parking lot. One suite with lake views has a queen-size bed in each of two bedrooms, two full bathrooms, and a large living room with a wet bar, refrigerator, and coffeemaker. The suite is large and as nice as you will find in any historic hotel.

The Annex has thirty-six rooms, which vary in size and configuration. All of the rooms have heat, private bath with shower, and telephone but no air-conditioning or television. Annex rooms cost about $50 per night less than nonview rooms in the hotel. Some Annex rooms have one double bed, while others have two. None of the rooms in the Annex offer particularly good views, although those on the east side look out at pine trees, while those on the west side overlook the parking area. The Annex also has five handicap-accessible rooms. The first floor has a very small lobby area, with several stuffed chairs and couches.

Frontier Cabin units are mostly constructed as duplexes, with rooms that back up to one another. The cabins are closely clustered in an area devoid of trees behind the hotel and away from the lake. Parking is available beside each cabin unit. The cabins vary in size, and come with either two double beds or two double beds plus a single bed. All the cabins have a private bath with shower only (one unit has a tub only). The cabins are plain but of adequate size. Some have paneled interiors, and all are carpeted. Cabin units rent for about half the price of a room at the hotel.

Lake Yellowstone Hotel is a quiet place to spend your vacation in Yellowstone National Park. The hotel captures the ambience of an earlier period and is reminiscent of Yosemite's even older Wawona Hotel. The airy and bright lobby area is a great place to read a book, with occasional glances out the windows at the lake. A pianist or string quartet play here in the evenings. The equally delightful dining room, just off the lobby, offers three meals a day. A small deli, just down the hall, serves sandwiches, ice cream, and beverages. The hotel and cabins are a short walk from a general store and Lake Lodge Cabins, which offers a cafeteria and laundry facilities. If you want an inexpensive place to stay, choose the cabins. If you want to experience Yellowstone in a grand old hotel, opt for a room in the main hotel.

*Construction on Lake Yellowstone Hotel began in 1889 in an area once populated by native tribes, fur trappers, and mountain men. The first guests arrived two years later. Additions engineered by the architect of Old Faithful Inn in the early 1900s nearly tripled the number of rooms at the hotel to 210. The East Wing, with 113 additional rooms, was completed in the early 1920s. The hotel had fallen into disrepair by the 1980s, when a decade-long renovation was initiated to return the building to its glory years of the 1920s.*

- **ROOMS:** Doubles, triples, and quads. A few rooms sleep up to six. All rooms, including cabins, have private bathrooms. Five handicap-accessible rooms are available in the Annex.

- **RATES:** Frontier Cabins ($83); Annex ($100); hotel: nonview ($150); view ($160); suite ($392). Children eleven and under stay free. Each additional person is $10 per night.

- **LOCATION:** East-central section of the park, on the north shore of Yellowstone Lake. The hotel is 30 miles from the park's east entrance.

- **SEASON:** From mid-May to first of October.

- **FOOD:** A 1920s-era hotel dining room serves breakfast ($4.00–$6.50), lunch ($5.00–$8.00), and dinner ($10–$19). A breakfast buffet ($7.00) is available. A deli on the first floor opens from 10:30 A.M. to 9:00 P.M. for sandwiches, soups, beverages, and ice cream. A cafeteria at Lake Lodge Cabins, a short walk from the hotel, serves three meals a day.

- **FACILITIES:** Hospital, restaurant, small deli, gift shop, ATM, post office. Nearby is a general store. Lake Lodge Cabins has a cafeteria and laundry facilities.

■ **ACTIVITIES:** Hiking, fishing, evening music in the hotel lobby. Nearby Bridge Bay Marina offers boat tours on Lake Yellowstone, boat rentals, and fishing guides.

## MAMMOTH HOT SPRINGS HOTEL AND CABINS

Yellowstone National Park, WY 82190 • (307) 344–7311
www.TravelYellowstone.com

*Mammoth Hot Springs Hotel*

If you have ever wanted to stay at an old Army fort, then Mammoth Hot Springs is your place. The hotel and some of the surrounding buildings were once part of a small military post that served as headquarters for the U.S. Army when it was in charge of this park. Some of the original Army buildings continue in use as administrative offices for personnel of the National Park Service. The current lodging complex at Mammoth comprises a four-story hotel plus 115 cabin units that together provide a total of 212 rooms. A separate and smaller lodge building adjacent to the hotel is open in winter months for guests but is used in summer for employee housing.

Registration for all lodging is in the first-floor lobby of the hotel. A covered porch runs across the front of the hotel. Bell service is available at the front desk. The cabin units are clustered in grassy areas behind the hotel. Each cabin has its own parking area, and adequate parking is available for the hotel. Mammoth Hot Springs Hotel and Cabins is located near the north entrance to Yellowstone National Park, 5 miles south of Gardiner, Montana.

The lodging complex offers various types of rooms, both in the hotel and in the cabins. No rooms available in summer are specifically designated handicap accessible. Ninety-six hotel rooms, all on the first, second, third, and fourth floors, each have steam heat and telephone but no air-conditioning or television (with the exception of the suites). An elevator is near the registration desk. The hotel has sixty-eight rooms with private bath that rent for about $25 per night more than twenty-nine rooms without private bath. Community bath and shower rooms are on each floor. Rooms without a bath have either one double bed and one single bed or two double beds. Regular hotel rooms with bath have a double and a single bed, two double beds, or two doubles and a single bed. Some bathrooms have a tub, some have a shower, and some have both. Corner rooms 230, 231, 330, and 331 each have a full bath and rent for the same price but are quite a bit larger than other rooms with a bath. The hotel has two suites, one each on the third and fourth floors, each about the size of two regular rooms. These have a bedroom and separate sitting room. Both are corner rooms that provide a view of the hot springs. The suites each have a television and coffeemaker, and guests receive a basket of fruit and a newspaper. The fourth-floor suite has two bathrooms, one with a shower-tub combination. The third-floor suite has one bathroom with a shower but no tub.

The cabins are either freestanding or two to a building. All cabins have a covered front porch with chairs. The least expensive lodging facilities at Mammoth are forty-seven Budget cabins without private bath. These cabins each have a sink, and have either two double beds or two double beds plus a single. Sixty-eight Frontier cabins have a private bath with a shower but no bathtub and rent for about $30 more per night than the Budget cabins without bath. Cabins in both these groups are virtually identical in size. Frontier cabins have either two double beds or two doubles and a single. Four of the Frontier cabins have a hot tub on a private porch and rent for about $40 per night more than the other Frontier cabins.

Staying in Mammoth seems a world apart from most of Yellowstone's other lodging facilities. The geography in this section of the park is unique, and the buildings are not what one usually expects in a national park. It's fun to walk around the area and view the buildings. An interesting dining room across the street, decorated in a kind of Art Deco style, serves three meals a day. Windows overlook the old military parade ground, which is in front of the hotel. A grill offering breakfast and sandwiches is next door to the dining room in the same building. A general store next door sells supplies and limited groceries, and a nearby stable offers horseback riding. A National Park Service visitor center in one of the old military buildings has exhibits on the park's early history. On the downside, Mammoth is at the extreme north end of the park, some distance away from Old Faithful and many of Yellowstone's other popular sites. This means that a stay at Mammoth is likely to result in additional driving.

- **ROOMS:** Doubles, triples, and quads. A few rooms can handle five adults. Some hotel rooms and cabins have private baths. No handicap-accessible rooms are available.

- **RATES:** Budget cabins ($52); Frontier cabins ($84); hotel rooms without bath ($63); Frontier cabins with hot tubs ($121); hotel rooms with bath ($89); suites ($261); winter only—Aspen Lodge ($114). Rates quoted are for two persons except suites, which are for up to four. Each additional person is $10 per night. Children eleven and under stay free. Special packages are offered during the winter season.

The hotel and cabins currently operating at Mammoth are only the latest chapter in a long history of lodging in this area. The first crude hotel in the park was built at Mammoth in 1871. The much larger and more elaborate National Hotel was constructed here in 1883. An annex that was added to the National Hotel in 1911 serves as the main lodging section of today's Mammoth Hot Springs Hotel. The remainder of the old National Hotel was torn down. The current hotel's front section containing the lobby, a map room, and a gift shop was added in 1936–1937, one year before the first ninety-six cabins were completed behind the hotel.

- **LOCATION:** North end of Yellowstone National Park, 5 miles south of Gardiner, Montana.

- **SEASON:** Summer season is from early May to the first week of October. Winter season is from mid-December to early March. During winter months, only the hotel and Aspen Lodge are open. The hot tub cabins are open to rent by the hour.

- **FOOD:** A large dining room across the street from the hotel offers breakfast ($4.00–$7.00), lunch ($4.00–$7.00), and dinner ($8.00–$14.00). A grill next to the dining room sells breakfast sandwiches, fast-food items, soups, salads, and ice cream. A general store sells limited groceries.

- **FACILITIES:** Stables, restaurant, cocktail lounge, grill, gift shop, general store, post office, nature store, National Park Service visitor center. Winter season: ski shop, ice-skating rink, and skate and snowshoe rental.

- **ACTIVITIES:** Walking on the boardwalk that winds through the hot springs area, walking through the historic buildings at Mammoth (printed guide available), hiking, horseback riding, evening programs. Winter activities include ice skating, guided snowshoe touring, cross-country skiing, snowmobiling, guided snowmobile touring, snowcoach rides.

## OLD FAITHFUL INN

Yellowstone National Park, WY 82190 • (307) 344–7311

www.TravelYellowstone.com

Old Faithful Inn is the most famous of all the national park lodges. The structure's unique appearance is so familiar that the Disney Company constructed a replica of the inn for its Disney World theme park. The older midsection of the inn, constructed in 1903–1904, contains the scenic lobby, a registration desk, a restaurant, a gift shop, and a number of lodging rooms. The East Wing was added a decade later, and the West Wing fifteen years after that. The hotel is well maintained, and all of the facilities, including the rooms, are clean and comfortable. The large lobby, with log beams and a vaulted ceiling that soars 85 feet above the first floor, has multiple overhanging balconies. A mezzanine with chairs, tables, and sofas wraps around the entire second floor. Oddly shaped logs are used as decoration and for support of the railings and log beams. A huge clock ticks away on the front of a massive four-sided stone fireplace that highlights the lobby. An attractive restaurant and lounge are entered from the back of the lobby.

The inn doesn't directly face Old Faithful, but arriving guests are likely to discover that the famous geyser is the first thing they see as they drive up to the front door to unload their luggage. Good views of Old Faithful are obtained from several locations in the hotel, including the large second-floor porch and some of the lodging rooms. All of the lodging rooms are in the older main section and the two attached wings. No cabins or separate buildings are part of the hotel, although two other lodging facilities with cabins are nearby. The registration desk for Old Faithful Inn is to the left as you enter the lobby. Bell service is available to assist with luggage. A large parking area is in front of the hotel, a relatively short walk from the entrance. Lodging rooms are on three floors, so some climbing of stairs may be required, especially in the older section. Each of the wings has an elevator. Old Faithful Inn

*Old Faithful Inn*

is in the southwest portion of Yellowstone National Park, 30 miles from the entrance station at West Yellowstone.

The inn offers 327 rooms that vary in size, views, bathroom facilities, and configuration. Accommodations range from Old House rooms without private bath in the original central log building to relatively large, recently remodeled rooms with private bath in each of the wings. Room rates vary accordingly. All of the rooms have heat, but none have air-conditioning or television. Only the rooms in the east and west wings have telephones. Pay phones are available in the building.

The least expensive rooms in Old Faithful Inn are in the original Old House section of the building. Although these rooms tend to be dark, and can also be noisy if they are located close to the busy lobby, the log walls provide the ambience of an old lodge. Only a limited number of Old House rooms have a private bath. Here you will find various room arrangements that range from single rooms with one double bed but no bath to two rooms with two double beds, a single, and a bath. The largest rooms at the inn are in the East Wing, which was remodeled in 1992–1993. These feature renovated bathrooms, and some offer a view of Old Faithful. Six semi-suites in the East Wing offer a larger room with a sitting area. Two suites have two queen-size beds, a separate sitting room, a coffeemaker, and a refrigerator. Sections of the West Wing have been renovated more recently, although unrenovated portions of the wing remain. Bedding in this section ranges from two twins to two double beds. Our favorite is room 8 in the Old House, which has two

> Old Faithful geyser's eruption intervals range from 30 to 120 minutes and average about 75 minutes. Estimates for the next eruption are posted inside Old Faithful Inn. This famous geyser, like other geysers, is caused when surface water seeps down porous rock to be heated under pressure to very high temperatures. As the superheated water rises and nears the surface, it converts to the steam you see when an eruption occurs.

rooms and a clawfoot tub in a bathroom that is almost as large as a bedroom. There is one double bed in one bedroom and a double and a single in the other.

Old Faithful Inn is a classic national park lodge. If you plan to visit Yellowstone, stay at least one night here. It is convenient to the geysers and a good base for exploring this section of the park. Be aware that, during the summer, the inn is a busy place and the Old Faithful area is congested. Both guests and visitors constantly roam through the lobby, the mezzanine, and the second-floor porch, so if you are seeking quiet, this isn't the place. On the other hand, you've got to see Old Faithful, so you might as well do it from where you are staying.

- **ROOMS:** Doubles, triples, and quads. A few rooms in the Old House can sleep up to six persons. Most but not all of the rooms have a private bath. Three handicap-accessible rooms are available.

- **RATES:** Old House rooms without private bath ($68); rooms with private bath ($91–$159), depending on size, location, and view; semi-suites ($251); suites ($334). Most rates quoted are for two persons, with the exception of the two-room units in the Old House, the semi-suites, and the suites, where the price is for four persons. Each additional person is $10 per night. Children eleven and under stay free when staying with an adult.

- **LOCATION:** Southwest section of Yellowstone National Park, 30 miles from the entrance station at West Yellowstone.

- **SEASON:** Early May through the third week of October.

- **FOOD:** A dining room on the main floor serves breakfast ($4.00–$7.00), lunch ($5.00–$8.00), and dinner ($10–$16); the snack shop offers sandwiches, fast-food items, and ice cream; a lunch counter in the adjacent general store serves breakfast, salads, sandwiches, soup, ice cream, and beverages. Other eating facilities are nearby.

- **FACILITIES:** Restaurant, snack bar, tour desk, gift shop, ATM. Many additional facilities, including a gas station, gift shops, stores, and restaurants, are in the immediate area.

- **ACTIVITIES:** Walking through nearby geyser area, tours of the inn, hiking.

## OLD FAITHFUL LODGE CABINS

Yellowstone National Park, WY 82190 • (307) 344–7311
www.TravelYellowstone.com

Old Faithful Lodge Cabins consists of a main lodge building and 97 cabins, constructed two to four to a building. The main lodge was constructed in the late 1920s and has no overnight accommodations. The cabins are behind and to one side of the main lodge, which houses the registration desk. The impressive lobby area has large windows that provide an excellent view of Old Faithful. A big stone fireplace is surrounded with chairs and sofas for reading, visiting, and relaxing. The main building also has a cafeteria, ice cream shop, bake shop, and gift shop. Old Faithful Lodge Cabins is in the southwest section of Yellowstone National Park, 30 miles from the west entrance at West Yellowstone. It is a short walk from the better-known Old Faithful Inn.

*Frontier Cabins at Old Faithful Lodge Cabins*

The lodge offers two classes of cabins that are similar in size but feature different bathroom facilities and interior decor. All of the cabins are relatively small and clustered closely together behind the main lodge in an area with few trees. All have heat and electricity. Adequate parking is beside each cabin.

The least expensive thirty-six Budget cabins have a sink but no bathroom facilities. Toilets and sinks are in a single bathroom building that can be a distance away from some of the cabins. Shower facilities are in the main lodge building, which is not particularly close to any of the cabins. Beds in these units are a double plus a single bed. The cabins are paneled and carpeted. Most are duplex units with connecting doors, a feature that may appeal to families. Sixty-one Pioneer cabins each have a private bath with a toilet, sink, and shower. Bedding varies from a double bed, a double bed and single bed, or two double beds.

Old Faithful Lodge Cabins offers basic but inexpensive accommodations. In fact, the Budget cabins are the least expensive lodging facilities in all of Yellowstone National Park. The main lodge has a large cafeteria serving lunch and dinner. Menu items include salads, pasta, hamburgers, and prime rib. A small bakery sells muffins, cinnamon rolls, and other baked goods, as well as coffee. Even though you won't want to do much other than sleep in your cabin, the lodge offers an attractive atmosphere for reading, talking, and relaxing. Staying at the lodge also allows you to enjoy nearby Old Faithful Inn.

- **ROOMS:** Doubles, triples, and a few quads. More than half the cabins have a private bath. None of the cabins are handicap accessible.

Boardwalks and unpaved paths meander through Upper Geyser Basin, near Old Faithful Lodge Cabins. A boardwalk that begins near the lodge leads around Old Faithful Geyser and through a large area of pools, geysers, and springs. One path is designated for both people and bicycles. One 3-mile loop leads to Morning Glory Pool and returns to the lodge. Both shorter and longer trails are in the basin area.

- **RATES:** Budget cabins without bath ($42); Frontier cabins ($65). Rates quoted are for two persons. Each additional person is $10 per night. Children eleven and under stay free with an adult.

- **LOCATION:** Southwest section of Yellowstone National Park, 30 miles from the entrance station at West Yellowstone.

- **SEASON:** Mid-May to mid-September.

- **FOOD:** A large cafeteria offers lunch ($4.00), and dinner ($10). Two snack shops serve bakery goods, ice cream, yogurt, and espresso.

- **FACILITIES:** Cafeteria, snack shops, tour desk, gift shop. Many stores and restaurants are in the immediate vicinity.

- **ACTIVITIES:** Walking through the geyser area, hiking.

## OLD FAITHFUL SNOW LODGE AND CABINS

Yellowstone National Park, WY 82190 • (307) 344–7311
www.TravelYellowstone.com

*Old Faithful Snow Lodge*

Old Faithful Snow Lodge and Cabins consists of a single three-story main lodge building plus thirty-four wooden cabins that are located near, but not immediately beside the lodge. The lodge offers a dining room, grill, cocktail lounge, two gift shops, and an impressive two-story lobby with huge wood beams and a large gas fireplace. A second-floor mezzanine with chairs and a table overlooks the lobby. Lamps and chandeliers throughout the building and the guest rooms feature animal motifs. Craftsmen created many of the furnishings in the lobby, lounge, and restaurant. Even much of the woodwork includes inlaid animal figures. The rustic design of the lodge fits in well with better known Old Faithful Inn, which is nearby. The entire complex is in the Old Faithful area of Yellowstone, 30 miles from the west entrance at West Yellowstone. The lodge is across a large parking area from Old Faithful Inn. Plenty of parking is available near the lodge and beside the cabins. Registration for the lodge and the cabins is at the main desk of the lodge building.

Snow Lodge is the first full-service hotel (dining rooms, lobby, gift shop, etc.) built in Yellowstone National Park since Canyon Lodge was completed in 1911 (and has since burned) and is one of the newest lodging units in any national park. The complex has one hundred similar but not identical rooms that are all rented at the same rate. The new lodge building replaces the previous lodge that was demolished in 1998. Each room in the new lodge is large, with two double beds, a desk and chair, and a built-in wooden closet. Heavy wooden shutters swing out to cover the windows. A padded window seat is in a few of the rooms. All rooms have heat, telephone, and full bath with a combination shower-tub.

The complex is in a relatively quiet section of the Old Faithful area, but the location does not lend itself to great views from any of the rooms. There are elevators in the lodge and porters are available to assist with luggage. We recommend that you try to book rooms 2037, 2039, 2041, and the three corresponding rooms on the third floor that are larger but rent for the same rate as all other rooms in the lodge. Rooms on the second floor have larger windows than first- and third-floor rooms. The lodge hallways are exceptionally wide, and seven rooms are handicap accessible.

Two categories of cabins are rented at Snow Lodge. All the cabins sit in a gravel area of sparse vegetation. The least expensive are the ten Frontier cabins with one or two double beds. The two cabins with one double bed are quite a bit smaller than the others. They all rent for the same price, so try to get two doubles if you book a Frontier cabin. These cabins are of modest size and nicely finished. They do not have a porch. Each cabin has a private bath with shower but no tub. Twenty-four Western cabins are much larger, nicer, and cost nearly twice as much as the Frontier units. They are about $20 less than rooms in the new Snow Lodge. These are constructed four to a building; each cabin has a small covered porch, two double beds, and a full bath with a combination shower-tub. One Western cabin is handicap accessible. We believe the Frontier cabins with two double beds are a better value than the Western cabins.

Old Faithful Snow Lodge and Cabins offers something for everyone. Those on a tight budget can choose a Frontier cabin. Others who are willing to spend more can sleep in one of the nicest lodging units in any national park. The lodge is only one of two Yellowstone lodging units (Mammoth is the other) open during the winter. The Snow Lodge complex is in a central location from which to explore a major thermal area of the park. It is also convenient to a National Park Service visitor center and various stores. A restaurant serves three meals a day, and a grill offers sandwiches and ice cream. Another restaurant in Old Faithful Inn and

*Old Faithful Snow Lodge and Cabins and Mammoth Hot Springs Hotel are the only two facilities that offer winter accommodations. Reservations should be made well in advance of your planned arrival. Only Mammoth is accessible by car. Old Faithful Snow Lodge is accessible only by over-the-snow vehicles from West Yellowstone, Mammoth, and Flagg Ranch on the south end. Skiing, snowshoeing, and ice skating (Mammoth) are popular activities. Ski rentals, waxes, trail maps, and other equipment are available at both locations.*

a cafeteria in Old Faithful Lodge are only a short walk from the cabins or main building of Snow Lodge.

- **ROOMS:** Doubles, triples, and quads. All rooms have a private bath. Seven lodge rooms and one Western cabin are handicap accessible.

- **RATES:** Frontier cabins ($65); Western cabins ($111); Snow Lodge rooms ($131). Rates quoted are for two persons. Each additional person is $10 per night. Children eleven and under stay free.

- **LOCATION:** Southwest section of Yellowstone, 30 miles southeast of the west entrance at West Yellowstone.

- **SEASON:** Summer season is from early May to mid-October. Winter season is from mid-December to mid-March. The cabins are closed in winter. No roads are open to this location during winter months.

- **FOOD:** An informal dining room serves breakfast ($4.00–$6.00), lunch ($6.00–$8.00), and dinner ($8.00–$16.00). A grill serves breakfast ($2.00–$4.00) and fast food for lunch/dinner ($3.00–$6.00). Another dining room, a cafeteria, and a store with limited groceries are nearby.

- **FACILITIES:** Restaurant, grill, cocktail lounge, and gift shops. Other nearby facilities include a service station, clinic, general store, visitor center, and post office. Winter sports equipment rental is available during winter months.

- **ACTIVITIES:** Hiking, walking through the nearby geyser area, and tours. Winter activities include snowcoach tours, guided ski tours, and snowmobiling.

## ROOSEVELT LODGE CABINS

Yellowstone National Park, WY 82190 • (307) 344–7311

www.TravelYellowstone.com

Named for an area that served as a favorite campsite for President Theodore Roosevelt, Roosevelt Lodge Cabins include a log registration and dining building and an adjacent small store. These two structures are surrounded on three sides by rustic wood cabins that were constructed mostly in the 1920s. The main building has a registration desk flanked on one side by a lobby and a large stone fireplace and on the other side by a family-style dining room. Chairs fill a covered front porch that runs the length of the building. The lodging complex is situated on a hill surrounded by pine trees and overlooking a valley with a background of mountains. The relatively isolated location places the lodge away from the congestion that plagues other such facilities in the park. Roosevelt Lodge Cabins is in the northeast corner of Yellowstone National Park, 23 miles southeast of the north entrance near Mammoth.

Roosevelt Lodge Cabins provides only rustic cabin accommodations; no overnight rooms are in the main lodge building. Two categories of cabins are available. None of the cabins have television, telephones, or air-conditioning. All of the units are closely clustered and provide basic lodging at economical prices. The least expensive option is the sixty Rough Rider cabins, which have a wood stove (manufactured logs provided) for heat but no water or pri-

*Frontier Cabins at Roosevelt Lodge Cabins*

vate bathroom. Nearby community bathrooms and shower houses are available. Rough Rider units vary in size and come with one to three double beds.

Fourteen Frontier cabins have electric heat, a full bath with a shower but no tub, and either one or two double beds. These are larger than the Rough Rider units.

Roosevelt Lodge Cabins offers relatively inexpensive accommodations for a stay at Yellowstone National Park. The lodging facilities are basic, and support facilities are limited in comparison to those at most of the other lodging complexes in the park. A nice dining room in the main lodge building serves three meals a day. A small store next door has limited supplies and groceries. A small lobby in the main registration building has chairs and benches surrounding a large stone fireplace. Horseback riding and stagecoach rides are available at the nearby stables.

- **ROOMS:** Doubles, triples, and quads. A few cabins hold up to six adults. Most of the cabins do not have a private bath. No handicap-accessible cabins are available.

- **RATES:** Rough Rider cabins without bath ($46); Frontier cabins ($84). Rates quoted are for two persons. Each additional person is $10 per night. Children eleven and under stay free.

- **LOCATION:** Northeast section of Yellowstone, 23 miles southeast of the north entrance.

- **SEASON:** Mid-June through mid-September.

- **FOOD:** A dining room serves breakfast ($4.00–$6.00), lunch ($5.00–$9.00), and dinner ($13–$19). An Old West Cookout ($32) via horseback or covered wagon is offered each evening, rain or shine. Limited groceries are sold at a small store.

- **FACILITIES:** Store, dining room, gift counter, stables, gas station.

- **ACTIVITIES:** Hiking, horseback riding, stagecoach rides.

The northeast corner of Yellowstone National Park is known as Roosevelt Country. This area of fir-, aspen-, and pine-covered rolling hills features 132-foot Tower Fall, which is a short drive south of the lodge. This area of the park offers some of the nation's best fly-fishing.

# ABOUT THE AUTHORS

DAVID AND KAY SCOTT reside in Valdosta, Georgia, where the winters are mild, the humidity is high, and the people are friendly. They have spent twenty-six summers touring the United States and Canada in a series of Volkswagen campers. The first VW bus they owned was a 1967 model that looked like a relic from World War II. During its first cross-country trip, in 1970, the VW was barely able to make headway against the wind blowing across a Wyoming interstate. Their two- and three-month trips have taken the couple through all the states, the Canadian provinces, and to nearly all the areas administered by the National Park Service. The Scotts drove from Georgia to Alaska and back during the summer of 1982. David and Kay have appeared live from Yellowstone National Park and Grand Canyon National Park on NBC's *Today* show, offering tips on visiting the national parks. In addition to their domestic travels, the Scotts spent four summers carrying backpacks while riding trains through Europe.

David Scott was born in Rushville, Indiana, attended Purdue University and Florida State University, and received a Ph.D. in economics from the University of Arkansas. During most of the year, he is a professor of accounting and finance at Valdosta State University. He has written numerous books on accounting, finance, and investing, including nine titles in Globe Pequot's Money Smarts series of personal finance books. In addition to travel, he is interested in amateur radio, computers, and the Atlanta Braves. His e-mail address is dlscott@ valdosta.edu.

Kay Woelfel Scott was born in Austin, Minnesota, and was raised in Yankton, South Dakota. She graduated from Clearwater (Florida) High School and earned degrees at Florida Southern College and the University of Arkansas. During the academic year, she is assistant principal at an elementary school in Valdosta, Georgia. She is interested in a wide variety of crafts, including making stained glass and designing and painting T-shirts. She drew all the maps that appeared in the earlier editions of this book.